VATICAN

II

VATICAN
II

A SOCIOLOGICAL ANALYSIS
OF RELIGIOUS CHANGE

Melissa J. Wilde

PRINCETON UNIVERSITY PRESS
PRINCETON AND OXFORD

Published by Princeton University Press, 41 William Street, Princeton, New Jersey 08540

In the United Kingdom: Princeton University Press, 3 Market Place, Woodstock, Oxfordshire OX20 1SY

Library of Congress Cataloging-in-Publication Data

Wilde, Melissa J., 1974–
Vatican II: a sociological analysis of religious change/Melissa J. Wilde.
p. cm.
Originally presented as the author's thesis—University of California, Berkeley.
Includes bibliographical references and index.
ISBN-13: 978-0-691-11829-1 (hardcover: alk. paper)
ISBN-10: 0-691-11829-9 (hardcover: alk. paper)
1. Vatican Council (2nd: 1962–1965) 2. Christian sociology—Catholic Church—
History—20th century. I. Title. II. Title: Vatican 2. III. Title: Vatican Two.
BX8301962 .W47 2007
262' .52—dc22   2006103370

British Library Cataloging-in-Publication Data is available

This book has been composed in Postscript Galliard

Printed on acid-free paper. ∞

press.princeton.edu

Printed in the United States of America

1 3 5 7 9 10 8 6 4 2

To Stephen

———————————

CONTENTS

TABLES AND FIGURES

ACKNOWLEDGMENTS

I OWE THANKS to many people for the help they gave me during the time it has taken to finish this project. I'll start with where it started, as a dissertation at the University of California, Berkeley. My dissertation committee—Mike Hout, Ann Swidler, and Kim Voss—my fellow graduate students, and other faculty and staff contributed to this work in countless ways.

Words cannot express my gratitude to Mike Hout, my chair, for the intellectual, methodological, financial, and emotional support he has given me. Besides being an incredible mentor, cheerleader, and friend, Mike generously provided me with a room of my own: an office at the Survey Research Center. There, I could work undisturbed, yet also pop into his office with countless questions, requests for recommendations, or just a joke. His support didn't just make writing the dissertation easier and more enjoyable; it made it possible.

This project was immeasurably strengthened by Ann Swidler's incredible sociological imagination, positive attitude, and (sometimes frightening) faith in my work. Early in our relationship I feared I could never satisfy the intellectual rigor of her demands. In retrospect, I see how valuable those demands were to my self-confidence as a scholar and to the strength of my work. Each chapter of the dissertation benefited from her careful editing and thought-provoking comments. Ann first alerted me to the possibility of an interesting paper that further explored my conclusion that conservatives developed inferior organizational forms because of their beliefs, which eventually became the first publication from this project, reproduced here in chapter 3.

Kim Voss's amazing ability to balance honest and rigorous comments with constant support is a talent I hope to develop myself as a mentor someday. The many challenging alternative hypotheses she posed as I was writing this dissertation infinitely strengthened it. Those I could not address in the dissertation I kept in mind through my additional data collection and seemingly endless revisions, and I hope that she will now, many years later, find that I have finally dealt with them!

At Berkeley I also benefited from the support and feedback of many people outside of the department and my dissertation committee. Peggy Anderson was a generous outside member. Claude Fischer's willingness to give me comments whenever I asked was truly remarkable. Much of the advice he gave during his article-writing course proved useful during the dissertation-writing process, as well as when I was revising the dissertation to produce this book. Jane Zavisca, Avri Beard, Carolyn Chen, Phillip Fucella, Iona Mara-Drita, Stephanie Mudge, Joseph Palacios, Jeffrey Sallaz, and Karolyn Tyson are just a few of my fellow graduate students who provided important feedback, emotional support, inspiration, or just plain relaxation through my years at Berkeley. Jane especially deserves recognition here; over the years she read countless drafts of my MA thesis, grant proposals, and dissertation. As I was finishing the dissertation, Sara Nephew, a UCB undergrad, provided valuable research assistance.

I have been fortunate to have had help from a number of scholars outside of Berkeley. Andrew Greeley read every chapter of the dissertation with enthusiasm and a critical eye. John Coleman, Mark Chaves, Michele Dillon, Roger Finke, Mary Ellen Konieczny, Bill Sewell, Jr., Chris Smith, and Robert Wuthnow have offered helpful advice and feedback over the years. Joseph Komonchak patiently helped me develop this project, corrected misunderstandings and misconceptions, and provided me with valuable contacts. Rocco Caporale generously allowed me access to his priceless interview transcripts with eighty of the most important bishops at the Council.

Archivists William John Shepard at Catholic University of America, Lucinda Glenn Rand at the Graduate Theological Union, Piero Doria, Marco Maiorino and Sergio Pagano at the Vatican Secret Archive, and Giuseppe Alberigo and Sylvia Scatena at the Institute for the Scientific Study of Religion in Bologna, Italy, provided assistance at various stages of this research.

I benefited from the translation assistance of Josh Davies, Frederic Merand, Callily Campos Diana, and especially Han Tran. Funding for this assistance was provided by an NSF Dissertation Improvement Grant (SES-0002409), a Charlotte W. Newcombe Dissertation Writing Year Fellowship from the Woodrow Wilson Foundation, a grant from the American Sociological Association's Fund for the Advancement of the Discipline, a Research Award from the Society for the Scientific Study of Religion, and research funds and a junior sabbatical from Indiana University, where I turned the dissertation into this book. Any flaws in the book are of course mine and do not reflect the views of any of these funding agencies.

Though the support I received at Berkeley made this project possible, the book would not exist if it weren't for the research support I received while at Indiana University as an assistant professor. Almost single-handedly, Shelley Nelson took the thousands of pages of Council votes I brought back from Italy and turned them into an enormous and enormously valuable electronic database. After two years of overseeing more than twenty people (graduate students Evie Perry and Paul Kim; undergrads Amy Allen, Samantha Barbera, Samantha Brooks, Kristin Chaney, Jalane Deckard, Jenna DiMartino, Laura Dunn, Amy Gardner, Wendy Hoffman, Jason Lillie, Andrea Knies, Amber Kotyuk, Katie Mccauley, Jessica Messer,

Sarah Milligan, Justin Novotny, Mike Peterson, Lori Smith, Morgan Smith, and Kelly Straw) entering, checking, and cross-checking the data and merging it with other sources, she still speaks to me. Her husband, Jim Nelson, also deserves many thanks for his able and willing programming assistance.

Once the database was up and running, Shelley was joined by Kristin Geraty, Emily Bowman, and Grace Yukich, who have helped contribute to both the database and my thinking. Jessica Sprague-Bunk provided important help with the references as I was finishing the final revisions to the manuscript.

Along with the essential research support IU provided, I am very thankful for the collegial support I received there. Bernice Pescosolido has been a terrific mentor and friend. I have received helpful comments, advice, and encouragement from Elizabeth Armstrong, Clem Brooks, Bill Corsaro, Tom Geiryn, IU's Junior Faculty Working Group (Art Alderson, Ho-fung Hung, Ethan Michelson, Fabio Rojas, Quincy Thomas Stewart, Leah Vanwey) Pam Jackson, David James, Scott Long, Jane McCloud, Eliza Pavalko, Brian Powell, Rob Robinson, Brian Steensland, and Pam Walters.

Realizing that we would surely overburden our colleagues with drafts upon drafts of our works-in-progress, Tony Chen, Isaac Martin, and I decided to develop a mutually burdensome society and help each other through the process of book writing soon after we departed Berkeley. This book has benefited enormously from their input. Tony forced me many times to articulate theoretical implications I was tempted to leave for the reader to draw. Isaac's analytical precision and carefully posed questions always left me with a great many things to fix, but feeling strangely confident as I started the repair process.

Other friends have contributed to this book or my life in many ways. Melissa Dinverno and Alejandro Meíjas-López went way above the duties of friendship and helped the track down an obscure Spanish source when all roads were turning into blind alleys (and all the while kept their wonderful hospitality flowing). And I continue to be blessed by the life-long friendship I have enjoyed with Lisa Trophia and Kelley Baker.

There is, of course, no way for me to thank my parents, Adele and Paul Wilde. I would not be where I am today without the self-confidence they helped me to develop. Though this book is a long way from the soccer and basketball games and track meets of my youth, their unwavering support remains as tangible now as their cheers were audible then.

Finally, I would like to thank my partner in life, Stephen Viscelli. From reading drafts, listening to my complaints, and helping me figure out the structure and implications of this book, to cooking me meals, being patient with my moods and obsessive work habits, and making my home an inviting, happy place, I thank him with all of my heart.

VATICAN
II

INTRODUCTION

ON NOVEMBER 29, 1964, the first Sunday of Advent, Roman Catholics walked into their parishes around the globe and, for the first time since the fall of the Roman Empire, participated in a mass that was given largely in their native tongue.[1] Not only did parishioners find themselves responding to the priest in words they spoke every day, but they spoke more often than they had at any Catholic service they had ever attended. Many Catholics saw the strange sight of their priest consecrating the Eucharist facing the congregation rather than the crucifix behind the altar, along with other new practices meant to make the mass and liturgy more participatory by incorporating the "people of God."

These were just the first of many changes that came out of the Second Vatican Council of the Roman Catholic Church.[2] Indeed, as the Church was busily figuring out how to incorporate the vernacular language into its services, Roman Catholic leaders around the world prepared for the Fourth (and final) Session of the Council. These preparations were intense and often contentious. Though the liturgical reforms had been approved at the end of the Second Session, many other, even more important reforms remained to be decided.

By the time it was finished, on December 8, 1965, the Council had turned the Church on its head. To name but a few examples: as a result of the Council, the Roman Catholic Church relinquished its claim to be the one true church, and with it, abdicated claims to power in relation to nation-states, by declaring that the only just form of government was one under which people were free to worship as they pleased. The Council relaxed dietary restrictions and requirements regarding confession and attire for the laity, eliminated the Latin mass, and forever changed the character and identities of Roman Catholic nuns and brothers—and their orders. Most importantly, Vatican II changed the way the Church understood itself, as its identity went from being a hierarchical authority to a church conceived of as the people of God.

Together, these changes have had far-reaching effects on the doctrine, practices, and identity of Roman Catholicism. Politically, the Council has been cited as a central factor in the development of liberation theology in Latin America; as an important theological resource for progressive Catholics in the United States; and as a reason why the Church began to engage more actively in public debates over war and peace, capitalism and economic redistribution.[3] Everyday life was affected too: the Council liberalized religious practices as varied as dietary restrictions (Catholics are no longer required to abstain from meat on Fridays), clothing requirements (Catholic women no longer have to wear head coverings during mass), and annulment procedures.[4]

Simply put, Vatican II represents the most significant example of institutionalized religious change since the Reformation. Though sociological opinion is unified in attributing great significance to the Council, few systematic attempts have been made to examine the forces that determined the character and extent of the changes it effected.[5] This is partly because the council was huge. It took four sessions, three years (1962–65), and the leadership of two popes to complete. More than three thousand bishops, cardinals, heads of religious orders, and theologians (for convenience, hereafter all of the Council delegates are referred to as bishops) from all over the world attended. The daily events of the Council could easily fill the pages of this book. However, such a history has been more than adequately told and it is not the intent of this study to tell it again.[6]

My goal is to take the rich and complex history of the Council, and re-examine it through a sociological lens—to discover the factors that explain its outcome and in doing so, identify the factors that determine religious change more generally. Ultimately, the goal of this book is to answer some theoretical questions about cultural change: Why do some religious institutions adapt to cultural change, while others do not? When religious institutions do change, what determines what changes and what remains constant? In essence: When, why, and how do religious institutions, which are arguably the most rigidly structured and codified institutions in the world, adapt as the societies around them march onward?

Though many theories in the sociology of religion make implicit assumptions about institutional change, and though founding sociologists such as Max Weber and Émile Durkheim examined it, there is surprisingly little theory available to explain how, why, or when religious change occurs.[7] This is mainly because the sociology of religion, with a few notable exceptions,[8] has not attempted to explain institutional change but has focused instead on individual participation and its effects, or on religious growth or decline. Such studies, though important, do little to help us understand the organizational resources, forces, and mobilization efforts involved in an event like the Second Vatican Council.

Consequently, though this analysis is informed by these and other important research in the sociology of religion, throughout this book I also draw from theories of historical events, organizational and cultural change, social movements, and even from economic sociology.[9]

Vatican II is an ideal case through which to examine questions about religious change. Change, at least of great magnitude, is not common in Roman Catholic history. Councils are rare events, convened only by the pope, and occur less than once a century on average. Vatican I, the Church's last council before Vatican II, ended prematurely in 1869 as a result of the Franco-Prussian War and did little of note besides declaring the pope to be infallible. Prior to Vatican I, the Church had not held a council since the Council of Trent closed in 1563.[10]

Furthermore, the changes that came from the Council were almost completely unexpected. To appreciate just how remarkable Vatican II was, one must understand that even once the Council had been called, change did not seem likely. The Roman Curia, the men in charge of the Church's administration, who did not favor change, seemed to be at the zenith of their power. For four hundred years, the Curia had determined the pronouncements on theology and doctrine that constituted Roman Catholicism. They frequently used their powers of censorship to curb theologians, ban books, and keep the Church "untarnished" by modern thought. Their vocation was protecting the Church from heresy, something which by all accounts they did quite well. Initially, even the bishops who would rise to the greatest prominence once the Council began expected little more from it than a "rubber-stamp" of the Curia's conservative views.

When Pope John XXIII announced that he was calling a council, he had only been in office for three months, was seventy-seven years old, and was expected to be an "interim" pope—a placeholder who mollified progressives but made conservatives feel secure because of his age and "simple" nature. The resources, power, and confidence of the Roman Curia had perhaps never been greater. Though upset by John's announcement, they had almost complete control over the Council's preparations, proceedings, and agenda.

Given this situation at the start of the Council, many saw the unexpected and sweeping changes that came from it as nothing short of miraculous. Popular explanations of the miracle focused on one man: Pope John XXIII. In 1962, before any Council reforms had yet been solidified, but after the First Session had already signaled that Vatican II would not rubber-stamp the policies and views of the Curia, *Time* magazine declared John "Man of the Year," with the following justification:

> [1962 saw] the beginning of a revolution in Christianity, the ancient faith whose 900 million adherents make it the world's largest religion. . . . It began on Oct. 11 in Rome and was the work of the man of the year, Pope John XXIII, who, by convening . . . Vatican II, set in motion ideas and forces that will affect not merely Roman Catholics, not only Christians, but the whole world's ever-expanding population.[11]

In contrast to such explanations of the Council, I do not see the pope as the primary reason why the Council took the turn that it did.

There is no question that Pope John XXIII is an essential part of why Vatican II happened at all; it takes a pope to call a council.[12] Thus, John provided the "political opportunity" necessary for reform to occur.[13] But he died just weeks before the Second Session of the Council was to start, after only one of the hundreds of reforms which would come from it had passed. Thus, the overwhelming progressive outcome of the Council cannot be attributed to John.[14] Furthermore, John's successor, Paul VI, proved to be more conservative than John.[15] In fact, it would become clear that, on a number of issues, the Council was disposed to make much more progressive reforms than Paul desired.

Thus, even though they were certainly necessary, neither of the popes is a sufficient explanation of how and why Vatican II became the watershed event that it was. This in is large part because though there were a number of ways that John and Paul could play a role in the Council,[16] there were few moments when either of them actively intervened. Intervening in the proceedings of the Council was difficult for the pope because the purpose of a council is to call all of the bishops of the world together so they can discuss their views with their colleagues. By definition, if such discussion was not needed, a council would not have been called. Once it was under way, the bishops expected to decide what issues needed to be addressed and how to address them, and anticipated doing so with some autonomy. Thus, though the pope provided the opportunity for change, with rare exceptions the bishops decided the direction and extent of that change. Ultimately, they decided to change a great deal. The purpose of this book is to figure out why.

What Does Not Explain the Council

The Council's overwhelmingly progressive outcome cannot be explained by such traditional sociological factors as power, resources, interests, or even popular pressure. At the beginning of the Council, conservatives had, through the Roman Curia, more formal power than did progressives[17] and more of almost every type of resource we can imagine: money, institutional access, staff, even printing presses. And they had these resources concentrated precisely where the central decisions about the Council would take place, namely, the Vatican. If power and resources could explain the outcome of the Council, nothing much would have come from it.

Interests, at least those associated with money, power, or keeping the laity happy, also cannot explain the outcome of the Council. The Declaration of Religious Freedom, a key reform that came from the Council, abdicated the preferential status the Church had enjoyed in many countries (and the money and power which came with it). It is difficult to envision an interest-based explanation which can account for such a move. Finally, as much as popular accounts of the Council emphasize its focus on the

"Church as the People of God," Vatican II is also not a story of a religious institution responding to pressure from below. Many of the reforms that came from the Council were almost entirely irrelevant to lay concerns, and the reform that was the most central to the daily lives of laypersons, birth control, was tabled.

PART I: EXPLAINING THE COUNCIL

The first part of the book presents my explanation of the Council's outcome through three distinct analytical chapters. Chapter 1 answers a research question which is necessary for all of the later chapters. That is: Given the way things looked at the start of the Council, with the Curia in control, how did any change occur?

The answer to this question lies in key moments of the First Session which helped to eliminate the initial disadvantages progressives faced. These events began on the very first day of the Council, when a few progressive bishops organized and decided to reject the Curia's agenda for that day by refusing to elect members to the conciliar commissions. These progressive leaders argued that they needed more time for deliberations among themselves and within their national conferences. And, to everyone's surprise, they won.

This unanticipated occurrence began a shift in expectations in which many bishops began to believe that real change was possible from the Council. This shift was furthered by the second key moment of the First Session: when it became clear that liturgical reforms—the first issue the Council debated—were supported by the vast majority of the bishops, and that the schema would have an easy passage. Though the issue was not contentious, it demonstrated to everyone that the vast majority of bishops were willing to undertake real changes and do more than rubber-stamp the Curia's opinions.

The possibilities for the Council were finally cemented during the contentious debate on the sources of revelation. In a very close vote, a majority, but not the needed two-thirds majority, voted to reject the conservative schema. Though it looked like the Curia was going to triumph, Pope John intervened and mandated that the schema be sent back to committee because such a large majority of the bishops rejected it. This act was interpreted by many as legitimating the power of the bishops' votes over the procedural rules and regulations established by the Curia.

Together, these occurrences are an essential part of explaining why, even though they had greater resources and power at its start, conservatives were not able to dictate the agenda or outcome of the Council. However, though the shift that occurred during the First Session is crucial to understanding why any change occurred at the Council, it is also true that Vatican II did not change everything it might have. Indeed, in the end it would become clear that the Council left some very important but difficult issues alone, in particular, birth control, priestly celibacy, and the ordination of women. And thus, a crucial question arises: Once the opportunity was present, what explains why some things changed and others did not? This is the comparative question which motivates the remainder of the book and is addressed by a very simple, but necessary, preliminary question in chapter 2. That is, who wanted what, and why?

When we examine the various priorities of the bishops at the Council, four distinct groups of bishops emerge: those from European Catholic monopolies such as Italy and Spain, who wanted no change; those from non-monopolistic countries (meaning either non-Catholic countries or Catholic countries with a formal separation of church and state) in Europe and North America, who prioritized ecumenism (or bettering relations with Protestants); those from Latin America, who prioritized economic justice and reaching the poor and unchurched in their countries; and those from Africa and Asia, who had a full range of ecumenical outreach and social-justice concerns oriented toward helping the Church grow in their missionary countries. Comparisons between these four groups of bishops allow us to isolate the factors that directed the bishops' priorities at the Council, and ultimately understand the factors that affect religious leaders today.

The fact that bishops from Italy and Spain steadfastly fought against any accommodation with the modern world is consistent with current theories in the sociology of religion, which argue that religious diversity creates more accomodationist religious organizations by creating competition. The complete lack of diversity left bishops from monopolistic countries unconcerned about losing constituents and unwilling to engage in changing their institution.

Though it initially seems difficult to explain within current theories, the fact that bishops from Latin America were overwhelmingly progressive despite the seemingly monopolistic situation of the Church in Latin America can be explained by the key difference between the Church in Latin America and the Church in Italy and Spain. The Latin American Church was in decline, their monopoly was unstable. Leaders of unstable monopolies make every attempt to staunch the flow of their losses and become much more open to change than their counterparts in stable monopolies.

Finally, while they were certainly more willing to change their church than their colleagues from monopolistic environments, the fact that bishops from non-monopolistic European countries prioritized bettering relations with Protestants suggests that current theories need some tweaking. It seems that religious diversity causes religious leaders not only to care about their constituents but also to care a great deal about legitimacy. This is the case because bettering relations with Protestants entailed addressing a number of important legitimacy critiques being made against the Church at the time. Ecumenically oriented bishops focused on addressing these critiques (two of which, the Church's stance on religious freedom and Catholic devotion to Mary, are described in detail in the case studies), even at the expense of their constituents' wishes, as their neglect of the issue of birth control, which is examined in chapter 6, suggests.

These findings provide insight into the factors that direct religious change more generally. In particular, they suggest that religious institutions, like other organizations, respond as much to concerns about legitimacy as they do to concerns about efficiency. Whether legitimacy concerns become paramount depends upon the characteristics of a particular environment, most importantly, whether it is stable and whether it contains other prominent institutions that can provide leaders with a reference point and with specific legitimacy challenges. Religious leaders who are insulated from other religions and the legitimacy concerns they pose, like the bishops from Italy and Spain during the Council, will most strongly and successfully resist change.

Chapter 2 also demonstrates that Latin American bishops initially had difficulty embracing their Northern European colleagues' goal of improving relations with Protestants. This finding thereby raises the final analytical question addressed in the book. That is, given the initial divisiveness ecumenical reforms created, but the overwhelmingly ecumenical tone of the Council in the end, *how* did progressive leaders from Northern Europe and North America develop compromise positions that the majority of the rank and file bishops would support?

This question is the focus of chapter 3, which argues that a great deal of the Council's progressive outcome can be explained by a relatively simple sociological fact: because progressives built a far more extensive and flexible organization than their conservative counterparts, they were more successful at developing compromise positions the vast majority of bishops could support. These organizational differences derived from different cultural understandings of the nature of authority in the Roman Catholic Church. Progressives believed in the doctrine of "collegiality," which stated that the bishops convening together have the same teaching authority as the pope—a doctrine that conservatives saw as threatening the authority and primacy of the pope. Consequently, while progressives built a highly effective, consensus-based organization as soon as the Council began, conservatives were much slower to mobilize, and when they did so, formed a hierarchical organization which never developed into much more than a letter-writing campaign to the pope.

Vatican II is thus a story of the process through which individuals changed their institution, and thereby history, by enacting their beliefs and cultures.

PART II: THE CASE STUDIES

The second part of this book, which consists of the three final empirical chapters, narrows the focus of the analysis to three specific Council proposals. Of these three, one passed, the Declaration on Religious Freedom, and two failed, conservative attempts to further elevate the status of the Blessed Virgin Mary and progressive attempts to allow the laity access to birth control. Together, these chapters illustrate how the eventfulness of the First Session explored in chapter 1, the variations in the bishops' priorities explored in chapter 2, and the progressives' organizational advantages explored in chapter 3 determined the success or failure of particular conciliar reforms.

Chapter 4 focuses on the Declaration on Religious Freedom, one of the most important reforms to come from the Council. The declaration in essence stated that the best form of secular government is one that allows people to worship as they please. The story of the declaration illustrates how legitimacy concerns were communicated to and understood by the bishops and theologians from Northern Europe and North America prior to the Council and ultimately led them to fight for the reform in the Council Hall.

Chapter 5 turns to the first of the two failed reforms examined in the book, an attempt by conservatives to further elevate and emphasize Catholic devotion to the Blessed Virgin Mary, long an essential part of Catholic worship in many parts of the world. A document on Mary that would assert her central and almost independent importance to Catholicism was proposed at the beginning of the Council. Further elevation of Mary's status within Roman Catholic doctrine would have essentially ended ecumenical dialogue. Progressive bishops therefore fought tenaciously to keep the Council from emphasizing Mary's importance, or indeed from officially bestowing on her any additional titles or accolades. In one of the hardest-fought battles of the Council, during which the pope was squarely allied with conservatives, progressives, largely because of their organizational advantages, succeeded in voting down the separate document and avoided most of the terms Protestants saw as problematic.

In the long run, the Council's decision about Mary resulted in a de-emphasis of Catholic devotion to her. Those most against de-emphasizing Mary (mainly bishops from Italy, Spain, and Portugal) claimed that doing so would be an affront to the laity in their countries. However, the final case study, presented in chapter 6, demonstrates that lay pressure was certainly not a definitive motivator for either conservatives from monopolistic environments like Italy and Spain or progressives from Northern Europe and North America. Both groups had ample evidence that their laity were very interested in birth control reform, but neither fought for it.

The fact that progressives from Northern Europe let the issue die, despite strong lay interest, demonstrates that ecumenical concerns really were at the forefront of their agenda. Protestants considered birth control to be a matter "internal to the Church." Feeling little ecumenical pressure to bring about birth control reform, progressives protested very little when Paul removed the issue from the Council's agenda.

The Data

A wide variety of primary and secondary sources helped me develop this explanation. Though the primary materials are described in detail in the appendices, because of their importance it is worth briefly describing them here. The first primary data source consists of transcripts of interviews with more than eighty of the most important bishops and theologians at the Council. The interviews were conducted by Rocco Caporale during the First and Second Sessions of the Council as part of his dissertation research in sociology at Columbia University. Using snowball sampling (and nine languages), Caporale asked respondents to identify five of the most important people at the Council and stopped when no new names were being volunteered.

I also use archival materials from six collections (see appendices A and B), which were in seven languages. The majority of these materials focus on progressive and conservative leaders and include formal minutes from meetings, letters and other personal correspondence, petitions, and other documents.[18]

Because both the archival and interview data admittedly omits the perspectives of the more than three thousand "rank and file" bishops who ultimately decided the outcome of Council reforms with their votes, I obtained the records of these votes from the Vatican Secret Archive (Archivio Segreto Vaticano), and had them entered into an electronic database. The vote tallies identify individual bishops, their dioceses, and their votes on ten of the most contentious council reforms. With these data I assess national trends that were previously obscured because the Vatican had only made summaries of the votes available to the public.

By the time it was over, the Council had enacted a wider variety of reforms than had ever been envisioned at its start. This is in no small part because a small group of progressive bishops stole the day, convinced the majority of bishops not only that change was needed but that it *was possible*, and, ultimately, turned Vatican II into the most significant religious event of the twentieth century. We now turn to the first few days, during which they accomplished this crucial goal and ensured that Vatican II would not be, as many had predicted, a rubber stamp Council.

PART

I

꩜

EXPLAINING
THE
COUNCIL

Chapter One

COLLECTIVE EFFERVESCENCE

AND THE HOLY SPIRIT

The Eventful First Session

Surely, we all have changed considerably . . . very much
so. The action of the Holy Spirit was very evident.
One could almost touch it everywhere.
—*Leo Jozef Cardinal Suenens, to Caporale*
after the First Session[1]

ON JANUARY 25, 1959, the Church and the world were taken by surprise when Pope John XXIII called "a general Council for the Universal Church" less than ninety days after his election.[2] This surprise extended to even the most prominent bishops, including the Council leaders interviewed by Caporale. Almost all of them echoed Bishop Thomas Roberts, who told him, "I never even dreamed of [a council] and never met anybody who did."[3] However, though surprised, Church leaders were not optimistic about the Council's potential.

Despite the fact that many bishops wished for change in the Church,[4] none really expected it to come about. They knew that though a council would be an exciting break from the ordinary, the fact that one was being held was no guarantee that change, especially progressive change, would occur. Most bishops were well aware that the most recent council, Vatican I, which had ended ninety years earlier, had done nothing but urge the Church in a more conservative direction by proclaiming the doctrine of papal infallibility.

Knowledge of this history combined with the current reality of Council preparations—which were almost completely controlled by conservatives in the Roman Curia—to make most participants less than optimistic that it would result in any significant progressive change, or that they would have any significant role in it. For example, American bishop Robert Tracy wrote:

I came to the Council not at all sure that I would have very much of an active part to play in it. I was not a professional theologian, canonist or Scripture scholar. Moreover, I had been brought up to regard with awe officials highly placed in the government of the Church. As an ordinary administrative bishop, I would not have been surprised to find that, at the Council, the Vatican experts would simply tuck the ball under their arms and run with it. . . . And so, I felt, that the subject matter of the Council had been fairly well settled in the Preparatory Commissions, over the past three years, and that we were called to Rome simply to exhibit our solidarity with the "approved authors" and with the Holy See.[5]

Neither progressive nor conservative leaders expected the Council to "last very long."[6] Most participants simply expected a "rubber-stamp council," as Archbishop Armando Fares, a conservative Italian, told Caporale: "At the first session, the majority of our bishops [were] unprepared. It was a new experience for us. . . . Many bishops . . . thought it would be a rubber-stamp council, something that would be read out to us, to be approved, a few decrees. . . .[7]"

Progressive leader Archbishop Marcos McGrath, a Domus Mariae representative for Panama who will appear quite often in later chapters, reflected on his initial low expectations for the Council:

> I well remember the perfunctory fashion in which our staff answered the first questionnaires sent . . . on what the Council might study. We simply did not take our participation seriously, nor that of most of the outlying Church. . . . We had become so accustomed to the highly centralized doctrinal and jurisdictional operation of the Church in our century, exercised by the Holy Father personally and through his Curia, that we could not awake quickly.[8]

What changed from the time that McGrath wrote his banal reply to the pope's request for direction and the time that he wrote this after the Third Session? The primary change was immaterial. It had nothing to do with the structure or organization of the Church. The Curia was still the central administrative office of the Church, the Church was still hierarchical, and the bishops still subject to the primacy of the pope. What had changed was his sense of the possibilities for the Council. Many bishops, whether progressive or conservative, began to believe that the Council could institute real changes in the Church, that indeed, it could be an "event."

EVENTFUL SOCIOLOGY AND VATICAN II

William Sewell, Jr.'s theories of historical events are essential to a complete understanding of the Council. In his seminal article, "Historical Events as Transformations of Structures: Inventing Revolution at the Bastille," Sewell defines a historical event as "(1) a ramified sequence of occurrences that (2) is recognized as notable by contemporaries, and that (3) results in a durable transformation of structures."[9] The Second Vatican Council certainly fits this definition.[10] Because it occurred over the course of three years and four sessions, the Council was, by its very nature, a "ramified sequence of occurrences." And, from the moment of John's announcement, it was recognized as notable by contemporaries. But all Roman Catholic councils have these two qualities. What differentiates Vatican II from most other councils is the number and magnitude of changes it wrought, what Sewell would call the "durable transformation of structures" it achieved.[11]

Sewell identifies three components to social structures: culture,[12] distributions of resources, and modes of power,[13] all of which were altered by the Council.

Culturally, the Council changed the very identity of the Church. José Casanova describes Vatican II as a "collective redefinition" that resulted in "the transformation of the Church from a state-centered to society-centered institution"; Michele Dillon calls it a "revolutionary event" that "redefined the church from a rigidly hierarchical, authoritarian, imperialist, antimodern institution to one that has become more relevant to and engaged in the modern world."[14] Perhaps the most well-known cultural change that resulted from the Council was the shift in the Church's identity from a "hierarchical teaching authority" to "the people of God"—with countless implications for the Church's doctrine, ritual, and practices.

Along with transforming the Church's culture, Vatican II, at least temporarily, profoundly altered the modes of power, and with them, the distribution of key resources within the Church. More than any other organization, the Roman Curia was the mode of power in the preconciliar Church. By specifying which doctrines "were legitimate, by determining which persons and groups have access to which resources, and by adjudicating conflicts that arise in the course of action,"[15] the Curia was in charge of "regulating" the Church.

By the time the First Session was over, the Curia's role in the Council had been significantly truncated, the authority of Council votes legitimated, and the Curia's hold on power greatly weakened. This chapter will demonstrate that if "we can speak of structures" when culture, resources, and modes of power "combine in an interlocking and mutually sustaining fashion to reproduce consistent streams of social practice,"[16] then the First Session inextricably changed the structures of the Roman Catholic Church.

None of these changes could have been predicted as the Council opened, under the steady hand and watchful gaze of the Curia. But a sudden rupture, "a surprising break with routine practices," changed the course of the Council by touching "off a chain of occurrences" and turned the Council from a likely rubber stamp of the Roman Curia's views to an historical event.[17] Ironically, this rupture was made possible by the Roman Curia's careful attempts during the preparation period to ensure that no change would come from the Council.

TRYING TO ENSURE A RUBBER-STAMP COUNCIL: THE CURIA ON THE EVE OF VATICAN II

After John's announcement, it took three years to complete the seemingly countless preparations needed to bring the almost three thousand bishops, cardinals, and theologians from around the world to Rome for the Council. Perhaps the most obvious issue that needed to be addressed was the absence of a concrete agenda for the Council. Now that the bishops were coming, what indeed should they discuss? During the first stage of preparations, Pope John XXII asked all of the Church leaders to write down their concerns and send them to the Vatican. Their letters were then condensed, categorized, and given to committees, which developed abbreviated statements of the Church's current stances on the issues raised in the letters.

On the surface, the plan seemed fair and efficient. Rather than arriving in Rome in a state of mass confusion, the bishops would come having already read documents which provided the platform for the Council's debates. If everything went as expected, they would be able to amend or approve the documents and return home within a few months. However, rather than providing a clear agenda for the Council, the preparatory documents (or schemas, as they were officially called) helped ensure that it would last for three years and four sessions rather than a few months.

The preparatory committees were comprised "entirely of acknowledged curialists," meaning members of the Roman Curia and their allies, individuals who were, by virtue of their positions as Church administrators, invested in keeping the Church as unchanged as possible. "Always hostile to councils," but faced with John's insistence that one be held, "the Curia had only one course open to it: to sabotage the Council; and they partly succeeded by securing the [preparatory commissions]".[18] Rather than assessing the possibilities for the Council, the preparatory documents simply reasserted Church doctrine and condemned those who had publicly questioned it.[19]

When progressive bishops received the preparatory documents, they were dismayed, finding that many of their ideas had been condemned or simply ignored, and they moved quickly during the very first day of the Council to counteract its conservative direction. Jan Brouwers, secretary and theologian to the Dutch episcopate, recalled this time: "Everyone deemed that accepting these documents would be fatal to the Council and the Church, and that this should be prevented from happening."[20]

In a tumultuous first few weeks, through a combination of protest events and hard-won votes, progressives succeeded in changing the course of the Council and building an organizational structure which would serve them well in the years ahead. The first of these events occurred on the day of the very first official assembly of the Council.

The Chain of Occurrences

The Motion for Free Elections: The Initial Rupture

On October 13, 1962, the 2,500 or so attendees converged on St. Peter's Cathedral, which had been completely revamped to provide seats and proper acoustics for the Council. (Approximately 2,500 bishops attended any given session, about 2,100 of whom regularly voted. The total number of bishops who ever attended a session and voted on an issue eventually reached 3,000, because of death and replacement over the three years of the Council.) The agenda for this first meeting of the Council was to elect the members of the ten key conciliar commissions, which would oversee drafting, revision, and promulgation of Council documents. Each bishop was to vote for sixteen members for each of the ten commissions, for a total of 160 places. Each bishop had been given ten cards, which contained sixteen lines for listing the names of those he wished to elect, and a list of the bishops who had served on the overwhelmingly conservative preparatory commissions that had drafted the "disastrous" preparatory schemas.

While each bishop could select other names from the booklet listing all of the more than 2,500 bishops serving at that time, the likelihood that a consensus could be reached that did more than mirror the preparatory commissions was not great. As the historians Guiseppe Alberigo and Joseph Komonchak note, each bishop "had to vote for 160 of his colleagues and it was not possible for each voter to come up with his own list out of so many possibilities. Given the lack of knowledge of particular bishops, each would have ended up reproducing to a greater or lesser degree the list of men on the preconciliar commissions."[21] Reelecting the preparatory commissions responsible for the conservative preparatory schemas would have essentially ensured the rubber-stamp council most progressives feared and to some degree expected, an outcome that was clearly the goal of the Curia, and, many felt, the reason why the elections were taking place so quickly.

As soon as the opening mass concluded, Pericle Cardinal Felici, the conservative secretary general of the Council,[22] and secretary of the Roman Curia, asked the bishops to cast their votes. His announcement was met with "great bewilderment" and "disorder" as the bishops attempted to get and give advice to and from their colleagues and write down their nominations. As this was going on, Achille Cardinal Liénart, a prominent French progressive leader who was a member of the Council of Presidents, and who had "great prestige among the bishops," turned to his colleague, Eugène Cardinal Tisserant, also French and chair of the Council of Presidents, who was seated on his right at the presidents' table, and said to him, "Eminence, it is impossible to vote in this way, without knowing anything about the best qualified candidates. If you will allow me, I would like to speak."[23]

Despite the fact that he was also dissatisfied with the plan and had "written to Felici the day before to complain," Tisserant refused Liénart's request, on the grounds that the agenda for that day did not include any discussion. Liénart, who was seated with the Council presidents and in the view of the vast majority of bishops, stood up anyway, took the microphone, and asked (in Latin)[24] "that the voting be postponed for a few days so that the fathers might have time to get to know one another." Liénart's motion was met with unexpected and "prolonged applause," and was immediately seconded by the prominent German cardinal Josef Frings, also a Council president, who stated that he spoke in the name of two other presidents.[25] The fact that Liénart's protest was immediately seconded by other powerful cardinals, and met by the assembly's vigorous applause,[26] helped to ensure that his actions would constitute a rupture, because the collective support made it difficult for his resistance to "be forcefully repressed, ignored, or explained away" by conservative leaders.[27]

After conferring with the Council of Presidents, Tisserant announced that the voting would be postponed for three days, until the following Tuesday. Because there were no other matters on the agenda for that day, the first meeting of the Council closed in less than fifteen minutes.

The importance of Liénart's motion cannot be overstated. In the end, the elected commissions were far more diverse, both ideologically and nationally, than they would have been had the preparatory commissions simply been reelected.[28] Not only did the postponement prevent conservatives from gaining control of the conciliar commissions but it had effects that would only become discernible in the months ahead. It indicated to all present that the Council might do more than simply rubber-stamp the Curia's agenda. At a very basic level, the Council could not be viewed as having revolutionary potential until it became clear that the Curia would have to yield to the authority of the bishops.[29] One American bishop described the effect Liénart's motion had on him:

It would be hard to overestimate the impact of what happened on the first day of business. . . . It was the first clear indication that the Council had no intention of allowing itself to be made a rubber-stamp for documents prepared in advance by Curia-dominated commissions; that, instead, it was to be a working Council insistent upon the adequate discussion of each item proposed for its consideration, upon full and free debate.[30]

Furthermore, by approving Liénart's motion, the Council of Presidents also legitimated an organizational form which would become crucial to progressives throughout the course of the Council, the episcopal conferences. Episcopal conferences (ECs) generally consisted of all of the bishops and members of the hierarchy in a given country, or even continent (as in the case with the Latin American episcopal conference, the Consejo Episcopal Latinoamericano, or CELAM), which met annually to discuss issues of common concern to the Church and nation or region. When the Council began, ECs were inchoate; most were not recognized by the Vatican, and some countries did not even have one.[31]

In his intervention, Liénart asked that the job of creating new lists of nominees be delegated to the episcopal conferences.[32] Thus, when the Council of Presidents approved his motion, ECs were officially given the function of nominating candidates for the Council commissions, an assignment which marked the beginning of their official and legitimate role in the Council.[33] ECs would prove to be an essential resource for the progressive leadership.

Though many heralded Liénart's decision to intervene on that first day of the Council as an impulsive act that was the work of the Holy Spirit, in actuality it was just the first and most public part of a larger progressive plan to circumvent the Curia's domination of the Council.[34] The second, and perhaps even more important, part of the plan was the result of French leaders' alliances with key Latin American bishops Manuel Larraín and Helder Câmara, both vice presidents of CELAM.[35] Together they decided to create an international group of bishops representing their ECs that would meet regularly to discuss Council procedures and proceedings, develop positions which could be supported by the majority of bishops, and strategize about ways they could bring their ideas to fruition. Their group, which is examined in detail in chapter 3, came to be named after the hotel where they met weekly, the Domus Mariae (House of Mary, DM hereafter), and quickly became a key part of the progressive organization and ultimate progressive outcome of the Council.[36]

As progressives were building their organizational strength and trying to elect more diverse drafting committees in order to prevent the Curia from having a lock on the Council proceedings and documents, the Council was turning to its main purpose: discussing, and supposedly approving, the preparatory documents. Thus, the final part of the progressive plan crystallized very quickly. In order to achieve any real changes, progressives needed to ensure that the preparatory schemas, which they felt "did not make the slightest positive contribution to the renewal of the Church," did not set the tone of the debates.[37] Given the pace at which events were moving forward, there was no time for any of the preparatory schemas to be revised significantly. But there was one that was much less problematic from their perspective than the rest: the Schema on the Liturgy.

The Schema on the Liturgy

The Schema on the Liturgy was different from the other preparatory schemas because the preparatory commission which drafted it was the only commission not dominated by curialists. Very few conservatives had any experience with liturgical reform, which was intended to make the Catholic mass more modern and participatory through a variety of changes, the most significant of which was eliminating the requirement that mass be said in Latin. Thus, when the commission was formed, it was dominated by individuals who had taken part in the movement for liturgical reform in Northern Europe, and the preparatory schema they wrote was quite progressive.

Though it was fifth in the bound copies of the preparatory documents the bishops received prior to the Council,[38] progressives quickly set about making sure that it became the first issue addressed by the Council.[39] The widely distributed Dutch commentary on the preparatory schemas reportedly called the liturgy schema "a very outstanding document" and proposed that it be discussed first, as it could be more expeditiously dealt with than the more problematic schemas.[40]

In what proved to be the second key moment of the First Session, and despite significant resistance from conservatives, the first, quite progressive draft, of the liturgical schema passed with overwhelming support toward the middle of the First Session.[41] Its relatively easy passage heartened progressive leaders, and thoroughly frightened conservatives. Some bishops felt that "the concession of the vernacular [language in the liturgy] alone could justify the Council as a great achievement."[42] Bishop Ramón Bogarín, a progressive leader from Paraguay, told Caporale: "The [constitution] on liturgy is marvelous. It gave . . . the bishops courage to speak because it was easy ground. . . . I don't know if this was planned or by chance. In any case, the Holy Spirit worked."[43] As it heartened progressives, the vote on the liturgy also seemed to prod some conservatives awake, as Italian Archbishop Fares told Caporale: "We were prepared to 'assist' at a council, not to participate actively. Then we saw that it was different with the discussion on the Liturgy."[44]

The Schema on the Sources of Revelation

After the discussion of the liturgy, the Council turned to a far more difficult topic, revelation. The key question was, To what extent were the
Church's traditions and teachings meant to interpret Christ's preaching as
it is revealed in the New Testament? In other words, how much authority
did the Church have to interpret Jesus' teachings? The Church had historically upheld its authority to interpret scripture by citing two sources of
revelation, scripture and tradition.

Progressives, particularly those for whom building bridges with the
ecumenical movement was a key concern, wanted to tone down the focus
on the two sources of revelation because Protestants had long argued that
the only valid source of revelation was scripture. As some Protestants
wrote in the *Ecumenical Review*, "The issue on Scripture and Tradition as
two distinct sources of revealed truth has been ardently debated ever since
Reformation times,"[45] and the proposed text "would have rendered the
ecumenical dialogue sterile on one capital point."[46] Other progressives,
some of whom had been involved in biblical archeology alongside Protestants, wanted the Church to allow historical, archeological, and anthropological research into discussions of the accuracy and origins of the Bible.[47]

To conservatives, even moderating the Church's stance on revelation was
tantamount to heresy. To them, the Bible was inerrant, historical or archeological research was risky and illegitimate, and God's word was clearly revealed through two sources: scripture and Church tradition. As Bishop
Domenico Valerii, an Italian conservative, told Caporale: "On Scripture,
some ideas are tantamount to a denial of the divinity of Christ. Little by little
they undermine the very faith in the Bible with all of these literary forms."[48]

The preparatory schema on revelation was wholly within the conservative framework, asserting two sources of revelation, stressing the inerrancy
of the Bible, and leaving no room for biblical archeology or other research. Progressive groups and theologians began writing responses, and
entirely new schemas, soon after it was distributed, and more than fifteen
hundred copies of these critiques were reportedly handed out to the bishops in Latin, English, and French as they began arriving in Rome.[49] By this
point in the Council, the DM had officially formed, and revelation was a
key issue at their very first meeting. The minutes state:

> It clearly appears that *De Fontibus Revelationis* [the schema on revelation] in
> its presentation and content, does not satisfy a large number of the bishops.
> It would be preferable if . . . a vote rejects it. A counter-schema, coming from
> a group of episcopal conferences, is submitted to all participants.[50]

After five days of sometimes heated and often repetitive speeches, the
Council presidents asked the assembly to vote on whether to continue the

discussion or to return the schema to the newly elected committees for revision.[51] Though the vote demonstrated that a substantial majority was in favor of significant revision (1,368 voted to send the schema back to the drafting table; 868 voted to continue discussing it), progressives were 105 votes short of the required two-thirds majority. At this point, many observers felt that "the Council seemed destined to be plunged into a crisis from which there was no return."[52] A majority of bishops had demonstrated that they were in favor of progressive reform, but that majority was not big enough for a decisive outcome.

However, in what would be his last, and perhaps most important, intervention, John rescued "the Council from this impasse." The day after the voting, Felici read a statement from the pope which stated that "yielding to the wishes of many," he had decided to refer the matter to a mixed commission made up of members from both the Doctrinal Commission (the committee in charge of drafting schemas on doctrine) and the Secretariat for Promoting Christian Unity, the SCU (the organization in charge of communicating with the Protestant observers at the Council).[53]

Along with allowing a much more progressive statement on revelation to come from the Council, John's intervention had a number of important effects. First, was a key "rearticulating action"[54] which validated the supreme authority of the Council once and for all in most participants' eyes and concretely established the rules that the Council would follow. Chief among these was the fact that the bishops could and would reject a schema if it was deemed unacceptable. Historian Jan Grootaers notes that the DM's "first concern" was "to improve the procedure and efficiency of Vatican II's working method"—above all, given the state of most of the preparatory schemas, by establishing "the possibility of giving the Council the means to reject a project discussed *in aula* [the Council hall]." This was an essential issue because the Curia "kept on repeating" that the preparatory "schemas had been approved by the Pope himself," and therefore "could not be rejected by the Council."[55] Thus, while the vote on the liturgy demonstrated that a majority of the bishops were progressively inclined, it was not until a majority *rejected* a schema that it became clear that their votes were binding, not just recommendations the drafting committees would "take into account" as many members of the Curia insisted.[56]

The Effects: Collective Effervescence and the Holy Spirit

Finally, and perhaps most importantly, the outcome of the schema on the sources of revelation heartened progressives and solidified the newfound sense among Council participants that change was possible. The extent to which this "chain of occurrences" affected Council participants became clearer as time passed and the Council progressed, with many participants reflecting on them as the Council drew to a close, as did Bishop Ernest Primeau, the American DM representative, who wrote:

> It is very difficult for me—I should really say nearly impossible—to compare my thoughts, my feelings and my hopes on the eve of my first trip in 1960 with those I experienced as I prepared to leave Rome five years later after the formal closing of the Council. As I prayed Pope John's beautiful prayer to the Holy Spirit for the success of the Council, I could not perceive, I must admit, not even darkly, the silhouette of the adaptation and renewal that was to come. . . . My memory is filled with highlights that made Vatican II what it is: the epochal intervention of Cardinal Liénart on the first day requesting a delay in the voting, the crucial debate and vote on the schema on Divine Revelation followed by the decision of Pope John. . . . Each event, one could almost say, each day, contributed to my development, my growth.[57]

As this statement from Bishop Primeau suggests, these events had a profound effect on Council participants. Bishop Roberts told Caporale that the first sessions of the Council[58] had changed him "from a pessimistic to an optimistic frame of mind."[59] American theologian Fr. Thomas Stransky wrote Bishop Primeau between the First and Second Sessions: "I am more optimistic than ever. Now there are enough excellently revised drafts . . . to offset discouragement and to prevent impatient rubber-stamping of the weak schemata. . . . The Vicar of Christ with his college of bishops is alert and the Holy Spirit blows strongly!"[60] The prominent German Catholic theologian Bernard Haring told Caporale, "The Council gave us all courage. If you are alone you do not trust in yourself, but if you see that you are not in the minority, because the whole Church is with you, then you have more confidence."[61]

By the end of the First Session, progressives were so confident that it became common to refer to conservatives in general, and the Curia in particular, as "the minority," as Bishop Bogarín did when expressing his optimism to Caporale: "By now, we could say that the minority is nonexistent. They are very few and present no danger because there is a strong majority."[62]

Certainly, the successive victories they had witnessed during the First Session were key to progressives' growing confidence. However, another important factor was often mentioned: by coming to the Council, they had realized that others also wanted change. As Bishop Bogarín told Caporale: "Last December I gave a press conference and nervously dared to say a few things that made me shake. Now those same things would be just plain common talk in everybody's mouths. . . . At that time, this was a scandal and my nuncio in Paraguay was very angry."[63] Bishop Warren Boudreaux, a newly appointed American bishop, told Caporale, "Although I hoped changes would take place, I thought it was impossible," but once the Council got underway, "I felt a new source of joy. *Above all, I feel that I am not alone any more.*" Boudreaux attributed his feeling of optimism to his "contacts with other bishops," which he said had given him "a new sense of strength and better understanding." He closed his interview with Caporale saying, "I am ready to help any bishop and give him all I can."[64]

Like Boudreaux, Câmara attributed his ability to deal with the events that unfolded early in the First Session to his increased contacts with other bishops:[65]

> There was a crisis in the Church. To begin with, we had wrong ideas of each other, and we did not know each other. Especially during the first few days of the Council this was very evident. Even the list of members for the commissions showed this. The contacts, the conferences, gave us a continental experience.[66]

Other respondents made similar statements, saying that face-to-face contacts with other bishops had given them a greater "sense of the Church" or made them feel the Church was more "alive."[67]

Though their descriptions varied, Caporale's data demonstrate that the bishops were experiencing an overwhelming sense of community, what Victor Turner refers to as *communitas*,[68] and Émile Durkheim called "collective effervescence." Collective effervescence is "the state in which men find themselves when . . . they believe they have been swept up into a world entirely different from the one they have before their eyes."[69] It is a euphoric state, a result of individuals gathering together, in this case, to worship, to discuss, and to engage in changing an ancient institution in which they all fervently believed. Summing it up well just after the Council's opening ceremonies, the progressive cardinal Giacomo Lercaro, archbishop of Bologna, wrote that he "certainly never felt so absorbed into the Church of God as I did today."[70] Most of the progressive leaders who benefited from their contacts with other bishops, like Câmara, were active in organizations like the Domus Mariae and those episcopal conferences where lively theological discussions were taking place.

One reason these interpersonal contacts were important was that it helped them to deal with the uncertainty that change brought with it. Sewell argues that when "articulations between different structures become profoundly dislocated," actors "are beset with insecurity: they are unsure about how to get on with life."[71] In a sense, the First Session, particularly the first few weeks, was, in the words of Victor Turner a "liminal period,"[72] a time of great potential and great uncertainty when "hierarchies momentarily evaporate and the celebrants experience a profound sense of community."[73] Bishop Michal Klepacz, a progressive from Poland, described his initial insecurity, and how it eventually gave way to confidence about the Council's direction:

> At first we did not know what we wanted in the Council, nor did we know the method to follow. There was hesitation, "How do you go about working with these people?" Nobody knew, not even the Pope or the Cardinals. There has been a great development and evolution in the thought and in the attitudes of the Bishops. They [have] now begun to think that . . . great fruit [will come from the Council]. Before they were somewhat skeptical about it. Now they have greater faith.[74]

It may come as no surprise, given that "symbolic interpretation is part and parcel of the historical event,"[75] that many bishops articulated these feelings in relation to the Holy Spirit, an extremely important part of Roman Catholic belief.[76] Often represented by a dove, it is everywhere and yet intangible. "The spirit, the personal center of the church, is the basis of the church's authority." It represents the idea that "the risen Christ is alive and powerfully present in human history." It is commonly believed that "the spirit operates in the world through the signs of the times."[77] As a result many everyday occurrences can be seen by the faithful as the work of the Holy Spirit. Therefore, it is not surprising that though Caporale never explicitly asked his respondents about the Holy Spirit, many of them (more than a quarter of his sample, approximately twenty bishops) invoked it during their interviews.

For example, French bishop Léon Elchinger told Caporale that the greatest gains of the first sessions had been "The sense of ecumenism, the catholicity of the Church. Now we understand the problems and difficulties of others, and we can perceive how the Holy Spirit animates the whole church."[78] Bishop Miguel Miranda y Gómez, the DM representative for Mexico, told Caporale that he was sure he was "not the only one to note that we felt the presence of the Holy Spirit very deeply."[79] Ecuadorien bishop Leonidas Proaño confidently told Caporale that "the Holy Spirit brings out the truth and makes it triumph."[80] Many attributed their experience of personal change to the Holy Spirit. For example, McGrath told Caporale that the views being "ventilated at the Council"

> . . . went from being the ideas of a few leaders to becom[ing] the ideas of the majority of the council fathers. I was one of those whose thinking was rather backward. *Now I feel very different: then I thought of them as "those crazy people." Now I have accepted their ideas.* This is the work of the Holy Spirit.[81]

The belief that the Holy Spirit was guiding the Council had an interesting twist. It seemed to have created a pressure for consensus, especially when progressives found themselves in the minority.[82] For example, Colombian bishop Pablo Correa León said:

> Yes, I have been defeated sometimes, but I believe that I must say what I feel in conscience. After voting, I accept the decision of the Holy Spirit and agree with the majority. I accept the decision naturally without internal conflict because I believe that God wants it.[83]

Moderate Italian bishop Luigi Rinaldi explained to Caporale: "The minority invariably thinks that they are right. However, after the results of the voting, each bishop questions himself: 'Am I with the Church or against it?' "[84]

CONSERVATIVES: WAITING FOR THE HOLY SPIRIT

By the end of the First Session, "in something like a *coup d'église*, those who had presided over the preparation [of the Council] were marginalized and those who had then been marginalized would emerge as conciliar leaders."[85] Though they would not attempt to remedy their situation by organizing in the way progressives had for many months, it was clear to the Curia and their allies that things were not turning out as expected. "Accustomed to speaking, while other listened with respect,"[86] the Curia now found that no one was listening at all, and even worse, some were explicitly questioning their authority to speak.

An official indication of this shift came with Paul's reform of the Curia just before the Second Session, which was met by a willingness to disparage the Curia and to rejoice in its loss of power among the bishops. For example, Indian bishop Leonard Raymond complained to Caporale about "a mentality born of the Curia system," and went on to explain that in the past "The Curia . . . thought of themselves as the people who would save the Church and protect it. All was tinged by this mentality. They understood that the Church is a beleaguered city to be defended. Now this situation is gone but these people will not change their mentalities."[87]

Such radical views of the Curia, so frankly expressed, would have been unthinkable prior to the Council, and it seems likely that the events of the First Session allowed Raymond to feel comfortable expressing them. As he told Caporale later in the interview, "I have observed the beginning of a change in leadership: The Curia is losing it and it [is] being transferred to a larger body of bishops."[88] Bishop José Vicente Távora, a progressive Brazilian, told Caporale that "the Curia is an instrument of coercion."[89] Bishop Adam Kozlowiecki, a progressive from Rhodesia, alluded to the Curia as "some bishops [who] . . . think they know everything."[90] By the end of the Second Session, the change was so complete that Henri DeLubac, a prominent French theologian, told Caporale,

"Above all, the main gain [of the first two sessions] was the dis-identification of the Curia from the Pope and the allowance of criticism of the Curia, and the abuses there, without touching the Papacy and its position."[91]

In sum, the three events of the First Session changed the Council from one that many thought would be a rubber stamp of the Curia's views to one in which the participants felt comfortable openly criticizing them. As a result of this shift, and in contrast to the euphoria and excitement progressive leaders described during and after the First Session, reports from conservatives were downright depressing. By the end of the First Session, conservative leader and member of the Roman Curia Alfredo Cardinal Ottaviani was reported to be "in terrible shape." Conservative leaders "had been told not to talk" and were reportedly "quite discouraged."[92]

It will come as no surprise that the Curia and their allies were neither feeling nor invoking the Holy Spirit at the Council. Only one conservative Caporale interviewed, the Italian cardinal Giuseppe Siri, mentioned the Holy Spirit. After stating that none of the theological viewpoints expressed were new or seemed valid to him, he remarked: "These are my impressions of the Council. The final word is truth and it can never lose. The Holy Spirit has a way of overcoming even these difficulties and situations, and you will see that, in the end, truth will prevail."[93] Archbishop Frane Franic, a conservative from Yugoslavia, made his frustration evident: "I am disappointed. I expected more from the Council. The periti [Council theologians] used too much propaganda and lobbying to get the vote of the Bishops."[94] In fact, rather than experiencing the Council as collective effervescence, Franic likened it to evil coercion. Caporale noted that during his interview, Franic "recalled the brainwashing and trials under the communists and said that this helped him to understand what was happening in the commissions and the Council, too."[95]

Given this perspective it is not surprising that almost none of the conservatives Caporale interviewed reported feeling conflicted about going "against the Church." For example, Valerii told Caporale, "Yes, sometimes I voted with the minority, but I feel neither guilt nor pain for it."[96] Because they did not see the events that transpired as the work of the Holy Spirit, conservatives generally felt no guilt over disagreeing with their fellow bishops.

CONCLUSION: THE TRANSFORMATION OF STRUCTURES

When John XXIII announced that there would be a council, most Church leaders, even those who had hoped and prayed for change, were fairly pessimistic about what it might achieve. These low expectations went through a metamorphosis during the First Session as a chain of occurrences shifted the modes of power in the Church, convinced the bishops that the Council could result in real historic changes, and created a collective effervescence that all but the very conservative bishops of the Curia embraced.

Just as French citizens adapted "an existing ritual form . . . to a very different situation" after they took the Bastille and marched in a traditional triumphal procession to indicate a new power had risen,[97] the bishops invoked the traditional symbol of the Holy Spirit to legitimate and embrace the changes taking place at the Council. Because their "interpretation of what was happening was a crucial ingredient of what happened,"[98] the fact that the majority of bishops saw these changes as a holy event was key to their legitimacy, and therefore to their profound consequences.

Conservative members of the Curia, however, rejected such interpretations of the events. To put it bluntly, they did not see the hand of God in them; they saw them as the work of men, men with political motives. Thus, *how* each group interpreted the events was crucial to their reaction to them, just as, of course, their initial predispositions determined that interpretation.

It is in the delegitimation of the Curia and in the legitimation of the authority of the assembled bishops that we can most clearly see the interwoven nature of culture, resources, and modes of power, a complex relationship Sewell calls the "duality of structure."[99] As the modes of power shifted from the Curia to the assembly, and the Curia lost and the assembly gained legitimacy, the resources that would matter changed too. When the Curia was in power, access to its members was a key resource. Once their power was checked, access to the voting bishops, the assembly at large, became the key resource for those who wanted to determine the outcome of the Council. It was this resource progressives focused on mobilizing, and it was to this same resource that conservatives attempted to deny legitimacy.

Just as the taking of the Bastille and its subsequent occurrences were but one, albeit very important and even crucial, part of the larger event of the French Revolution, Liénart's intervention and the chain of occurrences which followed during the First Session were but the first links in a much longer chain of events which would ultimately come to an end three years later. Because of the path-dependent nature of the Council, these initial ruptures changed the modes of power in the Church and were essential to creating the possibility for change. But they cannot, on their own, explain the direction or magnitude of the change. For that, we must turn to new questions, and new chapters.

Chapter Two

WHO WANTED WHAT AND WHY

AT THE SECOND VATICAN COUNCIL?

Toward a Theory of Religious Change

As the First Session closed and it became apparent that real change might come from the Council, progressives turned to the complicated task of figuring out what kind of change they most wanted. They quickly realized that though consensus had been fairly easy to achieve on the issue of modernizing the liturgy (after all, Latin was no one's native tongue), and though progressives were, by definition, open to accommodating the Church to the modern world in some way, there was little agreement among the different progressive groups about what should be accommodated and how.

The key bone of contention was to what extent they should prioritize rapprochement with Protestants in order to engage the ecumenical movement. The three distinct groups of progressive bishops had different views on this issue, particularly in regard to whether it should be prioritized over other concerns, such as social justice or reforms oriented toward helping to keep and attract more laity.

The first, and most well-known, group of progressive bishops at the Council, those from Northern Europe and North America, felt that building better relations with Protestants was the most important issue the Council would address and prioritized ecumenical concerns throughout the course of the Council. Their consistent and persistent calls for ecumenism, the backbone of the "new theology" they developed, ultimately became the "master frame" of the Council.[1]

The second important group of progressives at the Council, those from Latin America, initially saw this agenda as strange, if not downright foolhardy. Actively dealing with Protestant missionaries' increasingly successful attempts to win souls away from the Catholic Church, they were not inclined to better relations with Protestants and preferred instead to focus on a message of social justice, ameliorating poverty, and ministering to the poor and unchurched.

The third major group of progressive bishops at the Council, those from "missionary countries" in Africa and Asia, saw wisdom in both of their allies' priorities. As bishops in developing countries where the Roman

Catholic Church was actively trying to grow, missionary bishops prioritized reforms which they felt would make their admittedly foreign religion more accessible and intelligible to the populations in their countries and help alleviate poverty. And, as bishops working in diverse societies with missionaries from other, mainly Protestant, religious denominations, African and Asian bishops were supportive of bettering Catholic-Protestant relations.

Eventually, though the Northern European ecumenical agenda became the hallmark of the Council, these three progressively oriented groups formed an alliance that helped them achieve reforms which were important to all of them. Such collaboration took impressive organizational strength and many months, nearly the entire Second and Third Sessions of the Council, to achieve. However, before we get to the story of *how* they did this, we first must understand *what* was at stake for each group of progressives, and conservatives as well, and, perhaps most importantly, *why* each group's views of the Council, and indeed the Church, were so different.

This chapter explores the differences among the bishops at the Council (including the three groups of progressives and the staunch conservatives from Italy and Spain),[2] with the goal of answering a simple, but key, sociological question. That is, who wanted what, and why? In other words, what patterns can be observed among the interests and goals, or what I call *organizational strategies*, of the bishops at the Council? Understanding the forces and factors that shape religious leaders' orientations to religious change is crucial to understanding the paths different religious institutions ultimately take in their dealings with the modern world.

My answer to the question of who wanted what and why integrates theories from the sociology of religion with theories from organizational and economic sociology. I argue that in order to predict religious leaders' organizational strategies, sociologists of religion must broaden their understanding of the factors that affect them. In particular, sociologists of religion must recognize that, like other organizations, legitimacy concerns are at the heart of most organizational processes within religious institutions.

MEASURING ORGANIZATIONAL STRATEGIES

Throughout this chapter, I use two early and highly contentious votes from the Council as indications of the bishops' openness to various organizational strategies. I first analyze the vote on the Sources of Revelation, a key part of the eventfulness of the First Session described in chapter 1, and an issue around which progressives were united. The majority of Northern European, Latin American, and missionary bishops voted to reject the conservative preparatory schema.

I then analyze the first vote pertaining to the Blessed Virgin Mary, an issue which was much more contentious, in no small part because it deeply divided progressives. This vote, which occurred during the Second Session, centered on the general question of how the Council would address issues pertaining to Mary, namely, whether devotion to her would be emphasized by giving her own conciliar document or deemphasized by making the Council's main discussion of Mary appear as merely a chapter in the document on the Church.

Mary was a contentious issue (one which is discussed in much greater detail in chapter 5) because devotion to her "has been a hallmark of the Catholic tradition"[3] and has often served to differentiate Catholics and Protestants. At the time of the Council, conservatives wanted to further elevate Mary's status in the Church, but progressives from Northern Europe and North America resisted these efforts because their central goal for the Council was rapprochement with Protestants. Many Protestants already saw Catholic devotion to Mary as inappropriate, even verging on the heretical, her status among Catholics often seeming to equal, or even surpass, that of Jesus. Thus, "toning down" Catholic devotion to Mary was an important goal for Catholic ecumenists.

These two competing expectations for the Council (the conservative view, which held that the Council should reaffirm and uphold distinct Catholic doctrine and the progressive view, which wanted to deemphasize differences between Catholics and Protestants) confronted each other over Mary. Ultimately, this vote was the closest of all of the votes taken during the Council (1,114 to 1,074), with progressives winning by only 40 votes.[4]

Thus, together, the vote on the Sources of Revelation and the first vote on the Blessed Virgin Mary reveal important differences between conservatives and progressives, as well as within the three groups of progressives. However an important caveat is necessary. These two votes provide only a partial picture of the patterns that emerged during the Council; only those that determined who would vote for a particular measure once it made it to the table. But the issue of *what made it to the table* to be voted on is also an important part of a sociological explanation of the Council. However, the patterns affecting that issue cannot be clearly seen until we look at the case study of birth control in chapter 6. This is because Northern Europeans prioritized reforms with ecumenical implications over those, such as birth control, which were important primarily to their constituents. Thus issues without ecumenical implications were much more likely to "die in committee" and never make it to the table. While the evidence for this is not presented until chapter 6, the findings and implications from the case study of birth control informed my theoretical conclusions and are thus a part of the theoretical argument presented in this chapter.

The Four Groups of Bishops and Their Votes

Conservatives from European Catholic Monopolies: Unthreatened and Unwavering

Bishops from Western Europe, particularly those from Italy, Portugal, and Spain, as well as those from Ireland, were infamous for their staunch conservativism at the Council, and for in general being against any sort of accommodation to the modern world. Led by Italy and Spain (which together constituted more than 15 percent of the voting bishops at the Council), and dominated by the Roman Curia, these men were used to being the center of power in the Church.

As religious leaders in monopolistic religious environments, whose home churches were prospering and who were central to the administration of the universal Church, bishops from Western Europe cared deeply about primarily one thing: protecting the status quo. Irish bishop William Conway eloquently described monopolistic bishops' take on reform to Caporale:

> Ireland is deeply religious, 95% practice. . . . [It] has not been faced with problems of mass paganism and defections and new mores. Many suggestions brought up in the Council have been forced upon bishops [for these reasons]. In Ireland we don't feel the same pressure as in other countries; obviously our situation is different.[5]

Though relatively few in number, Catholic-dominated countries have long constituted the administrative center of the Church, and thus the hierarchy from these countries made up a sizable proportion of the episcopate, as table 2.1 demonstrates—approximately 20 percent of the voting bishops at the Council.

With close ties to the Roman Curia, bishops from these monopolistic countries presented a formidable group of opponents for the more progressively oriented bishops at the Council. This is in no small part because, as table 2.1 demonstrates, the bishops from these countries were nearly uniform in their conservativism, with the vast majority of them voting conservatively on the schema concerning revelation and the issue of whether the Blessed Virgin Mary would be accorded her own conciliar document.

Northern Europe and North America: Focusing on Colleagues, not Constituents

Bishops from Northern Europe, and to a lesser extent North America, distinguished themselves at the Council as the bearers of a "new theology."[6] This new theology had many parts, but its single unifying factor was

TABLE 2.1

Voting Patterns among Bishops from State-Supported European Monopolies[a] (by the Number of Bishops in Each Country)

Country[b]	Number of Bishops	Percent of all Bishops (n = 2,594)	Percent Catholic 1965	Change in Percent Catholic (65–55)	Percent Voting Progressively on Revelation[c]	Percent Voting Progressively on Mary[d]
Italy	367	14.0	99	0	19	12
Spain	89	3.4	100	0	33	5
Ireland[e]	32	1.2	94	0	40	42
Portugal	28	1.0	92	−4	32	5
Total[f]	519	20.0	97[g]	−1	23	12

[a] This table includes only those European countries where the Roman Catholic Church was the state religion or "principal" religion as of 1955. I have included Portugal in this category because, though it has had a formal separation between church and state since 1910, in practice Roman Catholicism still functioned as the established religion of the nation. This decision is supported by earlier versions of the *National Catholic Almanac*, which noted in 1942, for example, that "Catholicism is the principal religion" of Portugal.

[b] Country designations and the number of bishops in each country reflect the Church's categorization in the *Acta* (1960–61), and thus represent the total number of bishops serving in a given country at the beginning of the Council, not necessarily the number who went to the Council or who voted on any particular issue. Figures for the percentage of the population that was Catholic are from the *National Catholic Almanac* (1956 and 1966). See appendix B for more information on the voting data.

[c] First Session, November 20, 1962, *Suffragationes*, vol. 1, no. 5.

[d] Second Session, October 29, 1963, *Suffragationes*, vol. 19, no. 97.

[e] Includes Northern Ireland.

[f] To protect the bishops' anonymity (as per my agreement with the Vatican Secret Archive), all countries where 100 percent of the bishops voted one way (whether conservatively or progressively) were removed from the table, but these bishops and their votes were included in the totals. On this table, the totaled figures thus include three bishops from Malta.

[g] So that more populous countries did not skew the statistic, this figure was calculated by averaging the percent of the population of each country that was Catholic, not by adding the total Catholic population for all of the countries together and dividing by the total population.

the new and, some certainly felt, even heretical idea that Protestants and Catholics were both Christians and should be working together in the world rather than fighting with or competing against each other.[7] As Archbishop John Heenan of England stated in his intervention on the schema on ecumenism, "The renewal of the Church requires a true religious dialogue. Genuine interest in the mission of the Church demands that we undertake a fuller and frequent dialogue with all Christians of whatever denomination."[8]

Table 2.2 demonstrates that these ecumenically oriented bishops constituted fully a quarter of the voting episcopate and came from a variety of countries, all of which had two important qualities: they were (1) industrialized, politically and religiously stable countries (note in table 2.2 that the percentage of Catholics in these countries does not change greatly between 1955 and 1965), (2) in which the Roman Catholic Church was not the state religion, either because of formal religious freedom, as was the case with France[9] and the United States, or because the state religion was Protestant.

Table 2.2 demonstrates that, in the aggregate, exactly the same proportion of these bishops (78 percent) voted progressively on revelation and on Mary. On any issue connected to ecumenical concerns, in fact, more than three-quarters of these bishops always voted progressively.[10]

However, while these bishops were progressive, they were not equally interested in all issues. The case study of birth control presented in chapter 6 demonstrates that they prioritized reforms connected to the ecumenical movement at the expense of reforms that were important to the laity. Latin American and missionary bishops were more invested in reforming birth control policy than bishops from Northern Europe and North America, who simply let the matter drop, despite the fact that the laity in Northern Europe and North America were even more interested in this issue than laities in Latin America, Africa, and Asia. Thus, Northern Europeans and North Americans had a very clear agenda, the focus of which was bettering relations with Protestants.

Latin American Progressives: Saving the Poor and Their Church

With almost 600 bishops, or more than 22 percent of the voting episcopate, Latin Americans were an important group at the Council. Table 2.3 demonstrates that the Church enjoyed the same monopolistic advantages in many Latin American countries as it did in the European countries shown in table 2.1. In fact, in no small part because of the dominance of the Church in Latin America, many initially expected the Latin American bishops to be "a monolithic group of conservatives."[11]

However, despite their monopolistic situation, Latin Americans, unlike Italians and Spaniards, were progressive. Indeed, many Latin American

TABLE 2.2

Voting Patterns among Bishops from Non-Monopolistic Countries[a] (by the Number of Bishops in Each Country)

Country[b]	Number of Bishops	Percent of all Bishops (n = 2,594)	Percent Catholic 1965	Change in Percent Catholic (65–55)	Percent Voting Progressively on Revelation[c]	Percent Voting Progressively on Mary[d]
United States	216	8.3	23	+2	66	78
France[e]	131	5.0	83	−1	92	90
Canada	90	3.5	46	+1	79	65
Germany[f]	54	2.0	48	+2	94	98
Australia	39	1.5	23	+5	62	34
Great Britain	35	1.3	8	+1	67	81
Belgium	26	1.0	95	−3	86	85
Austria	17	0.6	85	−4	89	86
Switzerland	12	0.5	40	−1	71	60
Greece	5	0.2	1	NA	57	50
New Zealand	5	0.2	14	+3	75	67
Total[g]	663	25.5	36[h]	0	78	78

[a] This table includes only non-monopolistic countries where the Church had been long established. For the non-monopolistic countries where that was not the case, see tables 2.4 and 2.5.

[b] Country designations and the number of bishops in each country reflect the Church's categorization in the *Acta* (1960–61), and thus represent the total number of bishops serving in a given country at the beginning of the Council, not necessarily the number who went to the Council or who voted on any particular issue. Figures for the percentage of the population that was Catholic are from the *National Catholic Almanac* (1956 and 1966). See appendix B for more information on the voting data.

[c] First Session, November 20, 1962, *Suffragationes*, vol. 1, no. 5.

[d] Second Session, October 29, 1963, *Suffragationes*, vol. 19, no. 97.

[e] France, Belgium, and Austria are included on this table even though the majority of their population was Catholic because they had formal religious freedom at the time of the Council.

[f] Includes East Germany.

[g] To protect the bishops' anonymity (as per my agreement with the Vatican Secret Archive), all countries where 100 percent of the bishops voted one way (whether conservatively or progressively) were removed from the table, but these bishops and their votes were included in the totals. On this table, the totaled figures thus include twenty-four bishops from Cyprus, Denmark, Finland, Gibraltar, Holland, Iceland, Luxembourg, Monaco, Norway, and Sweden.

[h] So that more populous countries did not skew the statistic, this figure was calculated by averaging the percent of the population of each country that was Catholic, not by adding the total Catholic population for all of the countries together and dividing by the total population.

TABLE 2.3
Voting Patterns among Bishops from Latin American Countries (by the Number of Bishops in Each Country)

Country[a]	Number of Bishops	Percent of all Bishops (n = 2,594)	Percent Catholic 1965	Change in Percent Catholic (65–55)	Percent Voting Progressively on Revelation[b]	Percent Voting Progressively on Mary[c]
Brazil	167	6.4	93	−2	70	50
Colombia*	54	2.1	97	−1	65	33
Mexico	53	2.0	94	−2	55	17
Argentina*	50	1.9	88	−2	70	27
Philippines*[d]	40	1.5	86	+4	68	36
Peru*	36	1.4	95	−1	48	45
Chile	25	1.0	88	−3	79	86
Venezuela	24	0.9	93	−3	75	63
Ecuador	22	0.8	94	−2	27	33
Bolivia*	21	0.8	94	−2	64	59
Paraguay*	10	0.4	92	−3	70	64
Uruguay	7	0.3	67	−12	85	58
El Salvador	6	0.2	98	−2	33	50

Honduras	6	0.2	96	−1	50	40
Nicaragua	6	0.2	94	0	50	17
Costa Rica*	5	0.2	76	−21	67	17
Panama	4	0.2	73	−16	75	80
Total[e]	570	22.0	88[f]	−4	66	44

* Catholicism was the official state religion or given special status (*1956 National Catholic Almanac*; see also Schmidt, *The Roman Catholic Church in Modern Latin America*, pp. 11–16).

[a] Country designations and the number of bishops in each country reflect the Church's categorization in the *Acta* (1960–61), and thus represent the total number of bishops serving in a given country at the beginning of the Council, not necessarily the number who went to the Council or who voted on any particular issue. Figures for the percentage of the population that was Catholic are from the *National Catholic Almanac* (1956 and 1966). See appendix B for more information on the voting data.

[b] First Session, November 20, 1962, *Suffragationes*, vol. 1, no. 5.

[c] Second Session, October 29, 1963, *Suffragationes*, vol. 19, no. 97.

[d] Colonized by Spain during the same period, the Philippines shared more similarities with Latin America than with Asia, including a population the majority of which was Catholic and a government which granted "special status" to the Church (Godement, *The New Asian Renaissance*, 29).

[e] To protect the bishops' anonymity (as per my agreement with the Vatican Secret Archive), all countries where 100 percent of the bishops voted one way (whether conservatively or progressively) were removed from the table, but these bishops and their votes were included in the totals. On this table, the totaled figures thus include 34 bishops from British Honduras, Curacao, Dominican Republic, Guadeloupe and Martinique, Guatemala, Haiti, and Puerto Rico.

[f] So that more populous countries did not skew the statistic, this figure was calculated by averaging the percent of the population of each country that was Catholic, not by adding the total Catholic population for all of the countries together and dividing by the total population.

leaders became well known as progressive visionaries. A first indication of the progressive inclinations of the Latin American bishops is presented on table 2.3, which demonstrates that two-thirds of them voted progressively on the issue of revelation.[12]

Despite their progressive leanings, however, Latin Americans had difficulty supporting ecumenically oriented reforms, particularly those which watered down Catholic doctrines they thought were important to the laity in their countries. More than half of them voted to devote a separate conciliar document to the Blessed Virgin Mary—in short, they voted conservatively on this issue.

Their ambivalence toward ecumenism put them in conflict with other progressives, especially those from Europe. As Bishop McGrath of Panama, an active leader in CELAM and the DM, told Caporale: "For central European theologians the renewal of the Church is a preparation for reunion of Christianity, but in Central America the problem is quite different. Here, the question is to build a bridge with the modern world. This is our problem."[13]

The Missionary Church in Africa and Asia

In contrast to bishops from Latin America, bishops from "missionary countries" in Africa and Asia were progressive on all fronts. Their contingent was just as large as the Latin American, and, as tables 2.4 and 2.5 indicate, they constituted a central voting bloc during the Council, voting progressively on both revelation and Mary.

Missionary bishops' openness to both ecumenical reforms and those oriented toward social justice and the amelioration of poverty is well represented by the following quote from the African leader, Bishop Blomjous, from Tanganyika.

> The Church is not destined simply to save men for heaven but also to humanize man's social life, to inspire a sense of personal responsibility in all men, and to foster a social order that sins less flagrantly against divine justice. . . . There should be a common Christian confrontation with the modern industrialized world.[14]

Thus, there were four distinct groups of bishops at the Council, three of which were open to reform, but each with its own interests and priorities: Northern Europeans and North Americans were focused on ecumenical concerns, Latin Americans were focused on reforms that would help stem the tide of lay defections to Protestantism and Marxism, and missionary bishops were open to and supportive of both types of reforms. How do we make sense of these patterns? How can we explain the differences between the four groups, in terms of their general openness to reform as well

TABLE 2.4

Voting Patterns among Bishops from African Countries (by the Number of Bishops in Each Country)

Country[a]	Number of Bishops	Percent of all Bishops (n = 2,594)	Percent Catholic 1965	Change in Percent Catholic (65–55)	Percent Voting Progressively on Revelation[b]	Percent Voting Progressively on Mary[c]
Dem. Rep. Congo	40	1.5	37	+11	98	82
Occidental Africa[d]	33	1.3	3	0	92	88
South Africa	28	1.1	6	+1	72	69
Tanganyika	21	0.8	18	+7	86	68
Nigeria	19	0.7	6	+5	46	53
Rhodesia and Zambia	14	0.5	9	+3	92	57
Madagascar	13	0.5	20	+2	83	82
Egypt	13	0.5	1	−1	88	30
Equatorial Africa[e]	11	0.4	15	+8	92	93
Kenya	9	0.3	12	+4	56	63
Cameroon	8	0.3	22	+7	88	89
Ethiopia and Eritrea	7	0.3	1	0	88	38
Nyassaland	7	0.3	20	+6	50	60
Ruanda-Urundi and Burundi	7	0.3	26	+5	86	67

TABLE 2.4 (Continued)

Country[a]	Number of Bishops	Percent of all Bishops (n = 2,594)	Percent Catholic 1965	Change in Percent Catholic (65–55)	Percent Voting Progressively on Revelation[b]	Percent Voting Progressively on Mary[c]
Uganda	7	0.3	32	+7	55	70
Algeria	5	0.2	4	−6	83	57
Total[f]	289	11.0	19[g]	+5	80	67

[a] Country designations and the number of bishops in each country reflect the Church's categorization in the *Acta* (1960–61), and thus represent the total number of bishops serving in a given country at the beginning of the Council, not necessarily the number who went to the Council or who voted on any particular issue. Figures for the percentage of the population that was Catholic are from the *National Catholic Almanac* (1956 and 1966). See appendix B for more information on the voting data.

[b] First Session, November 20, 1962, *Suffragationes*, vol. 1, no. 5.

[c] Second Session, October 29, 1963, *Suffragationes*, vol. 19, no. 97.

[d] According to the *1956 National Catholic Almanac* (333), Occidental Africa, or French West Africa, includes Benin, previously Dahomey (13% Catholic in 1965); Burkina Faso, previously Upper Volta (4% Catholic in 1965); Guinea, previously French Guinea (0.1% Catholic in 1965); Ivory Coast (9% Catholic in 1965); Mali, previously French Sudan (0.8% Catholic); Mauritania (0.3% Catholic in 1965); Niger (0.4% Catholic in 1965); and Senegal (5% Catholic in 1965). Because the statistics for all of these countries were aggregated in the 1955 data, I had to reaggregate them in order to calculate the change in percent Catholic, despite the fact that Niger and Mauritania had no bishops representing them at the Council, and the very small Catholic proportions of their populations may be masking growth in percent Catholic in the other countries.

[e] According to the *1960 National Catholic Almanac* (342), Equatorial Africa, or French Equatorial Africa, includes the Central African Republic (14% Catholic in 1965), Chad (3% Catholic in 1965), the Republic of Congo (35% Catholic in 1965), and Gabon (46% Catholic in 1965).

[f] To protect the bishops' anonymity (as per my agreement with the Vatican Secret Archive), all countries where 100 percent of the bishops voted one way (whether conservatively or progressively) were removed from the table, but these bishops and their votes were included in the totals. On this table, the totaled figures thus include 49 bishops from Angola, Cape Verde, Gambia, Ghana, Libya, Liberia, Mauritius, Morocco, Mozambique, Portuguese Guinea, Reunion, Seychelles, Sierra Leone, Somalia, South-West Africa, Spanish Guinea, Sudan, Togo, and Tunisia.

[g] So that more populous countries did not skew the statistic, this figure was calculated by averaging the percent of the population of each country that was Catholic, not by adding the total Catholic population for all of the countries together and dividing by the total population.

TABLE 2.5

Voting Patterns among Bishops from Asian and all other Missionary Countries[a] (by the Number of Bishops in Each Country)

Country[b]	Number of Bishops	Percent of all Bishops (n = 2,594)	Percent Catholic 1965	Change in Percent Catholic (65-55)	Percent Voting Progressively on Revelation[c]	Percent Voting Progressively on Mary[d]
India	80	3.0	2	0	70	49
Lebanon	26	1.0	31	−6	80	63
Japan	18	0.7	<1	0	83	53
Vietnam	17	0.7	9	+3	75	56
UAR-Syria	15	0.5	3	−1	62	30
Iraq	12	0.5	3	−1	55	43
Pakistan[e]	10	0.4	<1	0	60	60
Korea	20	0.4	2	+2	38	63
Burma	8	0.3	1	0	57	43
Ceylon	6	0.2	7	0	83	50
Turkey	4	0.2	<1	0	43	29
Totals[f]	290	11.0	7[g]	+1	72	56

[a] I define a missionary country as a developing country in Africa or Asia in which the Church never had a monopoly.

[b] Country designations and the number of bishops in each country reflect the Church's categorization in the *Acta* (1960–61), and thus represent the total number of bishops serving in a given country at the beginning of the Council, not necessarily the number who went to the Council or who voted on any particular issue. Figures for the percentage of the population that was Catholic are from the *National Catholic Almanac* (1956 and 1966). See appendix B for more information on the voting data.

[c] First Session, November 20, 1962, *Suffragationes*, vol. 1, no. 5.

[d] Second Session, October 29, 1963, *Suffragationes*, vol. 19, no. 97.

[e] These figures include East Pakistan or modern-day Bangladesh.

[f] To protect the bishops' anonymity (as per my agreement with the Vatican Secret Archive), all countries where 100 percent of the bishops voted one way (whether conservatively or progressively) were removed from the table, but these bishops and their votes were included in the totals. On this table, the totaled figures thus include 98 bishops from Arabia, the Bahamas, Bermuda, the British Virgin Islands, Cambodia, the Falkland Islands, Guyana, Indonesia, Iran, Jordan, Laos, Malaysia, Melanesia, Micronesia, Palestine, Papua New Guinea, Polynesia, Taiwan, and Thailand.

[g] So that more populous countries did not skew this statistic, this figure was calculated by averaging the percent of the population of each country that was Catholic, not by adding the total Catholic population for all of the countries together and dividing by the total population.

as the types of reform that they prioritized? To do so, we must combine
theories from the sociology of religion with economic and organizational
sociology.

THEORIES OF RELIGIOUS COMPETITION

The "new paradigm"[15] in the sociology of religion offers some fruitful
insights about the factors that affect religious institutions. Rejecting the
field's long-held belief that religious diversity was bad for religious institutions, institutional competition theory, commonly called "supply-side"
theory, argues that religious diversity increases religious participation.[16]
Diversity causes religious institutions to feel more competition, and thus
they work harder to attract and keep members and "market" their religion more actively than religious institutions with monopolistic religious
economies.

Supply-siders define a religious economy as "a market of current and
potential followers (demand), a set of organizations (suppliers) seeking to
serve that market, and the religious doctrines and practices (products) offered by the various organizations."[17] Supply-side theorists argue that
three factors contribute to the overall level of religious competition in a
religious economy: (1) religious regulation, or the relationship between
religious institutions and the government,[18] (2) pluralism, or the variety
of religions, and (3) market share, or the percentage of the population be-
longing to a particular religion.[19] These three factors are often highly correlated: pluralism and market share depend to a large extent on regulation,
in that a country with a state-supported religion will almost certainly have
less religious pluralism, and if the government actually outlaws all other
religions, the official religion may enjoy up to 100 percent of the market
share.[20]

For supply-side theorists, religious diversity is the key independent variable because it determines the amount of competition religious leaders
feel, and thus how actively they market their faith. In supply-side terms,
"religious pluralism is important only insofar as it increases choices and
competition, offering consumers a wider range of religious rewards and
forcing suppliers to be more responsive and efficient."[21] As this quotation
should make clear, the key causal relationship for institutional competition
theory is the effect competition has on religious leaders (and thus the nick-
name, "supply-side" theory).

Despite this theoretical focus, however, proponents[22] and skeptics[23]
alike have concentrated on examining correlations between pluralism
and religious participation and have neglected to directly examine the
ways in which competition affects religious leaders—the key mechanism of

the theory. This study, by contrast, focuses on competition's effects on religious leaders and leaves the question of its ultimate effect on religious participation to others.

Applying Supply-Side Theory to Vatican II

Supply-siders argue that "Monopoly firms always tend to be lazy."[23] I choose not to use this terminology. The word "lazy" conjures up images of bishops lounging on divans, largely unconcerned about the state of their institution, and chapter 3 will demonstrate that the very opposite was true of these conservative bishops: they fought tenaciously and actively. However, I do borrow the insight that religious leaders in monopolistic environments will be less oriented toward change. In fact, supply-side theory's most basic insight, that religious pluralism creates religious competition and thus creates more active religious leaders, explains a very important part of the variation being examined here, that is, which types of bishops were more open to change. However, as I will explain below, supply-side theory leaves a key question about this variation unanswered, because it does not help us understand what kind of change each group of bishops prioritized.

Strictly speaking, according to the measures currently employed to examine competition (pluralism, market share, and regulation), the bishops who participated in Vatican II came from two types of religious economies: those in which the Roman Catholic Church was the predominant religion in the society numerically and legally (including Italy, Spain, Portugal, and those Latin American countries delineated by an asterisk in table 2.3), and those in which it was not (Northern Europe, North America, and the "missionary" nations of Africa and Asia). Overall, for at least three of these four groups, this dichotomy accurately predicts the openness of the bishops at the Council. Bishops from monopolistic environments in Europe were against accommodation with the modern world. Bishops from pluralistic or religiously free environments in Northern Europe, North America, and the missionary countries of Africa and Asia, most of which supply-siders would identify as competitive, were open to change.

However, in contrast to bishops from Italy and Spain, and despite their similar monopolistic status (by traditional measures), Latin American bishops were among the most progressive of all of the bishops at the Council. Though this somewhat unexpected finding can, to some extent, be explained within the supply-side framework, a complete analysis of the forces that created Latin American progressivism provides the first indication that supply-side conceptions of the factors that affect religious leaders need to be broadened, and the measures they use improved.

Latin America: A Monopoly in Crisis

In the decade or so prior to the Council, the Catholic Church in Latin America was experiencing increasing competition from both evangelical missionaries and Marxist political parties. Though this competition had not progressed far enough to be captured in many of the measures researchers currently use (such as static measures of the Church's market share, which still indicated that the Church had a strong majority, with an average of almost 90 percent of the population of Latin America), it had progressed far enough to be picked up by a different measure. Return to tables 2.1–2.5, and the column in each that presents data on the *change* in percent Catholic. This measure demonstrates that Latin America was the only place in the world where the Roman Catholic Church was in decline in the decade prior to the Council.

By the time the Council began, though the Church had only lost 4 to 5 percent of its market share in Latin America, this decline had created a "strong sense of institutional insecurity"[25] and Latin American leaders were searching for solutions. For example, the Chilean leader Raul Cardinal Silva Henriquez, archbishop of Santiago and leader of CELAM, told an interviewer that the Church was in decline in Latin America because "of a shortage of clergy, or because of the way the laity are neglected, or because the liturgy is unintelligible, or because our catechetical instructions are too moralistic and devotional, or because of the social injustices of some wealthy Catholics."[26] In sum, this religious leader had begun to realize that the Church had failed to provide for the religious needs of the multitudes in Latin America. Another Latin American leader, Bishop Leonidas Proaño Villalba, told Caporale that in order to stem this decline, "We cannot stay put and closed but must go out to attract masses to Christ. And this has to be done by sharing the beauty of Christian doctrine. Look at the attitude of the communists. They would even penetrate into our seminaries! . . . They would infiltrate everywhere." Proaño closed by arguing that the Church must make "greater efforts to give a solid [religious] formation for people," because by doing so, "we avoid the danger of them being conquered by others."[27]

The Church was in decline in Latin America, and Latin American bishops were concerned. Consistent with the history of Catholic Action[28] in many countries in Latin America from the 1920s and 30s,[29] Latin Americans developed a radical plan for renewing their Church.[30] This plan ultimately became the seed of liberation theology, which would blossom once the Council closed.[31] The plan focused, as Silva's statement implies, on ministering to unchurched populations and addressing social injustices, particularly those in which the Church had been implicated, all over Latin America.[32]

When a complete analysis of the Latin American situation is joined to analyses of the three other groups of bishops at the Council, it becomes clear that the presence of other religious institutions does indeed have powerful effects on religious leaders. Put simply, bishops from regions where their religious monopoly had become unstable were more open to reform than those from regions where it had remained stable. Thus, the Latin American case demonstrates that if we include measures of stability and incorporate an understanding of how it, along with religious competition as it is currently conceived, profoundly affects religious leaders, we can explain which bishops were more or less open to reform at the Council.

However, stability matters not only in terms of explaining why bishops from seemingly monopolistic environments in Latin America felt a great deal of competition, and were thus more progressive than Italians and Spaniards, it also explains the reverse process. Stability also explains why the bishops from diverse but quite stable societies, such as Germany or the U.S., seemed to be much less concerned about maintaining their competitive edge than they were with bettering relations with other religious leaders through the ecumenical movement. These ecumenically oriented bishops from Northern Europe and North America pose a problem for supply-side theory, because the theory simply cannot explain why bishops from the *most competitive* situations were the *least* interested in marketing their Church to their constituents, but were instead focused on bettering relations with the leaders of other institutions. In order to explain this, the sociology of religion needs to incorporate insights from economic and organizational sociology, particularly those which see legitimacy concerns at the heart of most organizational processes.[33]

THEORIES OF INSTITUTIONAL LEGITIMACY AND ORGANIZATIONAL CHANGE

Sociologists who study capitalist markets and organizations and have found that "organizations compete not just for resources and customers, but for political power and institutional legitimacy, for social as well as economic fitness,"[34] and thus that the success of organizations can be "explained as much by how well they resonated with their symbolic environment as by their technical efficiency."[35]

The symbolic environment most relevant to an institution is called its organizational field, "those organizations that, in the aggregate, constitute a recognized area of institutional life: key suppliers, resource and product consumers, regulatory agencies and other organizations that produce similar services or products." In sum, an organizational field includes the "totality of relevant actors" from an institution's point of view.[36]

Researchers have found that as organizational fields become more highly structured,[37] and the professionals within them more highly trained and credentialed, and the field more highly regulated and systematized, the organizations or firms within that field begin to resemble one another more and more closely. This increasing resemblance results from a variety of processes associated with the legitimacy concerns that arise from professionalization, education, government regulation, the desires of firms to mimic other firms they see as successful,[38] and "attempts to mitigate the effects of competition."[39]

Because "Economic worlds are social worlds . . . they operate according to principles like other social worlds. Actors engage in political actions vis-à-vis one another and construct local cultures to guide that interaction."[40] Thus, rather than viewing the actions of firms as continual attempts to outdo each other, economic sociologists such as Paul DiMaggio, Walter Powell, and Neil Fligstein argue that firms attempt "to erect social understandings whereby firms can avoid direct price competition and can solve their internal political problems."[41] They do so because

> Market actors live in murky worlds where it is never clear what actions will have which consequences. Yet, actors must construct an account of the world that interprets the murkiness, motivates and determines courses of action, and justifies the action decided upon. In markets, the goal of action is to ensure the survival of the firm. No actor can determine which behaviors will maximize profits (either a priori or post hoc), and action is therefore directed toward the creation of stable worlds.[42]

Just as these concepts help us to understand the actions of for-profit firms, they can also help us to understand the actions of religious organizations.[43] Religious leaders are also interested first and foremost in the survival of their firm, and thus are also oriented toward keeping stable organizational fields stable, stabilizing those which are not yet stable, and minimizing the risks of competition. We can see this in how easily many of the actions Fligstein argues that for-profit firms use to control competition translate into the religious field, and even to the ecumenical movement itself. Writing at the height of the ecumenical movement, sociologist Peter Berger attributed its growth to the desire of the mainstream Christian denominations to mitigate competition:[44]

> Every move made by the denominational organization carries with it substantial economic risks. Cooperation, as expressed in a rational limitation of cutthroat

competition, thus becomes an economic necessity. As one speaker put it in the writer's hearing at a meeting of denominational executives called to consider a more cooperative planning process: "Gentlemen, you may as well face it—you have a multi-million dollar investment to protect."[45]

Fligstein's theory does not only apply to religious institutions in competitive situations. He argues that firms attempt to "involve the state in regulation or protective legislation that increases the odds of firm survival." The Roman Catholic Church has historically been one of the most successful religious organizations at obtaining governmental support for itself—and indeed, as a result the Catholic Church's relationship with the state was a central issue at the Council for Protestants, something which will be discussed in much greater detail in chapter 4.

Fligstein identifies three types of markets or fields, those which are stable, emerging, or in crisis. In combination with concepts from supply-side theory, those categories of fields help to explain the variation apparent in the bishops' priorities at the Council. In stable fields "the identities and status hierarchies of firms (the incumbents and the challengers) are well known" and large firms share understandings of the field, organizational structures, and tactics.[46] Emerging fields are those in which "the roles of the challengers and incumbents have yet to be defined, and there is no accepted set of social relations."[47] Field "crisis is observed when incumbent organizations begin to fail," most often as the result of firms "invading" the field.[48]

COMBINING THEORIES

By combining organizational and economic sociology's understandings of the effects of field structure and stability with supply-side theory's focus on the importance of religious diversity, we can accurately predict the two key variations in the bishops' priorities, or what I call organizational strategies.[49]

Table 2.6 demonstrates that wherever there was significant religious diversity, bishops were open to the legitimacy pressures made prominent by the ecumenical movement. And, though the full ramifications of the Northern Europeans' neglect of marketing will not be apparent until chapter 6, table 2.6 also indicates that wherever the Church's organizational field was unstable, bishops prioritized marketing to their constituents more than their colleagues from stable fields. Thus, taken together, these two variables create a two-by-two table that allows us to explain the priorities of the four distinct groups of bishops at the Council by the characteristics of their organizational fields.

TABLE 2.6
Bishop's Organizational Strategies (by the Type of Field in His Country of
Service) at the Second Vatican Council

		DIVERSITY	
		Low	*High*
STABILITY	*High*	**Monopolistic Fields** (e.g., Italy, Spain) • Anti-Change • Not Ecumenical • Did Not Prioritize Marketing	**Stable Fields** (e.g., Germany, Netherlands, U.S.) • Pro-Change • Ecumenical • Did Not Prioritize Marketing
	Low	**Fields in Crisis** (e.g., Latin America) • Pro-Change • Not Ecumenical • Prioritized Marketing	**Emerging Fields** (e.g., Africa and Asia) • Pro-Change • Ecumenical • Prioritized Marketing

Monopolistic Fields

Monopolistic fields are, by definition, not diverse. But, importantly, to have
the characteristics of monopoly, they must also be quite stable. Bishops from
such fields were not ecumenically oriented, because the Church had virtually
no other religious institutions to deal with. In addition, the state in monopolistic fields was openly preferential to the Church. Thus, in monopolistic
fields, no institutions posed serious legitimacy challenges for the Church.

Bishops from monopolistic fields were also not marketing oriented.
Without any competition from other firms, bishops from monopolistic
fields were not under pressure to keep and attract more constituents.
Thus, bishops from monopolistic fields were, in general, opposed to the
vast majority of reforms that were on the table at the Council.

Fields in Crisis

When a monopolistic field becomes unstable, it becomes a field in crisis.
Thinking about Latin America as an unstable field allows us to explain why
a very small amount of religious diversity, as little as 4 to 6 percent, created

such active bishops.[50] Latin Americans felt such competition not because of the level of diversity but because that level of diversity reflected a very real *change* in the Church's market share, a change which "unsettled"[51] their formerly monopolistic field and introduced real instability into it. Fligstein argues that in fields in crisis, leaders are spurred to create inventive organizational strategies, and, as was the case with the Roman Catholic Church in Latin America, these strategies often resemble the invaders' tactics.[52]

Latin American bishops saw both Marxism and evangelical Christianity successfully taking away their constituents and developed organizational strategies which incorporated the tactics and critiques of both organizations by the time of the Council.[53] Realizing that a substantial part of the population was unchurched and needed more access to priests, they began to mimic the recruiting tactics of the evangelicals. And their focus on social justice and critiques of capitalism, especially their recognition of the Church's role in supporting monarchies and dictatorships that had done little to help the less fortunate in Latin America, was a direct outgrowth of powerful Marxist critiques of the Church.

Noticeably absent from the strategies of Latin American Catholic reformers was any attempt to better relations between Catholics and Protestants. The antiecumenical bent of Latin American bishops suggests that in fields in crisis, leaders remain hostile to the invaders, even as they are influenced by their strategies and tactics. Latin American bishops were very cognizant of this difference between them and the Northern Europeans and were quite aware that it stemmed from the very different relationships the two groups had with Protestants. The Latin American representatives continually compared their relationship to Protestants to the friendlier one that prevailed between Catholics and Protestants in Northern Europe and North America. For example, a Chilean leader told a reporter that "Protestantism in Europe today differs profoundly from Protestantism as found in Latin America, where it is daily growing."[54] The aggressive posture of Protestant missionaries in Latin America was recognized even by leading Protestant ecumenists. Lukas Vischer noted that "Many Protestant missionaries regard it as their obvious duty to draw live members away from the Roman Catholic Church."[55]

In sum, it is only when we understand that the bishops saw their Church in crisis in Latin America that we can understand the kind of reforms they supported and the kind they didn't.

Emerging Fields

Africa and Asia in the 1950s and 1960s saw enormous turbulence, with the vast majority of both continents changing from colonial to independent rule during this time.[56] Between 1955 and 1965, thirty African countries gained independence from their colonial powers, which consisted primarily of Belgium, France, Great Britain, and Portugal. (The smaller colonial holdings of Italy and Spain gained independence prior to and after this period.[57]) More than half of these transfers occurred in 1960 alone, just two years before the Council began.

This rapid decolonialization seriously affected religious organizations in many African countries, which had virtually flooded some areas of Africa since the beginning of the century.[58] As one indication of how pervasive the missionary presence could be, in the Belgian Congo "The mission establishment had virtually as many personnel as the state, and more than three times as many outposts."[59] However, unlike the white political commissioners, who left after independence was achieved, many white missionaries remained,[60] and with them, many remnants of precolonial rule. Among those who stayed were more than 250 Roman Catholic bishops (see table 2.4), living in countries with no dominant religion and alongside missionaries from many Protestant groups eager to win the souls of the native populations. It is difficult to imagine a more unstable, and indeed, more competitive, environment for religious leaders.

Though Asia's story differs from Africa's in many ways, the most significant difference certainly being the role of communism and Asia's central role in the Cold War, Asia was also very unstable during the fifties and sixties.[61] After a period of upheaval and Japan's colonization of many Asian countries, World War II marked the beginning of perhaps even greater instability, as most British, French and American colonies "were resurrected briefly, only to disappear again through negotiation or by force."[62] "By 1954, the only parts of Asia still under colonial rule were New Guinea, Borneo, Timor and Hong Kong."[63] Perhaps even more importantly, "A third of the Asian population was ruled by communist governments,"[64] and the United States fought throughout most of the 1950s and 1960s to prevent that proportion from growing, a fight which made Asia the battleground of the Cold War.

Thus, at the time of the Council, Asia and Africa were areas of great instability, in which the Catholic Church was not only fighting to win new souls, and to do so faster than the Protestant churches, but was also fighting to maintain the infrastructure it had developed in chaotic times.

Fligstein argues that competition exacts its greatest toll in emerging fields and that firm leaders are most actively entrepreneurial in these types of markets.[65] This observation holds true in relation to Vatican II. Bishops from emerging organizational fields were extremely responsive to their constituents, voting progressively on any reform which might help them make their admittedly foreign religion more attractive, or might alleviate poverty or other problems in these beleaguered areas.

African and Asian bishops' openness to ecumenism also suggests that leaders in emerging fields are much less hostile to other institutions than leaders in fields in crisis. As religious leaders working in diverse organizational fields, where the only other people who spoke their native tongue were often Protestant missionaries, many of whom were engaged in the same or similar humanitarian efforts as the Catholic Church (building roads, schools, hospitals, and so forth), missionary bishops were entrepreneurial, but open to ecumenical dialogue.

Stable Fields

Finally, and perhaps most importantly, the typology presented in table 2.6 helps us understand why bishops in what supply-siders would see as the most competitive religious economies were the least invested in reforms which would help them market to their constituents. Fligstein argues that incumbent firms in stable fields are risk averse, because their primary consideration is keeping the field stable and ensuring the firm's survival. Thus, they attempt to "mitigate the effects of competition with other firms,"[66] and "try to cooperate with competitors to share markets."[67] Cooperation necessitates conversation, and it is through these conversations that legitimacy concerns, concerns about fair and just ways of doing "business," are voiced and heard by firms.

A key organizational arena in which such a process was occurring at the time of the Council was the ecumenical movement, which had greatly increased both the density and interconnectedness of the networks within stable religious fields at the time of the Council. In order to understand the full implications of the ecumenical movement for the bishops who voted at Vatican II, we need to briefly review its history.

THE ECUMENICAL MOVEMENT

Though earlier theological and cultural precursors can be identified, scholars agree that the ecumenical movement, which stressed that all Christians, whatever their particular interpretations of the Bible, are baptized in Christ and share a common vision of the world and should thus put aside their differences, began in the United States in 1908, with the formation of the Federal Council of Churches.[68] In 1950, the Federal Council of Churches merged with a number of smaller American ecumenical organizations to form the National Council of Churches.[69]

Though officially born in the United States, the ecumenical movement was also strong in Europe, beginning with the First World Missionary Conference in Edinburgh in 1910.[70] After recovering from World War II, the international movement established the World Council of Churches (WCC),[71] the ecumenical body that was most influential at Vatican II, in 1948. The WCC grew in size and scope rather quickly, establishing out-posts in and receiving reports from every corner of the world by 1950,[72] though its backbone remained in the United States and other Protestant-dominated countries, such as Germany and the Netherlands.[73]

Initially, the Roman Catholic Church had little contact with the move-ment and the WCC, because relations between Protestants and Catholics in many countries, particularly the U.S. and the Netherlands, where the ecumenical movement was strongest, were cool at best until the mid-1950s.[74] In the U.S., Catholicism had been a "minority religion fighting desperately to meet the needs of impoverished immigrants."[75] As an immi-grant church, the American Catholic hierarchy was focused on keeping immigrants "in the church and away from the blandishments of Protes-tants," as they waited for them to assimilate into "a more American Catholicism," as Robert Orsi wrote in his study of Italian Harlem in the early twentieth century.[76] In the highly polarized Dutch society, Catholics and Protestants had separate institutions and little friendly contact until after World War II.

Since their relations with Protestants were in general somewhat antago-nistic, it is not surprising that Catholics had little contact with the ecu-menical movement, especially given that a major impetus behind the ecumenical movement was the stated desire of Protestants to have an or-ganization that could counter the institutional strength of the Roman Catholic Church.[77] In fact, since 1919, Catholics had been forbidden to participate in ecumenical congresses without the permission of the Vatican.[78]

Relations between Catholics and Protestants began to significantly im-prove around the early 1950s,[79] though they did so tentatively[80] and largely unofficially,[81] because the Roman Catholic hierarchy was initially reluctant to allow Catholics to take part in the WCC.[82] Though these improved re-lations were most apparent in the United States and, not coincidentally, came at a time when American Catholics had finally become fully "Amer-ican,"[83] a similar process of rapprochement between Catholics and Protes-tants was occurring in other Protestant-dominated countries, such as the Netherlands[84] and Germany. Sociologist Erik Sengers found that Roman Catholic tension with Protestant-dominated Dutch society "ended around 1945," after which Catholic "proselytizing activities" focused on building the Dutch Catholic Church "were changed into ecumenical ones, aiming no longer to attract members from other churches but to work together for the Christianization of Dutch society."[85]

As the networks between Catholics and Protestants became denser, exchanges between them became more common.[86] By 1955, as the ecu-menical movement gained ascendancy, Catholics and Protestants began to engage in ecumenical dialogue in earnest. A substantial literature on

Protestant/Catholic relations existed "in France, Holland and Germany,"[87] as well as the United States.[88] This literature makes it apparent that Protestants had increasingly come to believe that bettering relations with Catholics was a natural extension of the ecumenical movement, as Ernst Kinder, a German Lutheran theologian wrote in the *Ecumenical Review* in 1955:

> The very existence of the Roman Catholic Church as such prevents ecumenical thought from leaving it out. . . . The Roman Catholic Church is a fact, and it embraces a considerable number of the Christians of the world. That alone is sufficient reason for true ecumenical thought not to ignore it, whatever its own attitude may be. . . . If our thought and action are to remain truly ecumenical, we must bear the Roman Catholic Church constantly in mind.[89]

Kinder closed with a very positive assessment of the growing ecumenical dialogue between Catholics and Protestants: "There is a new spirit today in the relations between Protestantism and Catholicism. The old historical barriers between them have crumbled from within, and they are being drawn together by a renewal of the Christian spirit."[90]

Kinder's optimism was shared by other Protestant ecumenists writing in the next couple of years. In 1956 the *Ecumenical Review* noted that "We rejoice in the fact that . . . the number of Roman Catholic ecumenists . . . is constantly growing," a conclusion they drew from the growing "stream of Roman Catholic publications concerning ecumenical questions."[91] By 1957, Roger Mehl wrote in the *Ecumenical Review* that "the ecumenical movement today has valuable collaborators among Roman Catholic theologians," a fact which he interpreted (I think correctly) as an indication "that within a few years the WCC has succeeded in compelling recognition and acquired real and indisputable authority" in the world, and within the Roman Catholic Church.[92] That same year, the book jacket for the Danish Lutheran theologian K. E. Skydsgaard's well-known book *One in Christ* stated that "Protestants and Roman Catholics today are carrying on a more real 'conversation' with each other than at any time since the Reformation."

The increasing optimism apparent in the ecumenical literature at this time reached a crescendo with Pope John XXIII's sudden decision to call the Council, in October of 1958. After his announcement, the literature on Protestant/Catholic relations continued to expand so rapidly[93] that by 1962, just before the Council started, one author remarked that because of the growing "conversation going on between Roman Catholics and churchmen of other churches . . . the literature on this subject has become of . . . *overwhelming dimensions.*"[94]

John's announcement also improved formal relations between the RCC and the WCC. In 1962, five Catholic observers officially attended a

World Council of Churches meeting for the first time, and that same year, when Vatican II opened, Protestant observers were in attendance—the first time in history that Protestants had been invited to a Roman Catholic Council.

Thus, by the time of the Council, ecumenical dialogue between the Catholic Church and Protestant communions was "very intense" (as one German bishop told Caporale),[95] with some bishops reporting a great deal of experience with the movement. For example, American bishop Robert Tracy told Caporale at the beginning of the Council that he had "been very active in the ecumenical movement for the past ten years."[96] Canadian bishop Georges Pelletier told Caporale, "we have many organizations for the ecumenical movement. It is a permanent work well done."[97] American bishop John Wright told Caporale that he counted some of the Protestant observers "as personal friends of mine even prior to the Council because I usually went to conventions and meetings of Protestants."[98]

The three years of the Council strengthened these relations both formally and informally.[99] For example, American bishop Paul Hallinan told Caporale that though he had not known any of the Protestant observers before the Council, "here I have dinner with many of them," and that he had spoken at the World Methodist Council and eighteen other meetings of Protestants between the First and Second Sessions.[100] As the Council's ecumenical focus became apparent, both Catholic and Protestant ecumenists became more optimistic. So optimistic, in fact, that a Catholic observer at the 1963 Faith and Order meetings for the WCC wrote, "We have here undoubtedly an area of ecumenical triumph."[101]

In sum, we can only understand the overall ecumenical focus of the bishops from stable fields when we understand how their organizational fields were becoming more highly structured. By increasing "the extent of interaction" among religious organizations, creating "sharply defined interorganizational structures of domination and patterns of coalition" through the WCC and its national counterparts, and increasing "the information load" with which the organizations in the field had to contend through conferences and publications, the ecumenical movement helped to develop a "mutual awareness" among religious leaders that they were "involved in a common enterprise."[102]

As these fields became more structured, the bishops in them began to see Protestants not as competitors who might woo their faithful away but as colleagues who had similar goals and interests, a process which only accelerated once the Council began.[103] This shift explains why, ironically, religious leaders from the most competitive religious economies were, of the three progressive groups, the least focused on marketing concerns.

Conclusion: Competition from the Perspective of the Competitors

If we are to understand the factors that direct religious change, we must understand the factors that affect religious leaders. Sociologists of religion have begun to use organizational theory, but these efforts have not been completely incorporated into the powerful explanatory framework offered by supply-side theory.[104] This analysis of Vatican II demonstrates that we must examine not only the *presence* of other religious and political institutions in the Catholic Church's organizational field but the *relationships between* the Church and those institutions in order to understand the different priorities the bishops had at the Council. This is because, like other organizations, religious organizations are affected by legitimacy concerns as much as they are by the efficiency concerns pointed to by supply-side theorists.

Up to this point, the reader has not seen many examples of legitimacy concerns being communicated to the Church by participants in the ecumenical movement. Because these concerns are contextually dependent, and thus necessitate a great deal more information than I have the space for in this chapter, I have left them for the case studies on religious freedom, Mary, and birth control which appear in part 2 of this book.

This chapter also demonstrates that sociologists of religion need to develop not only a more complete picture of an institution's organizational field but a better understanding of how an institution's *position within* an organizational field is important to its actions. In all of the fields examined in this chapter, with the exception of the missionary countries, the Roman Catholic Church was an incumbent organization. Organizational theorists have noted that "incumbent firms pay attention to the actions of other incumbent firms, not challenger firms."[105] This distinction became particularly apparent when Latin Americans began wrestling with their Northern European allies' desire to improve relations with Protestants. While Protestants were incumbents in Northern Europe and North America, whom the bishops from these areas clearly saw as legitimate players, they were pesky challengers to Latin Americans. Latin Americans continually differentiated between the mainstream Protestant denominations that made up the ecumenical movement in Northern Europe and North America from the "sects" that "we have to deal with."[106] As Bishop Alejandro Olalia told Caporale, sects "are hostile."[107]

In contrast to incumbents, like the Catholic Church in Latin America, who became willing to engage in change because of a threat to their market share, challengers tend to be innovative and responsive from the get-go. Though it is perhaps a stretch to call the Roman Catholic Church in any organizational field a true "challenger," it was also not a true incumbent in Africa or Asia. As such, it was an innovative and active organization in these missionary countries.

Finally, this chapter has demonstrated that, especially at the start of the Council, the priorities of Latin American and Northern European bishops were vastly different. However, despite this, these two groups began looking for ways to bridge their differences as soon as the Council began. The next chapter tells the story of how and why they were able to do this, and thus how, in conjunction with the bishops from Africa and Asia, they turned Vatican II from a rubber stamp of the Curia's views into the watershed event it became.

Chapter Three

HOW CULTURE MATTERED AT VATICAN II

Collegiality Trumps Authority in the Council's "Social Movement Organizations"

CHAPTER 2 demonstrated that the various groups of progressive bishops at the Council initially had very different goals, and in particular, that Latin American bishops initially had difficulty embracing their Northern European colleagues' goal of improving relations with Protestants. How, then, did progressive leaders develop compromise positions that the majority of the rank and file bishops would support? And, just as importantly, given the initial divisiveness of ecumenically oriented reforms, how were the majority of bishops persuaded to vote in favor of them, so that these very reforms emerged as some of the Council's most prominent achievements?

These questions are the focus of this chapter. The answers to them demonstrate that a great deal of the Council's progressive outcome can be explained by a relatively simple sociological fact: because progressives built a far more extensive and flexible organization than their conservative counterparts, they were more successful at developing compromise positions that the vast majority of bishops could support. These organizational differences derived from different cultural understandings of the nature of authority in the Roman Catholic Church. Progressives believed in the doctrine of "collegiality," which, in essence, stated that the bishops, when convened as a council, are as infallible as the pope—a doctrine that conservatives saw as threatening his authority and primacy. Consequently, while progressives built a highly effective, consensus-based organization as soon as the Council began, conservatives were much slower to mobilize, and when they did so, formed a hierarchical organization which never developed into much more than a letter-writing campaign to the pope.

Progressives' greater organizational strength would not be predicted by an examination of the two groups' resources at the beginning of the Council, and their greater success would not be predicted by most studies of consensus-based organizing.[1] These findings suggest that consensus-based organizations are not necessarily ineffective or inefficient, as is often claimed; rather, their effectiveness depends upon the fit between activists' cultural understandings and the environment in which their organization is enacted.[2]

This chapter is structured as follows: I first describe how theories of social movements and culture may be linked to this case of religious change.
I then describe the contrasting models of authority in contention at the
time of the Council. After presenting evidence that progressives and conservatives were polarized in their views about the nature of authority in the
Church, I then turn to the contrasting strategies and organizations of
the two groups that are the focus of this chapter: the progressive group of
twenty or so bishops who met weekly at the hotel called the Domus
Mariae (DM) and the far less successful group of approximately ten to sixteen conservative "Council fathers and theologians" known as the Coetus
Internationalis Patrum (CIP).[3]

Organizational Effectiveness and Culture at Vatican II

This chapter is about two groups—one built by progressives and the other
by conservatives—that are widely cited as the most important of all the informal groups at Vatican II.[4] Because they were not official organizations
but were formed solely at the behest of activist bishops, they strongly resemble traditional social movement organizations. Thus, in this chapter I
rely mainly on social movement theory for analytical leverage.

Though Vatican II is obviously different from traditional social movements, I am not the first to notice the importance religious organizations
have had for many social movements,[5] to use social movement theory in
relation to pressures for change within religious organizations generally[6]
or the Roman Catholic Church specifically,[7] or to describe Vatican II as a
social movement.[8] The story presented here demonstrates that though the
Council was not a case of grass-roots mobilization, it became the arena
where activist bishops attempted to, and eventually did, radically change
their institution. In fact, many researchers cite Vatican II as an important
resource for, and even partial cause of, more traditional social movements
which took place after the Council.[9] In this sense, Vatican II is a clear case
of the "contentious politics" that social movement theorists seek to explain,[10] and I will show that social movement theories may benefit from a
systematic study of the factors that explain the progressive outcome of the
Council.

Social movement theory helps us understand many aspects of the Council. For example, the DM was far more successful than the CIP at mobilizing a heterogeneous population of bishops to support a variety of causes,
despite the fact that many bishops initially regarded ecumenism with suspicion. In other words, the DM was more successful at "framing" their issues in terms that a wide variety of bishops could support.[11] In contrast,
conservatives failed to ever develop an overarching frame that the majority

of bishops could support and were left drawing on different populations of bishops from issue to issue.

Recent developments in social movement theory also help us to understand the success of the DM and point to reasons why they had a far greater "strategic capacity" than the CIP.[12] In his study of the Farm Workers Movement, Ganz lists the attributes that enhance an organization's ability to devise successful tactics:

> Strategic capacity is greater if a leadership team includes insiders and outsiders, strong and weak network ties, and access to diverse, yet salient, repertoires of collection action, and also if an organization conducts regular, open, authoritative deliberation, draws resources from multiple constituencies, and roots accountability in those constituencies.[13]

The analysis presented below will demonstrate that the DM possessed virtually all of these attributes and the CIP almost none.

In her study of six social movement organizations, Francesca Polletta finds definite advantages to consensus-based, or what she calls "participatory democratic," organizing.[14] She argues that a focus on the deliberative process allows groups to build leaders, be more tactically innovative, own the decisions of the group, and create group solidarity. The analysis that follows highlights the fact that one of the greatest strengths of the DM was their focus on consensus-building and communication.

When the Council opened in 1962, few observers would have predicted that an informal organization of progressive bishops would prove to be far more successful than an organization of conservative bishops closely allied to the Curia. Indeed, in many ways this case illustrates how resources are not the sole explanatory variable for social movement success. Activists use models or strategies of action, "cultural toolkits," "organizational repertoires," "political logics," or cultural "schemas" which are available and familiar, and these ideas and beliefs hold explanatory power.[15] This study of the DM and the CIP demonstrates that more than any other variable (resources, status, prestige, etc.), what explains the type of organization each group built, and therefore ultimately their effectiveness, was deeply cultural.[16] These cultural differences hinged around each group's view of the locus of just authority in the Church, namely, whether the doctrine of collegiality was valid.[17]

COMPETING VIEWS OF AUTHORITY IN THE ROMAN CATHOLIC CHURCH

Progressive and conservative bishops were able to hold very different opinions on the nature of authority in the Church because the Church's stance on the issue was officially undecided. The First Vatican Council

(1869–70) was closed prematurely by the Franco-Prussian War, with the declaration of papal infallibility as its primary accomplishment.[18] Papal infallibility refers specifically to doctrinal statements made by the pope, which are not only considered exempt from error but even "from the possibility of error."[19]

The doctrine of papal infallibility is not without controversy. Critics at the time it was promulgated argued that "neither a fallible individual nor a collection of fallible individuals can constitute an infallible organ."[20] Most analysts agree that had Vatican I continued, it would have augmented the doctrine of papal infallibility with a corresponding decree asserting that the college of bishops, when acting as a body in concert with the pope, share his teaching responsibilities and authority. However, without any corresponding decree about the importance of the college of bishops, the Curia focused on the primacy of the pope and his infallibility in the century between Vatican I and II.[21]

This accentuation of papal primacy and infallibility was of great concern to progressives, especially those oriented toward ecumenism. For example, American archbishop Lawrence Shehan acknowledged in a speech that "one of the main sources of difficulties which non-Catholics find in Catholic teaching is the definition of the Pope's infallibility," particularly where they have "misconceptions . . . of the nature and extent of papal infallibility."[22] Philippe Nabaa, archbishop of the Melchite Church, told an interviewer that the infallibility and primacy of the pope were the "greatest obstacles" to union and stressed the importance of balancing these doctrines with a decree about the importance of the college of bishops, or collegiality.[23]

Augmenting the doctrine of infallibility with a decree about the importance and authority of the college of bishops, or collegiality, thus became an important issue on the progressive agenda at the Council, and therefore an issue which came to deeply concern conservatives.[24] Table 3.1 demonstrates that collegiality, though a contentious issue among bishops from monopolistic countries, unified the three groups of progressive bishops from Latin America, Northern Europe, and missionary countries, the vast majority of whom voted progressively on the most contentious vote on collegiality during the Second Session.

The sides were divided by one simple question: Was the doctrine of collegiality, which in essence states that when acting together, the bishops have an authority equal to that of the pope, legitimate Roman Catholic doctrine? Did it, in some way, hinder or qualify the primacy and infallibility of the Roman pontiff? Progressives and conservatives had sharply differing beliefs about the answer to this question, beliefs which would color their views and actions throughout the Council and which strongly directed the organizations they built and the strategies they used to achieve their divergent goals for the Council.

TABLE 3.1
Support for Collegiality by Organizational Field

	Percent Voting Progressively on the Fourth Point on Collegiality[a]
Monopolistic	
European Countries	53
Latin America	83
Africa and Asia	91
Northern European and	
North American Countries	93
Total	81

[a] n = 2,039. Second Session, October 30, 1963, *Suffragationes*, vol. 20, no. 104.

The DM's Belief in Collegiality

Early in the Council, the DM wrote the following petition, demonstrating that they saw collegiality as a central priority for the Council:

> The undersigned Fathers of the ecumenical Council of Vatican II, taking into consideration that the first Council of the Vatican, after it had defined the primacy and infallibility of the Roman Pope, parted without having been able to deal with the origin and powers of the Bishops, successors of the Apostles, find that the determination of the origin and powers of bishops is of special importance for the discussion of other questions to be dealt with by the Council. . . . [We therefore] propose that the schema [on collegiality] be studied and decided upon first.[25]

Though progressives were successful in ensuring a vote on collegiality during the Second Session, and the most progressive statement on the issue passed with majority support (see table 3.1), the DM was not happy with how the drafting committee summarized the issue after the votes. The members of the DM noted that "Although the Fathers keenly expressed what they felt . . . in regards to collegiality, [these progressive views] have still not been confirmed in the least in the [official Council] text. . . . Not a few deem that we must proceed to the end, for they consider collegiality to be, as it were, a truth that has been demonstrated and established."[26] Already acting collegially, DM members were distressed when their views of collegiality were not initially incorporated into Council documents. When it became clear that the Council would come out with an acceptable statement in the Fourth Session, the DM's minutes stated: "Everyone rejoices at the thought that this decree of greatest importance will be promulgated by the most Holy Father."[27]

The CIP's Suspicions about Collegiality

In contrast to the progressives' strong prioritization of collegiality, conservatives, especially those involved in the CIP, adamantly opposed the less hierarchical view of the Church promoted by the doctrine. Indeed, in the minutes from the first official CIP meeting, CIP theologian Berto stated that the group's primary purpose was to form and support "opposition to the idea of collegiality . . . adopting as a banner the defense of the rights of the Supreme Pontiff and, secondarily, those of each individual bishop."[28]

CIP founder Bishop Luigi Carli told Caporale, "collegiality . . . unless we define it properly is going to be a terrible headache for future councils and theologians. . . . They say they don't want to define new dogmas and here they are defining a new dogma of the utmost consequences. What is this?"[29] Another CIP founder, Brazilian archbishop Geraldo de Proença Sigaud, gave a forceful speech against the doctrine of collegiality prior to the first votes on the issue during the Second Session. When his speech failed to convince the majority of bishops to vote against collegiality, CIP leaders were dismayed. Cardinal Giuseppe Siri, a conservative Italian and key ally of the CIP, had harsh words about those first votes on collegiality. He told Caporale: "The famous vote on collegiality is not valid and I have proved it to them and to the Pope. . . . I felt like walking [up] to the four [Council] moderators and tear[ing] the IBM [punch] card right in their faces. . . . Of course, I voted no and make no secret about it."[30]

Letters from Berto to Carli referred to the votes as "disastrous," "peculiar," "unhappy," "hasty," and "secretive," and to the doctrine itself as a "false question" which rejects "the divine rights of the Roman Pope"; as "that detestable, unrealistic . . . pseudo-theology"; and as "bad faith" which is "refuted by the Sacred Scriptures, . . . Tradition, 'theological reason'—common sense itself."[31] His primary concern was collegiality's threat to the primacy of the pope. Less than a week after the votes, Berto wrote to Carli on this point:

> The "so-called college" (at least as it is now argued) is "deadly" for the . . .
> Pope, for it shatters his Fatherhood. . . . If the Pope is the head of the Church
> only because he is the head of the "College of Bishops," then the true Sovereign of the Church is that College. . . . I consider this view to be false . . . logically . . . the very name of "Holy Father," which was granted to the Pope, is
> not befitting; the true "Holy Father" is the "College of Bishops!"[32]

These competing views about the nature of just authority within the Church led the two groups of bishops to develop very different strategies, and build and enact very different organizations—one of which was much better suited to a council environment.

The Domus Mariae

As the Council opened amid uncertainty and with conservative preparatory schemas as its only guide, two Latin American leaders and a few progressive French bishops decided to create an organization that would allow them to communicate with all of the bishops present at the Council. French theologian Roger Etchegaray, who would become the DM's secretary, told the story of this decision years later:

> Cardinal Liénart asked me at the opening of the Council, to make "useful contacts" with bishops of other countries. There had been little mutual contact, and meetings were even up to that point discouraged by Rome. . . . Thus, stimulated by the two bishops I met the first evening (Manuel Larraín and Helder Câmara . . .), I was so bold as to invite a few bishops, as I met them, to meet regularly for an exchange of views on the proceedings of the Council.[33]

From the beginning, their strategy was to assess the concerns of bishops from diverse places and develop an organization and platforms to address them.

The DM's Strategy: Building Collegiality through Consensus

Early in the Council, Câmara told Caporale, "My dream is the formation of a collegial organization of bishops at the national and international level."[34] Their belief in the importance of collegiality, taken to a practical level, had important strategic and organizational implications for the DM. Those who believed in the doctrine of collegiality had to believe in the holiness of consensus building—in creating agreement among knowledgeable bishops.

The agenda for their third meeting stated that the members would discuss "what is felt by anyone concerning the meetings in the *Domus Mariae* and what results are expected from them."[35] Rather than coming together with a concrete agenda, the progressives who started the DM seemed open to figuring out the best course of action, form, and function of their group. In effect, they decided to build a "participatory democracy"[36] within the hierarchical and nondemocratic structure of the Church.

The DM's focus on participatory democracy seems to have lasted throughout the Council. At the beginning of the last session, Etchegaray sent this flyer to the members:

> It seems that it would be very useful for us to resume our weekly meetings without delay. We shall therefore meet together as one in the Domus Mariae,

Saturday, September 17th 1965, at 5 p.m. precisely. There is a sufficient variety of questions that seem to require discussion at the beginning of this session. We intend to list them and to devise a better way to inform and help each other.[37]

The DM ensured that they would be able to "inform and help each other" by attempting to generate consensus on the issues they were discussing. This focus on consensus was vital to the DM because of the complex, but highly effective, organizational form within which it arose.

The DM's Organizational Structure: Using Episcopal Conferences

The linchpin of the DM's organization was the episcopal conference.[38] Though the extent to which each national episcopal conference was organized, and the frequency with which they met, varied from country to country, they provided a natural solution and a preexisting organizational structure for the DM's conflicting desires to communicate with the bishops at the Council openly, but subtly and quickly.[39]

Beyond that, ECs were important to the DM in a number of other ways. Recall that when the Council began, ECs were inchoate; most were not recognized by the Vatican, and some countries did not even have one. This changed during the Council's first few weeks: as a result of Liénart's intervention on the opening day of the Council, ECs were officially given the function of nominating candidates for the Council commissions. The Council's approval of ECs helped the DM to gain validity, just as preexisting ECs, especially CELAM, provided organizational models or repertoires for the group.[40]

Furthermore, ECs were seen as a way of enacting collegiality, so progressives made better use of them than conservatives did. While bishops from France and CELAM, who founded the DM, had been meeting in their conferences for years, bishops from Italy never had a conference meeting until after the Council began and such meetings were mandated by the pope. Just as conservatives saw collegiality as threatening to the primacy of the pope, they saw conferences of bishops acting "independently" of the pope as potentially heretical. By avoiding the ECs, the CIP in effect handed over to the DM an important resource that helped to offset the conservatives' greater institutional resources.

Most importantly, the ECs linked the twenty-two DM members[41] to the vast majority of bishops at the Council who would ultimately decide its outcome through their votes. Figure 3.1[42] depicts an estimate of how many and which bishops the ECs helped the DM to reach, calculated by including those ECs which met at least once a week (the vast majority

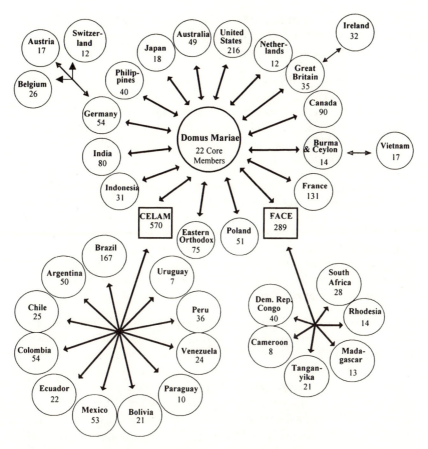

FIGURE 3.1. The Organizational Structure of the Domus Mariae. Estimated Number of Bishops Reached Weekly: 1,900.

did so; see tables 2.2–2.5 for a complete list of the countries and the number of bishops in each) or were closely connected to a DM representative,[43] and excluding those countries who had dysfunctional or anticollegial ECs. The countries excluded were Italy, China, Spain, Portugal, Yugoslavia, and Hungary.

The DM's wheel-like organizational structure allowed them to quickly and efficiently gain consensus about their agenda and strategies in a small group of twenty-two, and convey that information to more than nineteen hundred, or almost three-quarters of the bishops, within a week.[44] In their next meeting, the DM could get feedback from each EC representative and tailor their strategies accordingly.

Etchegaray described how he saw the relationship between the DM and the ECs in a letter he wrote to Cardinal Suenens, a prominent progressive theologian, during the First Session:

> I send you the list of the 22 regular participants . . . all [of whom] more or less represent their own episcopacy according to the structure and degree of "collegial conscience" of their EC. While they are naturally not able to engage their colleagues in debates, they nevertheless reflect the more general thought of their episcopacy and in turn . . . report on all that is said in the meetings of the Domus Mariae.[45]

Communication between the DM and the ECs lasted throughout the four Council sessions. At the beginning of the Fourth Session, the DM again summarized their impressions of this relationship in their minutes:

> Almost all the delegates have been able to consult their own Conferences on a weekly basis, to gather suggestions about the tasks to be accomplished. . . . Those who did not hold a meeting have sought the opinions of several members from their conference.[46]

Many of the leaders interviewed by Caporale identified their DM representative or told him that they knew someone from their conference was attending the DM meetings. The American hierarchy received weekly reports from their representative, Bishop Ernest Primeau, who summarized the DM's meetings and recommendations for votes or other action. These reports often closed by stating that points covered in the report "are submitted to the Bishops for study, discussion and decision at the next [EC] meeting,"[47] in the hopes that by getting feedback from their ECs, DM members would be able to provide "suggestions that are more thought-through and clear."[48]

If the ECs represented at the DM did nothing more than meet and inform their members on Council issues, they would still have provided the DM with an opportunity to better inform approximately three-quarters of the bishops about the ramifications of various issues, thus bettering the chances of a progressive victory when issues came to a vote. (Early documents had to be approved by a majority of the bishops—and final documents by at least two-thirds.) Yet such a structure would not have helped the DM to "develop suggestions that are more thought-through and clear." To do this, they needed feedback. A central resource which ensured that the DM did get useful feedback was that many ECs tried to reach consensus themselves, or at least polled their members about Council issues. Their EC's position was then communicated to the DM through their representative, as Bishop DeProvenchères, a progressive from France, told Caporale: "I was charged with the liaison task with other episcopates. . . . First [we] consulted among ourselves . . . to decide what position to take and what to say at the international meeting."[49]

The ECs that worked to develop a consensus were also those that believed in collegiality. Bishop Elchinger, a French progressive, told Caporale that the French EC had "organized a research committee of bishops in order to study the ways and means to realize and put into practice the idea of collegiality, and thus, reorganize the EC."[50]

This collegial consensus-building within the ECs allowed the DM to develop compromise positions that they could be relatively sure would be supported by the diverse episcopates they represented. As the DM decided on their agenda and strategies, each episcopate's representative could communicate these to all of the bishops from their country, gauge their reactions, and estimate support for progressive reforms when they came to a vote.

The DM benefited not only from its relationship to individual episcopal conferences, but also from strong links between episcopal conferences. Returning to figure 3.1, note that the English representative also communicated the news to the Irish episcopate, and that Germany's representative communicated to the Austrians and the German-speaking Belgians and Swiss.[51] Two supraepiscopal conferences (depicted as squares in figure 3.1) were crucial in providing both a large number of contacts and models for enacting collegiality: the Latin American bishops, who were organized under CELAM prior to the Council, and the African bishops (Federation of African ECs, or FACE) who began meeting during the First Session.[52] Through these two organizations alone, the DM was able to reach approximately 860, fully a third, of the bishops who might vote on any given reform.

Bishop Blomjous, one of the two FACE representatives to the DM, described to Caporale how FACE worked, and its relationship to the DM:

> We started the Federation of African ECs in order to help the Council. At the meetings of the individual conferences we discussed topics which later turned up at the Federation [meetings]. [FACE] is a board of twelve bishops representing different ECs. . . . Two bishops [Zoa and myself] act as secretaries. . . . We participated at the meetings of the intercontinental conference at the Domus Mariae, every Friday. . . . The purpose is mutual information.[53]

African leaders actively worked to ensure good communication between the national ECs, FACE, and the DM. A similar relationship existed within the larger and thus arguably more powerful CELAM. (As Câmara told Caporale, "There are nearly 600 bishops from South America."[54]) For example, the peritus for the Brazilian EC told Caporale:

> The Brazilian bishops met twice a week. The four periti would analyze and study selections and brief them on what position to take. *A trial vote would be taken to feel the attitude of the crowd and a decision would be made as to the total voting trend of the Brazilian Episcopate.*[55]

No doubt because of this deliberative process many felt that CELAM and FACE were "absolutely monolithic" during Council votes, as Bishop Raymond, a progressive from India, told Caporale.[56] Just like the DM's focus on consensus building, the focus on deliberation and democracy in CELAM and FACE stemmed from a deep belief in collegiality. Jean Cardinal Zoa, the other FACE representative to the DM, told Caporale that, "The concept of collegiality was for me the consecration of my most cherished idea. . . . We felt very seriously about it."[57]

Their beliefs in collegiality led DM leaders to enact a consensus-based form of participatory democracy: in a small group of twenty-two bishops, they discussed their own concerns, listened to Church leaders from areas with problems quite different from their own, and developed compromise solutions to disputed issues. This resulted in a learning experience that DM members felt both intellectually and spiritually. The Philippines representative to the DM, Bishop Olalia, told Caporale: "Personally, I widened my horizons of ideas. I came with my own little ideas, thinking that they were the best. Instead, I saw that others had better ideas than I had."[58] Reflecting on the Council, Bishop Primeau, the U.S. representative to the DM, wrote:

> Contact with the bishops of the world has widened my horizons, made me more appreciative of the ideas and problems of others, more sensitive to their needs, spiritual and material. . . . Before collegiality [was formally approved by the Council] . . . I had already profoundly experienced [it].[59]

More than simply a voting machine or political mobilizing structure (though those functions should not be discounted), the DM was, in effect, a school where bishops went to learn about issues and returned to their episcopates with greater knowledge and understanding than they had before, and thus an even deeper belief in collegiality. In fact, DM member Bishop McGrath, wrote that CELAM and the DM were "a formative school for our bishops" that provided "a practical lesson" in "episcopal collegiality."[60] As the DM developed its positions, each representative was able to communicate them to the bishops who were members of their EC sincerely and help the DM develop and employ effective tactics. These tactics and their successes will be examined in detail below, after the reader is introduced to the strategy and organization of the CIP.

THE COETUS INTERNATIONALIS PATRUM

In contrast to the DM's quick decision to institute an extensive, collegial organization, conservatives were slow to organize outside of the official structures of the Church and Council. This hesitation was in large part due to their already substantial resources and their access to the centers of power in the Church—the Roman Curia and the pope—at the start of the Council, as well as to the overwhelmingly conservative tone of the preparatory schemas, which many conservatives were confident would simply be approved.[61] However, as the Council progressed, and conservative schemas were defeated or watered down time and time again, conservative leaders grew increasingly alarmed.

Sometime early in the Second Session, three prominent conservatives, Brazilian archbishop Geraldo de Proença Sigaud, French superior general Marcel Lefebvre,[62] and Italian bishop Luigi Carli, began corresponding with each other and with their personal theologians with the intention of slowing down, if not stopping, the progressive momentum of the Council.[63] This correspondence provides an interesting picture of their growing concern and the strategies these conservative leaders devised and eventually implemented in their organization.

CIP Strategy

Two months into the Second Session, Lord Berto, who would eventually become one of the CIP's main theologians, wrote to Carli that he felt "dreadful sorrow" at the First Session's defeat of the conservative schemas, and complained that progressives seemed to have a "monopoly" on Council "discourse."[64] Once the Second Session was over, however, Berto began to feel more than sorrow and frustration. He and other conservatives began to see that their numerous defeats were the result of some kind of progressive organization:

> I cannot avoid a frightening question: "who stands behind the curtain? . . . Who is the author of this colossal deception? How is it that all the texts of the new "schemata" have been written according to . . . the "progressive" direction? Is there a "mafia" within the Church?" I certainly do not ask for a response from your Excellence! But the question is on my mind and I cannot drive it away.[65]

A few months later, just before the Third Session was to begin, Berto wrote Carli that the progressives' plan to impose "a *substantial* change of Catholicism" was making "itself more manifest each day."[66] Their increasing concern was in no small part due to the progressive statement on religious freedom, written by the Secretariat for Promoting Christian Unity, which they had just received.[67] By the time the Third Session was over, CIP leaders were certain that they were "faced with an enterprise of subversion of the doctrine of the Church of a kind that the Church has never seen throughout its history. Fortunately, God inspires brave defenders of the faith."[68]

Conservatives had realized that their schemas were being defeated and their views ignored because "progressives" had a plan and some kind of organization (whether mafialike or not) through which to implement it. This realization encouraged them to develop their own organization, with which they hoped to foil this plan.[69] They eventually organized under the name Coetus Internationalis Patrum (International Group of Fathers, or CIP), hired office staff, bought a printing press, and held weekly meetings that were attended by a core group of sixteen bishops.[70] Yet even though they became a full-fledged organization, they never figured out a way to communicate with the majority of bishops at the Council without seeming too "collegial." A central reason for this failure had to do with the CIP's relationship to ECs.

The CIP's Organizational Structure: Anticollegial, Suspicious of ECs, and Isolated

In contrast to the DM, for whom the ECs were essential, the CIP was, for two reasons, not able to utilize them. First, the ECs that most closely aligned with the CIP agenda (Italy and Spain) were less effective conferences for such purposes because they were not deliberative. Second, the CIP had little contact with the ECs that were deliberative because they viewed such organizations as a direct threat to the pope's authority.

The only complete CIP petition left in the archives,[71] which sought a conciliar condemnation of communism, circulated two weeks into the Fourth Session.[72] The petition gives a good indication of the nationalities of CIP sympathizers and demonstrates that though a wide variety of countries were represented, more than a third of the 435 signers were serving in, or were originally from, Italy or Spain, though bishops from those two countries constituted less than a quarter of all of the bishops at the Council. While such support from Spanish and Italian bishops could be seen as a CIP advantage, characteristics of the ECs of these countries hindered communication, and therefore CIP effectiveness.

Descriptions of the Italian and Spanish ECs suggest that they were far less communicative or vital than ECs more closely affiliated with the DM. In fact, though it was the largest national conference at the Council, "Prior to the Council, the Italian episcopate, nearly 400 strong, had never known what an EC was."[73] Bishop Valerii, an Italian who participated in the DM, told Caporale, "The Italian EC is very disorganized. . . . The Italian bishops did not meet many foreign bishops. I did, because I was here at the DM. . . . The other Italians stay at home and meet nobody. . . . The Brazilians, on the other hand, are very well organized."[74] CIP leader Carli told Caporale, "The Italian Episcopate delegated some participants to other conferences, but they never reported to us."[75] Bishop Calabria confirmed Carli's impressions:

> [Italian links to other ECs were] a great deficiency. We appointed commissions of representatives to other episcopates, but they never reported to us in our general session . . . [and] we never exchanged impressions . . . [or] reported or heard any report, although theoretically all the ECs were covered by our delegations.[76]

Though the Spanish EC, which met at least twice a week, was one of the most active, frequent meetings were not enough to ensure good communication, or to mobilize votes. Like the Italians and unlike bishops from other countries, none of the four Spaniards interviewed by Caporale mentioned the DM or their DM representative. When explaining the structure and function of his EC to Caporale, Bishop Morcillo, a progressive Spaniard, told Caporale: "Never did one bishop speak for all the Spanish bishops. I did it once, but exaggerated representation, [and] I spoke only in the name of 'many' Spanish bishops."[77]

The fact that Spain and Italy did not achieve this level of consensus by the Second Session (when most other ECs had, at least on occasion)[78] is indicative of a central weakness of their ECs for the CIP's purposes. There was simply less "exchanging of impressions" (as Bishop Calabria put it) when they met.

These characteristics were rooted in a central ideological characteristic of the Italian and Spanish ECs. Recall that when Etchegaray wrote to invite Cardinal Suenens to attend a DM meeting, he noted that the participants' ability to represent their episcopacy depended upon the "structure and degree of 'collegial conscience'" of their EC.[79] There is no doubt that the Italian EC was foremost on Etchegaray's mind when he made that qualification, and that Spain was close behind. Simply put, these ECs were suspicious of collegiality.

Some indications of this are presented in the voting data. Of the 408 bishops who voted no on the most progressive statement on collegiality, more than half were from Italy. Italians were infamous for their anticollegial stances. Bishop Raymond, a progressive from India, told Caporale that "with regard to collegiality, we have mostly Italians against us."[80] Together, bishops from Italy and Spain made up more than 60 percent of the bishops who voted against collegiality (results not shown), though again, bishops from those two countries constituted less than a quarter of the voting bishops. In other words, bishops from Italy and Spain were two and a half times as likely as their proportion in the episcopate would indicate to vote against collegiality. No other countries came close to such a disproportionate showing.

However, and more importantly, conservatives were hurt not only because the bishops in their sentiment pool[81] were from less collegial ECs but because CIP members were reluctant to use the structure of the ECs at all because the idea of collegiality within ECs was particularly troubling to the CIP bishops. All three of the CIP leaders made disparaging comments about ECs in and outside of the Council Hall. Lefebvre told an interviewer that he regarded ECs "as a threat to the teaching authority and pastoral responsibility of individual bishops," and referred to the tendency of some ECs to issue joint statements as "a new kind of collectivism invading the Church."[82] And during the Second Session, the two other major CIP leaders, Carli and Sigaud, made formal interventions in the Council Hall against further institutionalization of ECs. Carli's primary concern about ECs was their institutionalization of collegiality. Speaking for a number of CIP leaders and sympathizers, he argued that ECs "should not be based on the supposed principle" of collegiality, "even if the 'alleged' collegiality" was approved by the pope and the Council.[83] Sigaud stated that ECs could limit "the powers of individual bishops" or "even destroy them."[84]

Despite their negative feelings toward ECs, CIP leaders eventually did recognize their utility for any group wishing to communicate with the "rank and file." Sigaud reportedly wanted to establish a "Conference of Presidents of ECs," because he thought the CIP would "gain in vigor and size if it were based on pre-existing structures."[85] However, there is no record of Sigaud or any other CIP leader attempting to communicate with the bishops through the ECs. It seems that, ultimately, they were simply too disturbing a form of organization for these conservative leaders to deal with.

Instead, CIP leaders regularly communicated with what seems to have been only a select few allies. For example, the CIP's commentary on collegiality was disseminated only to those they knew to be sympathetic to their cause. Lefebvre closed the form letter seeming to recognize that such communication was less than ideal:

> Perhaps you may be able to find even other Fathers who agree with these principles, and who will be able to undersign them and who thus may confer the greatest authority on this petition. On this we congratulate you.[86]

Writing to Sigaud a few months later, just before the Third Session, Lefebvre again stated, "I am sending these documents to you with the hope that when possible you will give them *to the Council fathers who will look upon them favorably.*"[87]

Communicating only with sympathizers was a flawed strategy because it seems that the CIP often failed to bring their various sympathizers together. Table 3.2 compares the bishops who signed the CIP petition asking the pope to condemn communism and their votes on collegiality.

TABLE 3.2

Support for CIP Communism Petition Compared with Support for Collegiality

Support for CIP Petition on Communism[a]	Vote on the Fourth Point on Collegiality[b]		
	Conservative	Progressive	Total
Did Not Sign	296	1,492	1,788
row percent	17	83	100
column percent	**73**	87	84
Signed	112	225	337
row percent	**33**	67	100
column percent	27	13	16
Total	408	1,717	2,125
row percent	19	81	100
column percent	100	100	100

[a] FSig 3.7.

[b] Second Session, October 30, 1963, *Suffragationes*, vol. 20, no. 104.

Only one-third of those who signed the CIP petition voted conservatively on the issue of collegiality. Perhaps even more telling, nearly three-fourths (73 percent) of the bishops who voted conservatively on collegiality *did not sign the communism petition*. In contrast to the DM, who brought diverse groups of bishops together to support its causes, the CIP was left appealing to fractured populations from issue to issue. This finding will be reaffirmed in relation to the issue of how the Council would treat the Blessed Virgin Mary, which is examined in chapter 5.

As a consequence, the CIP's regular meetings were usually attended by only "five or six Council fathers" and "four to six theologians." Though they occasionally opened their meetings to all the bishops, the highest turnout reported at any of those meetings was eighty Council fathers.[88] CIP leaders seemed to recognize that their organizational choices had left them isolated. Caporale wrote notes after his interviews summarizing his impressions of his respondents. What he wrote about Carli is fascinating:

> What impressed me was his good sense of humor, his readiness to talk and he did so very extensively, his realization that he was considered reactionary, and yet his feeling of doing his duty even at the cost of martyrdom. He was very open and frank, but it was evident that he had had very few contacts and was at the margin of life at the Council.[89]

Even after the CIP had formed, Sigaud, in a statement that highlights the importance of regular feedback to an organization's strategic capacity,[90] complained to Lefebvre that "Here in Brazil we have little news on the process of [Council] work and for that reason we cannot plan anything for the Third Session."[91]

Sigaud's lack of information may have partly been due to the fact that the CIP was simply never as well organized as the DM. This is supported by the fact that after the close of the Third Session, Lefebvre wrote Carli, "Regarding sending it to the 200 Fathers who are not Italian, I hope that you will be able to obtain the list through [the Cardinal's secretary]. . . . They must, I think, have kept the names of those who signed the documents at the end of the last [session]."[92]

It is difficult to imagine a DM member making similar statements at any point during the Council. Indeed, as Sigaud was complaining about a lack of information, and Carli and Lefebvre were looking for lists of potential supporters, the DM was busily corresponding, drafting schemas, and making plans for the Third Session, plans which included communicating with more than three-quarters of the bishops at the Council.

Tactics in Common: Petitions, Votes, and the Modi

In many ways, especially in their strategies, the DM and the CIP could not have been more different. Yet these differences should not obscure their many similarities: both held weekly meetings, corresponded between Council sessions, consulted theologians, and had substantial administrative help, including staff and presses or other organizations willing to print their materials.

In addition, certain Council rules dictated the tactics available to both groups. Council documents would be drafted by Council commissions, voted on in intermediate stages, and eventually ratified or not by the more than the approximately 2,100–2,200 bishops who regularly voted. Correspondingly, both groups attempted to influence the Council agenda, the membership of the drafting committees,[93] the tone of documents to be voted upon, and the voters. There were two primary tactics used by each group to achieve these: they wrote and submitted petitions to the Council moderators and the pope, and they authored amendments (modi) for Council documents which they attempted to get their supporters to submit along with their votes.

Petitions

Both the DM and the CIP used petitions, or formal requests to the pope or Council moderators, to indicate their displeasure, usually when they felt an issue had been inadequately addressed or had been kept off or removed from the Council's agenda. The DM submitted a number of petitions over the course of the Council. Their use of petitions illustrates the advantages the ECs gave them, as well as how their views on ECs and collegiality freed them to employ tactics more efficiently than the CIP. For example, during the Third Session, the DM grew concerned that important schemas were not going to receive the attention and debate they deserved due to time constraints. However, rather than circulate a petition to all of the bishops at the Council, the DM was comfortable allowing Veuillot, as moderator of the group, to write "in the name of the Bishops *representing twenty-seven conferences or groups of ECs from the five continents.*"[94] They saw themselves as legitimate representatives of almost all the bishops at the Council.

In contrast, and because they could not stomach such reliance on ECs and were not a collegial organization themselves, when the CIP wanted the weight of the entire episcopate behind them, they disseminated petitions to all of the bishops at the Council through the mail.[95] Just before the Fourth Session, Lefebvre wrote the following to Carli, which illustrates how and why they eschewed the more collegial, and efficient, petitioning method used by the DM:

> It is clear that the Holy Father thinks [we are] an organization or a highly organized association with members that are enrolled . . . , a Council, a president, etc. We are, however, far from this organization and it seems to me of little import . . . now that we know each other, whether we have a title or not. Instead of saying "international meeting" we can say "some Fathers in various nations". . . . We have no official or public organization. *What we do together has value only through the signatures of the Fathers who are very willing to grant them to us,* when we ask them; more often even, they ask us.[96]

Their two petitions were the only occasions on which the CIP attempted to communicate with the entire episcopate.[97]

The Modi

Another important tactic employed by both groups were the modi. When a bishop was voting on Council documents, especially those in their final stages, he had three options. He could vote to reject the document outright, accept it, or accept it with certain conditions. These "conditions" were called the "modi," as the proper term for such a conditional acceptance was *juxta modum* (with modifications). If more than one-third of the episcopate rejected or submitted modi on a document, the drafting committee had to take the bishops' suggestions into account during revision. The DM and the CIP both recognized the value of the modi and tried to use them to their advantage.

Mobilizing enough bishops to submit modi was an effective tactic for the DM when they risked losing because they could not muster enough votes, when a document was not bad enough to reject entirely but needed revision, or when they were simply running out of time. DM minutes from the Fourth Session note modi being prepared on nine separate schemas. The following press release reveals how well this tactic could work for the DM:

> ROME, Nov. 16—This correspondent has learned that as many as 400—if not more—of the 712 affirmative votes with modifications submitted five days ago on the vital Fifth Chapter of the Missions schema contained an identical amendment. . . . The amendment was recommended by five leading cardinals from North America, South America, Africa and Europe, and by six high ranking bishops and archbishops, four of whom are presidents of extensive ECs. As a result of this amendment, [the document] received less than the necessary two-thirds straight "yes" ballots required, which means that the Missions Commission must revise the paper in view of the various amendments submitted.[98]

This is only one of many instances where the DM was successful (the schema on missions had been a very contentious one) but kept their role in the victory obscured, so that not even the conservative author of the press release seemed aware of the careful planning and mobilization behind it. Instead of attributing the modi to the DM, which was surely behind them, he attributed them to the individual efforts of some prominent leaders, and while an alliance between them on this one issue was obvious, their overarching agenda and efficient organization remained behind the scenes.

Like the DM, the CIP authored modi which they gave to the bishops to submit when they were voting on schemas.[99] However, because they tended to only give them to those whom they knew to be sympathizers on particular issues, they always failed to muster the necessary number of bishops to submit modi, and thus send the document back to committee.[100]

It is important to point out that the CIP's continued failures on the modi were not due to a lack of sympathizers. Though one petition is incomplete[101] and therefore leads to a low estimate of sympathizers, the two CIP petitions I obtained from the archives indicate that they had more than enough supporters to sink almost any reform through the modi. Six hundred and eighty-two bishops signed at least one of the CIP petitions—only ten to forty bishops shy of the one-third needed (of the 2,100–2,200 bishops who voted on any given issue) to sink a reform.

However, the two petitions alone by no means provide a complete picture of CIP sympathizers. Another 250 bishops who voted conservatively on collegiality *did not sign either petition*. Given that a conservative view on collegiality was a very good indicator of overall conservativism, these 250 bishops represent an important group of conservatives that were likely never reached by the CIP. Together with those the CIP was able to mobilize for at least one of the petitions, this is evidence that somewhere between 880 and 930 bishops, or between 33 and 44 percent of the total episcopate, were in some way a part of the CIP's sentiment pool. Thus, the CIP apparently failed not because their opinions were so out of line with the rest of the episcopate but because they did not mobilize all of their supporters.

CONCLUSION: INSTITUTIONAL RULES, MODELS OF AUTHORITY, SEMI-MARGINALITY, AND ORGANIZATIONAL EFFECTIVENESS

When the Second Vatican Council opened in 1962, few observers would have predicted that an informal organization of progressive bishops would prove to be far more successful than an organization of conservative bishops with close alliances with the Curia. Indeed, in many ways this case illustrates how resources are not the sole explanatory variable for social movement success. If they were, conservatives should not have even needed an extraconciliar organization, given the normal workings of the Church.

Institutional Rules

But things were not normal; real changes in both the institutional rules and the legitimate power structure of the Church began the moment the Council opened. As researchers have noted, "changing environments generate new opportunities—and constraints,"[102] which can lead to "collective creativity" and new organizational forms,[103] generated within the confines of preexisting cultural schemas and symbols.[104]

Conservatives, particularly those within the Curia as well as CIP leader Bishop Carli himself, insisted at the start of the Council that votes were not binding, but were "recommendations" that the conservative drafting committees could take into account, and that the agenda had already been approved by the pope as set forth in the preparatory schemas.[105] There was no historical precedent for such an argument—council votes had always been binding (although this was easy to ignore because councils were such rare events)—and conservatives quickly lost that battle. But their refusal to recognize that the normal institutional rules in which the Curia had the last say had changed once the Council was underway provided the first window of opportunity for progressives, who immediately recognized that they *needed* an organization if their concerns were going to be heard.

By organizing around the new institutional rules surrounding votes, progressives were able to make up for their initial lack of resources, at least to some extent, and equalize their position vis-à-vis the conservatives.

This provides support for Ganz's argument that organizational "newness can be an asset."

> Traditional union organizers selected for reasons that had little to do with the needs of the environment within which they were to work, developed strategy within an organizational setting better equipped to reproduce past routines than to innovate new ones. Ironically, the abundance of internal resources to which well-established groups have access may make it harder to innovate by making it easier for them to keep doing the same thing wrong. New groups, on the other hand, often lack conventional resources, but the richness of their strategic capacity—aspects of their leadership and organization . . . —can offset this.[106]

Because it formed at the time, and for the purposes, of a Council, the DM was well adapted to a council environment where votes were binding, and where, in contrast to the normal operations of the Church, more mattered than the Roman Curia's and the pope's opinions.

Cultural Models of Authority

On the other hand, the CIP actually formed later than the DM, and not until Council rules and debates were much more crystallized. If strategic capacity solely depended upon temporality, then the CIP should have been better adapted to the Council environment than the DM. The fact that it was not suggests that regardless of when an organization is formed, its culture can harm its strategic capacity if that culture conflicts with the environment in which the organization is acting, as studies of movements as diverse as women's liberation[107] and New-Left homeschoolers[108] have illustrated.

The CIP's paralysis in the face of the progressives' continuing success provides a powerful example of how culture can constrain the actions of individuals and groups. Even though they knew they were losing and were aware of an alternative, effective organizational structure, they simply could not stomach using it. The ECs' collegial organization directly contradicted their deeply held beliefs in the holiness of the hierarchical structure of the Roman Catholic Church and the primacy of the pope—and thus their beliefs about the way things are, and the way things should be, within the Church, and by extension within the world.

In fact, their cultural model of authority hurt conservatives not just by limiting the strategies of the CIP but in other ways as well. This becomes obvious when the following question is posed: if the DM was so successful in communicating with the ECs, why did the CIP and the conservatives in general, who were themselves members of ECs, often seem less than fully aware of the extent of the DM's organization and agenda? There are three reasons this was the case.

First, conservatives from deliberative ECs had a different understanding of their ECs than their progressive counterparts did. For example, though Bishop Orlando Chaves, a prominent Brazilian conservative, and his progressive Brazilian colleagues agreed about the frequency of their EC meetings, Chaves told Caporale that the Brazilian EC "had no relations with other Episcopates."[109] When the connections between the Brazilian EC, CELAM, and the DM, are considered, it is almost hard to believe Chaves was a member of the same EC as Helder Câmara. This suggests that even if the CIP had designed to work through the ECs, they may have proved less useful to conservatives, because their sympathizers were less engaged in them, or simply did not go to any "extraconciliar" meetings. Chaves implied that such organizations, even those he felt allied with theologically, were simply not a priority. He told Caporale, "I was invited to join a group of those who are . . . more conservative (with a little smile) from all countries, but I never went because I am too busy."[110] Most conservatives did not recognize the necessity of working beyond the formal groups of the Council.

Second, those involved in the DM kept as low a profile as possible. They deflected criticism by simply never claiming any victories.

Third, even though they were careful not to claim victory, conservatives did recognize that the DM existed and even knew who was involved with it. Furthermore, they recognized that it was dangerous to their own cause: during the First Session they attempted to shut down all informal groups and speeches by theologians.[111] However, while they recognized the threat the DM posed, conservatives simply could not grasp how or why the DM was so successful, or respond to tactics that were not contingent upon hierarchical authority. Collegial organizations were both mysterious and even sinister to conservatives. In other words, they were like "mafias." Thus, the DM was able to stay out of the limelight partly because conservatives were not sure exactly how it was doing what it seemed to be doing.

Their low profile and conservatives' failure to grasp why they were being so successful also gave the DM an advantage by protecting their semi-marginal status.

Semi-Marginality

In her study of the growth of interest-based politics, Clemens argues that successful groups have members who are marginal, but not too marginal, to the institution they are trying to change.[112] As well-known and powerful bishops outside of the Roman Curia, the members of the DM were uniquely positioned, and benefited from their semi-marginality in a number of ways.

As the rules by which the Council would proceed were being established, the structure and embodiment of authority in the Church were being questioned. As chapter 1 demonstrated, the First Session radically changed the sense of legitimate authority in the Church. By the time they were interviewed by Caporale (by the end of the Second Session), most of his respondents openly disparaged the Roman Curia's power and refusal to embrace change, and called for radical revision to the structure of the Curia or its elimination altogether. Because they were entirely outside of the Curia, the DM bishops were unharmed by this shift in legitimate authority, and were in fact well placed to be seen as leaders of the newly legitimated episcopal conference structure. One indication of this: more than three-quarters of the DM's twenty-two members were recognized as one of the "five most important" people at the Council by Caporale's respondents. Furthermore, it is no coincidence that the founding members of the DM were not Italians but French and Latin American individuals who were geographically, administratively, and theologically marginal to the Church.

Organizational Effectiveness

On the surface this account contradicts most studies of consensus-based organizations, which have found that they are less efficient and effective than other kinds, particularly those that are more hierarchical.[113] For example, Mitchell Stevens found that the conservative, hierarchical Protestant homeschoolers were more successful then the consensus-based hippie homeschoolers:

> Sluggishness in decision making and unpredictable resource commitments are the downside of organizational forms that lend a lot of discretion to the individual. . . . Pure democracy can come at the cost of organizational survival. . . . Hierarchical divisions of labor and authority make the completion of complex tasks more efficient.[114]

Barbara Epstein found that the direct-action movement's reliance on consensus, aversion to hierarchical leadership, and distrust of power produced strong feelings of solidarity among members but led to unresolved conflicts, short-lived organizations, and a lack of strategy.[115]

The DM's ability to avoid these problems was rooted in certain qualities of their organization. First, as Francesca Polletta notes, the most successful participatory democratic organizations seem to be those which combine "aspects of collectivist forms with aspects of more conventionally bureaucratic ones."[116] As an organization *of leaders* of episcopal conferences, the DM carefully incorporated hierarchy (a familiar "organizational reper-toire") into a framework of mutual cooperation and participation. This al-lowed them to benefit from "the *solidary, innovatory* and *developmental* benefits of participatory democracy,"[117] but to avoid the problems associ-ated with not having clear tasks and leaders.

This careful melding of organizational forms was made more successful by a number of policies that ensured good communication. They made sure that the core group did not grow too large and that no ECs were overrepresented in it—two conditions which could have hampered discus-sion and created unfair power differentials.[118] They stressed the impor-tance of regular attendance, mandating "that anyone who could not per-sonally be present at the meeting must be replaced by some designated person."[119] Not all ECs met according to the same schedule or functioned in identical ways, so DM members gave presentations on the organization and decision-making process of their respective ECs and how their confer-ences performed "[their] tasks in the course of a week."[120] Finally, they at-tempted to ensure not only frequent but *accurate, concise, and consistent* communication, by providing bullet points for the representatives to read or disseminate to their ECs.[121]

The DM was not able to generate consensus on all issues.[122] Yet even when they failed to achieve consensus, they actively worked toward com-promise positions that everyone in the group could support and were careful to record divergent views in their minutes.[123] In contrast, no diver-gent views were recorded in CIP minutes or correspondence. Compro-mise was not an option and consensus not the goal for the CIP: their pri-ority was to assert the Church's hierarchical teaching authority and the primacy of the pope. For the DM, give-and-take was key to their participa-tory democratic form of government, while for the CIP and conservatives in general, to *compromise* on their views of the Church was to compromise the Church itself. These contrasting cultures led one group to organiza-tional success and the other to failure—and ultimately profoundly altered Roman Catholicism.

The ways in which these organizational and strategic differences, as well as the factors identified in chapters 1 and 2, mattered at the Council are best illustrated in relation to particular Council issues. Part 2 of this book examines three key conciliar issues, one of which led to perhaps the most important reform to come from the Council, the Declaration on Religious Freedom, and two of which—conservative attempts to further accentuate the importance of the Blessed Virgin Mary and progressive attempts to liberalize Catholic teachings on birth control—failed.

PART

II

~∾ම∿~

THE CASE
STUDIES

Chapter Four

THE DECLARATION ON RELIGIOUS FREEDOM

Ceding Power, Gaining Legitimacy

I do not think there is a single direct thing the Council
can do that will have more *immediate* effect in bettering
Catholic-Protestant relations than a forthright and
unambiguous statement favoring full religious liberty for
all . . . the Catholic Church is not fully trusted on this
point. Whether rightly or wrongly, non-Catholics . . .
are fearful that the church may still espouse a position
of intolerance, persecution and penalty for the
exercise of a faith not Roman Catholic.
—*Robert MacAfee Brown, Protestant observer
at the Council, after the First Session*[1]

The Declaration on Religious Liberty (or Freedom) was an unprece-
dented statement from the Church that the best form of government is one
which allows people to worship as they please. This declaration radically
changed the Church's relationship to the world, since for centuries the
Church had been intimately tied to governments in many countries. Many
governments had established Catholicism as their national religion (see
tables 2.1 and 2.3), a situation which, though not unproblematic for the
Church, had given it great financial and ideological advantages. Sometimes the Catholic Church and the state were so intertwined that the ruler
of a country actually could and did appoint the bishops for that country,
as Franco did in Spain.

The declaration changed all of that. It undercut the power of the
Church in many countries where it previously had monopolistic state ties
and support, removed centuries-old justifications for war or colonializa-
tion based on Catholic supremacy, and highlighted an old theology that
only "free" individuals can truly find religious truth. Many sociologists,
historians, and theologians have referred to the declaration as one of the
most important and radical reforms of the Second Vatican Council. José
Casanova, who studied the effects of the declaration, notes:

> From a world historical perspective, the Declaration on Religious Freedom,
> *Dignitatis Humanae*, is perhaps the most consequential and the most radical

departure from tradition. It establishes the very conditions of possibility for a *modern* type of Catholic public religion. Without this declaration every other document would have been for all practical purposes meaningless. The recognition of the inalienable right of every individual to freedom of conscience, based on the sacred dignity of the human person, means that the Church abandons its compulsory character and becomes a "free church." Truth can no longer be imposed, nor is it permissible to coerce individual consciences to follow external dictates. The immediate historical consequences of the declaration were (a) the acceptance of the modern principle of disestablishment and separation of church and state; (b) the contestability of any Catholic party of political movement officially sponsored by the Catholic church; and (c) in the long run the incompatibility of a dogmatic conception of authoritative tradition and the principle of freedom of conscience.[2]

This chapter examines the factors behind the bishops' interest in making such a declaration, an analysis which demonstrates that, contrary to the assumptions in supply-side theory, religious leaders, even those in very diverse organizational fields, are as concerned about addressing the legitimacy concerns raised by other religious leaders as they are in marketing their own institution to constituents. Affirming the Church's support for religious freedom was primarily of concern to Catholic theologians living in stable fields far away from the places where the alleged abuses occurred, which tended to be in majority Catholic countries like Spain and Colombia. Protestants from stable fields openly criticized the Church's preferential status in these countries, claiming that the Church had a tendency to promote religious "liberty when she is in the minority and suppress . . . it when she is in the majority."[3] Thus, Catholic leaders from stable fields prioritized the issue of religious freedom at the Council, virtually above all others, and steeled themselves for a long and hard fight on behalf of it.

CRITIQUES OF HYPOCRISY: ILLEGITIMACY BEFORE THE COUNCIL

Protestants had long been wary of the RCC's perspective on church-state relations because of the commonly held belief that the Vatican wanted to control national and even global politics and would attempt to do so if it was at all possible, even in countries with a formal separation of church and state. These beliefs were brought into high relief in the 1928 American presidential election, in which Al Smith, the United States' first Roman Catholic presidential candidate, lost in a landslide to Herbert Hoover after a campaign during which Smith was subjected to rampant anti-Catholic prejudice.[4]

Though he lost decisively, Smith's candidacy seems to have worried Protestant church-state watchdogs. Books and articles that specifically addressed the Roman Catholic Church's stance on church-state relations appeared in ever greater numbers after Smith's campaign, achieving great visibility by 1949, with the publication of Paul Blanshard's *American Freedom and Catholic Power.*

The majority of the publications critical of the Catholic stance on religious liberty justified their suspicions by focusing on "a series of discriminatory actions taken . . . against Protestant groups in Spain and Italy."[5] Spain in particular was notorious for "persecuting the Protestant Churches in its territory"[6] and was often accused of abuse and intolerance by leaders of the ecumenical movement.[7] For example, an article in the very first issue of the *Ecumenical Review* criticized the fact that "public manifestations" of non-Catholic places of worship were outlawed in Spain.[8] An article in *Liberty* magazine catalogued the religious repression Spanish Protestants experienced in detail:

> In Spain, Protestants are forbidden to (1) identify their churches by any outward sign, (2) advertise their services either by press or radio, (3) circulate Bibles or portions of the Bible without Roman Catholic notes, (4) distribute tracts and other evangelical iteration on the streets, (5) have private schools to educate their own children, (6) teach in public schools, (7) be officers in the armed forces, (8) operate their own hospitals, (9) establish old folks' or orphans' homes, (10) broadcast the gospel over Spanish radio stations, (11) rent public halls for "special gatherings," and (12) operate public evangelistic bookstores.[9]

A number of other majority Catholic countries, particularly those in Latin America,[10] were also often criticized for intolerance toward Protestants.[11] The complaints varied, from special privileges that were granted informally to the Roman Catholic Church, despite formal and legal religious freedom, in countries such as Guatemala,[12] to serious violence (116 Protestants were reported killed and 66 churches burned in Colombia by 1961).[13]

Though always a prominent Protestant concern, Protestant critiques of the Church's stance on religious freedom ramped up in both frequency and severity after John announced that there would be a council, probably because it suddenly seemed much more likely that these critiques might actually have some effect on the policies of the Church. Between 1948, when it first began publication, and October 1958, when John announced that there would be a council, the *Ecumenical Review* published six articles or commentaries that focused on the Roman Catholic stance on, or abuses of, religious liberty—about one-third of all articles it published on the Church. In the next three years, between 1959 and 1962, the years of Council preparations, it published thirteen. Seven of these articles appeared in the same issue in 1961, which focused solely on religious liberty.[14] In total, the articles that focused on religious freedom constituted more than 50 percent of the articles that dealt with the Roman Catholic Church in any way in the *Ecumenical Review* during the years of Council preparations, and in 1961, the year prior to the Council's start, 100 percent.

By 1960, it was clear that religious freedom had emerged as the central concern about the Roman Catholic Church for Protestant members of the ecumenical movement. In that year, the executive secretary of the Lutheran World Federation issued a formal statement urging " 'all [Protestants] who have occasion to express opinions of the non-Roman churches' about the forthcoming meeting of the Catholic bishops, which is to be known as the Second Vatican Council, should underline the importance of the matter of religious freedom."[15]

As the number and proportion of articles written on the topic increased, the descriptions of their grievances and suggestions for remedying them became more forceful. For example, in October 1959, one year after John's announcement, one prominent Protestant commentator catalogued acts of Catholic religious discrimination as well as the papal pronouncements he saw as promoting religious intolerance:

> The Roman Catholic Church seems to have always acted, in practice, against the principles of religious liberty. The Inquisition, the historical fact of "Sacral Christendom," the bloody persecution of heresy, the confabulation of Church and State to oppress non-Catholic citizens, all seem to point toward *an intolerant attitude* which should necessarily correspond to *an intolerant doctrine*.[16]

This intolerance was often called hypocritical. For example, the same author wrote in another article:

> There is a common interpretation of the Roman Catholic attitude towards Religious Liberty which can be summed up as follows . . . where Roman Catholics are in the minority, they ask for religious freedom. On the contrary, where they are in the majority, they oppose the external freedom of other religious beliefs.[17]

ROMAN CATHOLIC REACTIONS

Roman Catholic theologians in many countries began responding to these critiques well before the Council began, and their responses indicate that they took them very, very seriously. The most innovative theologians on the issue were French, as one Protestant noted with approval: "French Roman Catholic theologians are, of course, leading in this movement 'pro libertate.' "[18] Alongside the French were theologians from a variety of countries, most notably Germany and the United States. By 1961, an article in the *Ecumenical Review* catalogued the "voluminous" Roman Catholic literature on religious freedom with approval.[19]

All of these progressive Catholic theologians had two things in common. First, as one French theologian put it quite clearly, they wanted the Church to officially support the principle of religious freedom without conditions:

> Can the state approve the principle of religious freedom in the civil sphere, or does Catholic doctrine compel it . . . to grant the Catholic Church a position of privilege? *The only answer* which is fully in keeping with the free nature of faith is the promulgation of religious freedom, *not as a lesser evil*, to be borne out of unwilling tolerance, or as a relative good as long as we are living [as minorities], but *as a principle, permanently and finally established.*[20]

Second, these progressive Catholic theologians were clear that their interest in Roman Catholic support for religious freedom was about salvaging the Church's tarnished legitimacy. As an American theologian put it:

> The harm caused by adopting two different norms for action . . . [one for when Catholics are in the majority and one for when they are not] is due not so much to the fact that the inferior legal status of Protestant groups in a Catholic country may lead to discrimination against Catholic minorities in Protestant countries. *The real trouble is that it affects the whole Church, which appears to the rest of the world to be insincere and unjust and loses respect, interest and the power to convince.*[21]

German theologian Max Pribilla's statement on the issue also highlights legitimacy concerns:

> It can therefore only be to its advantage if the Church concedes liberty of conscience and religion and of its own accord renounces the imposition of state restrictions upon people with different beliefs, even where it could still impose them. *What it loses in external power, it will gain in moral force.* However, it would lose much of its prestige, and would carry on a useless struggle if its acts of tolerance were merely concessions made against its will and liable at any moment to be revoked.[22]

Among the reasons these legitimacy critiques struck such a chord at the time were the concurrent growth of communism, the consequent "Cold War," and, in 1960, the election of the first Catholic American president, John F. Kennedy.[23] Many Roman Catholic members of the hierarchy deplored communism or openly condemned it. But, by doing so, they opened themselves up to critiques of hypocrisy, as a French commentator noted:

> I have often received letters from Protestants—who are unknown to me—and who say: "You protest rightly against the infringements of religious freedom which cause your co-religionist behind the iron curtain to suffer, but

why do you say nothing about the sufferings of our Protestant brothers in some countries, which are not under Communist rule?" These reproaches are right. We claim liberty for our faith. We claim it *in every place and for everybody*. . . . We want it now for our Protestant brothers and for our Orthodox brothers, wherever such liberty is infringed, compromised or menaced.[24]

Protestants responded to progressive Catholic theologians such as this with approval and encouragement. For example, one American Protestant wrote:

It is important to realize that a very able and earnest attempt is being made by Roman Catholic scholars in this country, with much support from Catholics in Western Europe, to change the principles as well as the practice of the Church in this matter. . . . American Protestants should realize that the Roman Catholic Church is not a vast international machine designed to overturn their liberties if this were to become politically possible, and that they have many allies in the Catholic Church who share their belief in religious liberty in principle.[25]

An article reviewing Roman Catholic theology on religious liberty in 1959 closed quite positively:

There is evidence enough of the fact that: (a) Many Roman Catholic theologians, in many countries, defend a new theory in favour of complete religious liberty *in principle*, which is quite different and even opposite to the old doctrine . . . (b) This theory has in no way been condemned but, on the contrary, is supported by very important members of the Roman Catholic Hierarchy; and (c) This theory is not a tactical variant of the old doctrine for reasons of opportunism, but another radical and irreducible doctrinal position which is very sincerely and fiercely fighting the old one.[26]

This Protestant author's assessment of Roman Catholic doctrinal changes on religious freedom was perhaps a bit optimistic, and definitely premature. In fact, French and American theologians were criticized,[27] and even openly censored, by the Vatican. Just four years before John convoked the Council, the Vatican determined four propositions "considered to represent" the views of the American Jesuit theologian John Courtney Murray to be erroneous. Though Murray wrote a long reply to the indictment, his Jesuit superiors advised him to "cease writing on the subject."[28] Murray did as he was told and did not write or teach on religious liberty until the Council, when he would become an important figure in relation to the declaration.

Thus, though Catholic theologians, in some circles, were taking progressive stands that were much to the liking of Protestants, by the time of the Council it was clear to everyone, as a Protestant writing in the *Ecumenical Review* put it, that "Only a statement by the Vatican Council" could truly clarify "the position of the Roman Catholic Church" on religious liberty.[29] And, as a Catholic writer accurately predicted just before the First Session, "the issue may generate as much heated discussion as the 'infallibility' question did at the First Vatican."[30]

THE STORY OF REFORM

The First Session

At the start of the Council, the topic of church/state relations was relegated to chapter 9 of the extremely conservative schema *De Ecclesia* (On the Church), which essentially stated that "the state has an obligation to support only the Catholic Church and prohibit all others."[31] In fact, insofar as the schema referred to religious freedom, it did so only to condemn current treatments of the subject authored by Murray and other progressive theologians.[32]

The progressive Secretariat for Promoting Christian Unity (SCU),[33] the key organizational location for Protestant/Catholic dialogue during the Council, had drafted a separate schema on religious liberty. However, the Curia, which had been responsible for stifling previous statements on the issue, including Murray's, did not promulgate the SCU's schema to the assembly. Murray had not been invited to the Council.

As the Council started, no one knew how long it would actually take, or indeed, whether there would be additional sessions, and a declaration on religious freedom seemed like a distant and unlikely accomplishment. Though the preparatory draft of *De Ecclesia* was the subject of serious criticism in the numerous alternative schemas and commentaries drafted by theologians such as Schillebeeckx, Phillips, and Rahner, and chapter 9 was not spared, the time allotted for the First Session was melting away and it soon became clear that there would not be enough to cover even a tenth of the issues on the agenda. Religious freedom would have to wait for the next session.

With nothing achieved during the First Session, Protestants kept up the pressure. In his summary of the First Session, Protestant observer Robert McAfee Brown wrote:

> [A] forthright and unambiguous statement favoring full religious liberty for all [is needed for two reasons]. . . . There is the past history of the Catholic Church, in which there have been notable instances of persecution by the Church, particularly when it was in positions of political power. It is unnecessary to detail this, for we are all familiar with it. And it must be reported that the images conjured up by a word like "Inquisition" still linger in many non-Catholic hearts. . . . In addition to past Catholic history, present Catholic

practices in certain parts of the world lend credibility to the notion that the Church does not really believe in religious liberty. It is perhaps unfortunate to always use Spain and Colombia as whipping boys here, but the fact is that in present times in these and other countries, non-Catholics have serious penalties and liabilities visited upon them because of their espousal of a different religious faith.[34]

Another article published after the First Session (one which Catholic ecumenists seem to have been reading, because I found a copy of it in O'Hanlon's archive)[35] asked two "of America's outstanding Protestant leaders . . . if Catholics formed a majority of the population in the United States at some distant date, [would this] curtail the freedom of non-Catholic Americans? Their answer: It very well might. It would be foolish to deny certain facts, or dismiss them too lightly."[36]

However, though Protestants were keeping up the pressure, and though bishops friendly to ecumenism continued to take these Protestant critiques seriously, it was also clear by this time that a progressive statement on religious liberty would meet serious resistance in some circles.

Resistance to the Religious Freedom

Bishops from majority Catholic countries, even very progressive bishops, had strong opposition to the Council making any definitive statement on religious freedom. As Bishop Manuel Fernández-Conde, a progressive Spaniard, told Caporale emphatically, "Fr. Courtney Murray has no idea of the Church-State relations the way we understand them."[37]

Most commonly, those opposed to the declaration justified their resistance by emphasizing the danger of allowing "sects" to come in and proselytize. For example, Conde continued, "In Spain we cannot let sects come in and work—this is a problem of religious freedom. We cannot let our faithful be taken away by these fanatics."[38]

When he told Caporale that "ecumenism in some countries is more dangerous than useful,"[39] Bishop Valerii, a conservative Italian, was likely thinking of those countries where the Church was experiencing the most competition from Protestants, namely, the countries of Latin America. Despite their overall progressive posture and awareness that the issue was important to their Northern European allies, Latin Americans admitted openly that religious freedom posed problems for them because of the aggressive posture of Protestant missionaries in their countries. For example, Bishop Eugênio de Araújo Sales, a progressive Brazilian, told Caporale: "We have to deal with sects. We suffer a lot of competition at the hands of the Baptists and the Pentecostals."[40] Sales was implying what Peruvian bishop

Fidel Tubino Mongilardi told Caporale explicitly: "Our Protestants are on the offensive. . . . Not all Protestants are the same. The Anglicans do not proselytize."[41]

Accepting the principle of religious freedom was more difficult for Latin American bishops because their relationship with Protestants was completely different from that of bishops in stable, and even emerging, fields. As Bishop McGrath of Panama, an active leader in CELAM and the DM, told Caporale: "In Central America [ecumenical dialogue] is non-existent because we have only sects and they are not capable of a dialogue. They are hostile to the Church and not willing to dialogue."[42]

Rather than seeing each other as colleagues, Protestants and Catholics in Latin America saw each other very much as competitors. It was thus difficult for Latin American churchmen to support religious freedom, despite the importance of the issue to their allies from stable fields.

Thus, though nothing definitive transpired during the First Session to either advance or impede the cause of religious liberty, it was clear that there would be fierce opposition from bishops in Spain and Italy, and that Latin Americans were far from supportive, especially initially. It was also clear that Protestants would continue to emphasize the issue as central to bettering ecumenical relations, and that as a result, bishops from stable fields needed to keep up the pressure if the Council was going to make a progressive statement on religious freedom. Bishops friendly to the ecumenical movement set to work between the First and Second Sessions to bring the topic to the floor of the Council.

Between the First and Second Sessions: A New Pope and a New Schema

By the last two weeks of the First Session, "rumors . . . had been circulating regarding the Pope's health."[43] Though Pope John's health improved enough for him to participate in the closing ceremonies of the First Session on December 8, it was to be the only session of the Council that he would lead.[44] He died on June 3, 1963, just weeks before the Second Session of the Council was scheduled to start.

His death could have marked the demise of the Council had conservatives succeeded in electing a pope who would not see fit to continue it. However, the College of Cardinals elected Cardinal Montini, one of John XXIII's closest advisors. Montini was the first cardinal John appointed after his election, and he wrote in his diary that he hoped Montini would be his successor.[45] Montini had publicly stated prior to his election that he hoped the new pope would continue the work of the Council, and indeed, made it clear as soon as he was elected that he would do so. So, while delayed, Vatican II was not derailed by John XXIII's passing.

As John was declining, various conciliar commissions had been engaged in revising the documents discussed during the First Session.[46] *De Ecclesia* underwent significant revision, and the ultraconservative chapter on church-state relations was dropped from the schema. While progressives had a difficult time securing a place for the more progressive statement that had been written by the SCU, through a series of negotiations religious freedom became chapter 5 of the Schema on Ecumenism being written by the SCU.[47]

However, though progressives had gained a foothold in important commissions, and significant confidence as a result of the events of the First Session, they remained outsiders in terms of the power structure of the Vatican. Two months prior to the start of the Second Session progressives learned that "the question of religious freedom had been purely and simply suppressed from the agenda" by the Curia-dominated commission in charge of promulgating documents to the assembly.[48] About this time, the secretary of the SCU wrote to American bishop and DM representative Primeau:

> De Libertate Religiosa—is supposed to be in the printing stage, although I will not be surprised if it still rests on Archbishop Felici's desk, and deliberately will be kept there until the last moment. The De Lib. Rel. draft is a gem and will rejoice the American bishops and many others—that is what Card. Ottaviani fears, that may be the reason for the delay.[49]

The Second Session: A First Look

As the Second Session of the Council convened on September 29, 1963, and a statement on religious liberty was nowhere to be seen, promoters of the declaration kept up the pressure. A month into the session, American Francis Cardinal Spellman presented the following petition to the Council moderators and the pope:[50]

> The Hierarchy of the United States of America, meeting Monday, October 21, 1963, having in mind—that there is world-wide and urgent interest in and a demand for a Conciliar Declaration on the right of the individual freedom of conscience and specially in what pertains to the profession and practice of religion; and that such a declaration is logically related to and would serve the interests of the faith; did unanimously vote to ask *instantissime* . . . that the question be treated on its supremely important merits at the earliest possible moment and with emphasis proportionate to its basic, world-wide moral urgency; [and] that, therefore, the Schema *De Oecumenisme* already prepared for discussion in the Council be presented to the fathers.[51]

Another statement released by the American EC illustrates clearly that their interest in the declaration stemmed from legitimacy concerns.

> The accusation is frequently made against Catholics that their doctrine and policy are machiavellian. The charge is that, when Catholics are a political minority, they demand full religious liberty as their right; when, however, they are a majority, they refuse to others the right to the free profession of faith according to the dictates of conscience. Hence Catholics fall under suspicion in the political order. And this suspicion is an obstacle to the spiritual apostolate of the Church. From a pastoral and ecumenical point of view, it would be a misfortune if no statement were to be made by the Council on the issue of the free exercise of religion. *A leading American Protestant theologian, Dr. Robert McAfee Brown, who is an observer at the Council,* has said, "I do not think there is a single matter on which more good could be done in terms of the relationship between Catholicism and Protestantism, than by some authoritative message from the Council about toleration and religious liberty." If no statement is made, the suspicion referred to above will be confirmed, it will be thought that the Church does not acknowledge, or at least calls into question, the personal right of religious freedom. In consequence, there will be a serious deterioration of the good relations which have recently begun to exist between Catholics and non-Catholics.[52]

In response to these and other pressures, Paul ordered the Doctrinal Commission to convene and make a decision, and the chapter finally made its way to the Council floor, but with only two weeks left in the time allotted for the Second Session.[53] Belgian bishop Emile De Smedt, when introducing the chapter, implored the assembly to accept the statement as the basis for a declaration:

> The whole world is waiting for this decree. The voice of the Church on religious liberty is being waited for in universities, in national and international organizations, in Christian and non-Christian communities, in the papers, and in public opinion—and it is being waited for with urgent expectancy.[54]

Like De Smedt's, other commentaries on the declaration's first public appearance demonstrated that its proponents were well aware of the importance the issue held for the Church's legitimacy in the eyes of non-Catholics. American cardinal Ritter "considered religious liberty to be a basis and prerequisite for ecumenical contacts with other Christian bodies."[55] American cardinal Albert Meyer told the assembly that he supported the document because it "would show that the faith was not to be spread by violence, conquest, or propaganda, but through freedom; and because a statement was necessary because of its implications for the ecumenical movement."[56] American archbishop Karl Alter told the assembly that the

Church should come out with a statement in favor of religious freedom because

> Among many Catholics as well as non-Catholics there still exist doubts as to whether the Catholic Church recognizes full religious freedom to worship God . . . for Catholics only or also for others. It is fitting to dispel these doubts, that Christian unity, according to the mind of Our Lord Jesus Christ, may be promoted and that both truly fraternal charity and good relations may increase, day by day, among Catholics and non-Catholics.[57]

This active lobbying on the part of the Americans was supported by bishops from other stable fields, particularly those from Belgium, England, Germany, and the Netherlands. For example, the English EC released a press statement which said that the Council should make "a basic assertion of a vital freedom—religious freedom," and English archbishop John Hennas argued that the Church "must put an end to the accusation that the Church claims liberty when she is in the minority and suppresses it when she is in the majority."[58]

In sum, as the declaration was first introduced in the Council Hall, proponents emphasized its importance to bettering relations with Protestants and solving the legitimacy problems current Church doctrine presented. However, to the dismay of these reformers, hopes that the document would be approved in the Second Session did not materialize. This seems to have been due to the serious time constraints being felt by the end of the Second Session, and to the fact that Paul was preparing for his visit to the Holy Land around this time. The statement, and chapter IV, on the Jews, which had been tabled along with it, held important implications for his visit. Rynne surmises that because Paul was unwilling to risk having the statements weakened by conservatives prior to his trip, he decided to withhold both chapters until the Third Session.[59]

After it became clear that there would not be a vote on religious liberty during the Second Session, Protestants continued to emphasize the importance of the issue.[60] After the close of the Second Session, a prominent Protestant commentator wrote:

> It is quite obvious that a forthright and unambiguous statement by the Vatican Council on religious liberty would be crucial in defining the posture of the Roman Catholic Church towards non–Roman Catholics. Every ecumenical "move" of the Catholic Church will be completely fruitless and void of any real meaning unless that Church states clearly and authoritatively that it will respect the liberty of other believers, even when it has the power or the occasion to do otherwise, and that it condemns intolerance, persecution and discrimination on the grounds of religious beliefs.[61]

Meanwhile, the DM made sure that it was doing its homework. About one month after the close of the Second Session, Etchegaray wrote

Primeau that the French bishops had been studying the question of religious liberty and "are currently translating the article published by Murray in *America* on November 30, 1963." He asked Primeau to keep him informed of any "other articles on this topic" which Primeau might "deem worthy of circulating."[62] Such preparation would come in handy during the next two sessions of the Council.

The Third Session: A Vote, Revision, and Black Thursday

Early in the Third Session, Bishop De Smedt, again acting as *relator*,[63] presented an amended document to the assembly. Debate ensued, in what was by now a quite familiar form, with conservatives arguing that the document "should be entitled 'On Religious Tolerance,' not 'Liberty,' because those in error had no rights . . . as the Catholic Church was the one and only true Church, it should be supported by governments; [because it] . . . was God's will that the Catholic Church should prevail."[64] Declaration supporters responded to conservatives by continuing to emphasize the importance of the issue for the Church's legitimacy, as did Cardinal Meyer in his intervention:

> This affirmation of religious freedom is essential for fruitful dialogue with non-Catholics. For unless it is perfectly clear to our separated brethren that we sincerely acknowledge their freedom, their personal dignity, the profound religious convictions, that same freedom, I say, and that same personal dignity, and those same profound religious convictions which we claim for ourselves, all of our efforts to deal with them will rightly be suspect.[65]

This time, declaration supporters were also joined by vocal support from bishops from behind the iron curtain, many of whom wanted the Council to condemn communism and were aware that doing so without a Council statement on Religious Freedom would only make the Church look more hypocritical. Yugoslavian bishop Smiljan Čekkada argued that "Religious Freedom is the problem *par excellence*," because "Marxist regimes were so actively engaged in the business of suppressing religion."[66] Later in the Council, exiled Yugoslavian cardinal Josef Beran, in a powerful speech just after he was released from prison, argued that the Church needed such a declaration in order to acquire, "greater moral force,"[67] because "Everywhere, and always, the violation of liberty of conscience gives birth to hypocrisy in many people," and that "In my country the Catholic Church . . . seems to be suffering expiation for defects and sins committed in times gone by in her name against religious liberty."[68]

Statements such as these, especially when they came from bishops who had themselves been subject to religious persecution and repression, reinforced reformers' arguments that the Church would continue to be seen as hypocritical if it did not come out with a declaration in favor of religious liberty. Furthermore, they helped to dispel the impression (right as it may have been) that religious liberty was largely a "Protestant issue."

On Friday, September 25, 1964, after three days of deliberation, the prominent progressive Dutch cardinal Suenens abruptly called for a standing vote on whether to end the debate. This proposal was carried overwhelmingly, and the declaration was sent back to committee with largely favorable reviews.[69]

As the end of the Third Session approached, and it became clear that a Fourth Session would be needed, the whereabouts of the declaration was something of a "mystery."[70] During the second-to-last meeting of the Third Session, the DM wrote a letter to Pope Paul, part of which stressed that "All participants wish that a declaration of this type, which has been expected by all so fervently, be submitted to a vote before the end of this session."[71] Though few knew it at the time, proponents had decided to "keep the document under cover until the last possible minute," to prevent the conservatives from being able to campaign against it,[72] or use their substantial bureaucratic power to suppress or defeat it, as they had recently tried.[73] It wasn't until the Tuesday of the last week of the session that the Council members finally saw the revised document, at which point they were informed that there would be a vote on Thursday.

However, the day that should have marked the greatest progressive victory yet became known as "Black Thursday." After receiving the schema, conservatives had submitted a petition to the Council presidents and moderators, signed by approximately 200 prelates, invoking a Council rule which specified that "adequate time must be allowed for considering the texts of schemata."[74] Thus, on the day everyone expected to vote on the schema, Cardinal Tisserant announced that there would be no vote on religious liberty during the Third Session.[75]

Though this move by conservatives took reformers by surprise, they quickly went into action, immediately drafting a petition in protest on which they gathered "more than 800 signatures . . . within the span of half an hour."[76] Despite these efforts, proponents would return home from the Third Session, after more than two years of Council debates without a declaration, with only a promise from Pope Paul that religious freedom would be the first order of business at the Fourth Session.[77]

Their victory on "Black Thursday" seems to have inspired confidence in conservatives, particularly those involved in the CIP. Just before the start of the Fourth Session Lefebvre wrote to Carli that "The schema on religious freedom . . . is contrary to the entire tradition of the Church. . . . It seems to me that the minority will be less minor at the next session."[78]

However, such optimism would prove to be unfounded, in no small part because progressives continued to plug away at the issue. As a member of both the SCU and the DM, Bishop Primeau was an important focal point of this activity, corresponding actively with other proponents of the declaration during the intersession, attending meetings in Rome where the final draft of the declaration was hammered out, and keeping DM members abreast of any developments.[79] For example, he told Cardinal Meyer that he was "sending the text of your memorandum to the . . . [DM, because] I am quite sure that the Secretariat will want to send your observations to all the hierarchies."[80]

Proponents of the declaration did not rest, at least in part because Protestants were open about the fact that the last days of the Third Session had created a sense of "mounting apprehension" among them and continued to stress that the "failure of the Council Fathers to adopt the religious liberty statement will be a disaster for the ecumenical movement."[81] As another Protestant observer wrote:

> [M]ajor interest in the whole Christian world will be focused on the reformulation, revisions, and final disposition of the Schema at the fourth session of Vatican Council II. To be sure an early concern will be the final disposition of the statement on "Religious Liberty" which is a prerequisite . . . to the whole future of ecumenical relations and of the effective presence of the Roman Catholic Church in the modern world.[82]

However, as much as they were concerned, just before the Fourth Session, Robert Macafee Brown predicted:

> There will be resistance among a good many Italian and Spanish bishops, a few (though not as many as I would have thought) from South America, and scattered bishops here and there. But the Americans, the British, the missionary bishops from the ends of the earth, and the solid group of French-German-Belgian-Dutch bishops will be very much in favor of a clearcut stand [on religious liberty].[83]

The Fourth Session: A Declaration

Brown's prediction was correct. Not only did the vast majority of bishops (fully 90 percent) vote in favor of the declaration when it was finally brought to a vote one week after the Fourth Session opened,[84] but the draft they approved was a stronger statement than the one handed out at the end of the Third Session.

And, though conservatives attempted to tone down the statement by authoring modi which enumerated eighteen specific flaws in the document, and which they asked (only those they knew to be) their supporters to submit with their votes on specific sections of the schema,[85] once again, the CIP's limitations were key. Only 543 modi were submitted, 170 less than the 715 needed in order for their recommendations to be taken into account.[86]

Conclusion: The Power of Legitimacy

Protestants heralded the declaration. One observer wrote, "The passing of the 'Declaration on Religious Liberty' marked one of the most significant milestones, not only of the Council, but of the whole history of the Church . . . to the great joy of all Christians and men of good will throughout the world."[87]

Such statements will come as no surprise, since religious freedom became an issue at the Council because of the serious legitimacy critiques Protestants had leveled at Church doctrine prior to the Council. I refer to the fields in which these critiques were made and heard as stable fields, not because they were unchanging (indeed, they were changing in a very important way by becoming more structured with the growth of the ecumenical movement), but because the position of the Roman Catholic Church had stabilized within them. It had become comfortable as an incumbent organization.

As incumbents in stable fields, bishops and theologians in Germany, the Netherlands, France, Belgium, and the United States were more aware of and disturbed by the legitimacy critiques from the leaders of other religious organizations in their fields. They thus fought throughout the entire course of the Council to change Church doctrine on religious liberty (as well as a host of other issues, one of which, Protestant critiques of Catholic devotion to Mary, will be addressed in the next chapter) and ensure that the Church did not appear "to be insincere and unjust."[88] They were convinced that whatever the Church would lose "in external power, it will gain in moral force" by coming out in favor of religious liberty.[89]

My examination of this process has a number of theoretical implications for the ways in which legitimacy concerns are raised and responded to by religious leaders. The first of these has to do with the importance of *genuine* responses to legitimacy critiques. Both Protestants and Catholics continually insisted that the declaration had to be sincere, that the Church had to make a declaration on the basis of belief, not expediency. As a German Catholic theologian wrote before the Council, the Church would be carrying "on a useless struggle if its acts of tolerance were merely concessions made against its will and liable at any moment to be revoked."[90] This suggests that for legitimacy concerns to be addressed effectively, organizations must accept the most basic principles of the legitimacy critique and not appear to be simply giving it lip service.[91] As bishop Primeau wrote when the fate of the declaration was uncertain, "we should drop the whole question unless we enunciate fundamental principles."[92]

Secondly, it was quite clear at the time of the Council that the legitimacy concerns to which proponents of the declaration were responding came from elites, arguably, elites who were just as well educated and powerful as the bishops who participated in the Council. As Bishop Primeau told a reporter before the Third Session, "the Protestant intelligentsia are always asking for a definite statement on Church and State."[93]

Though the elites with the most influence were those from other religious, particularly Christian, institutions, another important consideration should be noted. The same countries in which the ecumenical movement was prominent also had modern, secular states which rejected, and were often openly leery of, the political role played by the Roman Catholic Church in other parts of the world. Furthermore, these same states were among the most powerful in the world, and important allies in the Church's fight against "atheistic communism." Three weeks after the Fourth Session began, and two weeks after the first vote on the declaration, Pope Paul gave a speech to the United Nations. Though I cannot argue that he would not have appeared there had the Council rejected the declaration, it does seem that his visit was aided by the possibility of a declaration, and that his pending visit in turn likely aided the declaration's approval.

Finally, religious freedom was such a contentious issue because both progressives and conservatives were aware that, no matter how many previous statements in support of it could be cited by theologians and historians, any formal declaration about it represented a very real change in Church doctrine. Many bishops, especially conservatives, felt that the Church's unchanging nature was one of its major strengths. (Cardinal Giuseppe Siri argued against the declaration because, "If we bring about changes in doctrine and do not restrict ourselves . . . then, I believe, we are diminishing the theological sources of authority, and we are weakening our own authority.")[94] Ultimately, this case demonstrates that religious institutions can change fundamental doctrine, especially when *not doing so* means that institution might "lose much of its prestige" within the world, and among the leaders of other incumbent religious organizations.[95]

However, it is important to note that legitimacy concerns did not always result in the sort of radical changes to doctrine that the declaration represents. Sometimes, as in the case of how the Council would deal with the Blessed Virgin Mary, legitimacy concerns led the bishops oriented toward ecumenism to try merely to tone down and deemphasize "embarrassing" parts of Catholic devotion and doctrine. The question of how the Council should treat Mary, which more deeply divided the bishops at the Council than any other, is the topic of the next chapter.

Chapter Five

THE BLESSED VIRGIN MARY

THE TOUGHEST FIGHT OF THE COUNCIL

The [original] Schema [on Mary] . . . began to arouse
suspicions in the minds of some of the [Protestant]
observers when it began to speak of her as "not only
Mother of Jesus, the one and only divine Mediator and
Redeemer, but also joined with him in carrying out
the redemption of the human race." Suspicion grew
when it went on to speak to her as "administrator and
dispenser of heavenly graces" and finally as
"mediatrix of all graces."
—*John Moorman, Anglican observer at the Council,
after the First Session*[1]

WE NOW turn from the story of why and how Council documents like the
Declaration on Religious Freedom came into existence and were ultimately approved by the Council, to the story of why and how some documents failed. The case study examined in this chapter, the fight over how
the Council would treat the Blessed Virgin Mary, shares an important sim-
ilarity with all of the other issues dealt with in the preparatory schemas, because conservatives' views as expressed in those schemas were ultimately
largely rejected, either by vote or by fiat, early in the Council. Thus, in a
sense, Mary is representative of the many other conservative "reforms" attempted at Vatican II that tried to condemn or prevent change, or, as was
the primary goal in relation to Mary, further differentiate the Catholic
Church from other, particularly Christian, religions.

However, the issue of Mary is different from the other conservative efforts
represented in the preparatory schemas in two important ways. The schema
on Mary stayed alive longer and received more support from the episcopate
than any other preparatory schema. Indeed, in terms of issues brought to
a vote, no other issue so deeply divided the episcopate. In other words, the
fight over how the Council would treat Mary represents a conservative
failure that was almost a conservative victory, and thus the ideal case study
through which to examine why most conservative Council schemas failed.

In doing so, we find that, though in many ways the issues of religious freedom and Mary could not have been more different, the factors which determined why progressives fought so hard for a Council declaration on religious freedom also determined why they fought against the proposed Council schema on Mary. In a nutshell, both were the consequence of legitimacy concerns raised by the ecumenical movement. Furthermore, because Mary was the most contentious and divisive issue addressed by the Council, she allows us to compare conservatives' and progressives' organizational strength and strategies and tactics better than any other. The story of the CIP and DM's fight over Mary illustrates not only how advantaged progressives were by their organization and beliefs but, more importantly, how paralyzed conservatives were by theirs.

CATHOLIC AND PROTESTANT VIEWS OF MARY

Mary, the mother of Jesus, has held a special place in Catholicism for a very long time. As one Catholic theologian puts it, "Devotion to Mary the mother of Jesus has been a hallmark of the Catholic tradition."[2] Both popular and official devotions to Mary flourished in many places, especially Ireland, France, Spain, Italy, and Latin America.

Protestants have historically seen Catholic devotion to Mary as inappropriate and even verging on the heretical, because it often seemed to be more intense than Catholic devotion to Jesus.[3] Though Protestants accept Mary as the human mother of Jesus, and most also believe that she was a virgin when she conceived him, two particular Catholic doctrines about her have caused problems. First, since 1854, the Church has taught that Mary was conceived without original sin (this event is called the immaculate conception), so that she would be worthy to bear God's son. Secondly, in 1950, Pius XII declared that Mary was "assumed"—that is, taken up—body and soul into heaven, unlike all other humans, whose bodies remain on earth (this is referred to as the Assumption of Mary).[4] As one Protestant commentator acknowledged during the Council, many Protestants felt "that the Marian dogmas of 1854 and 1950 were without scriptural support."[5]

However, though these doctrinal differences were significant, the primary point of conflict between Catholics and Protestants was devotional rather than doctrinal. Protestants were disturbed by what seemed to be an overly intense devotion to Mary. Many Protestants felt that "Mary had been so elevated to a semidivine status [that] either she was given titles that parallel those given to Christ or she functioned like the Spirit."[6]

In 1955, three years prior to John's announcement that there would be a Council, a prominent German Protestant wrote the following in the *Ecumenical Review*:

> [T]here has been a violent growth of veneration of Mary in the dogma, theology, and general practice and worship of the Roman Catholic Church during the last few years. Veneration of Mary now plays an important part in its life and doctrine, and will probably occupy an even more important place in the future. All that is quite foreign to us, so that many of us can no longer see any basis for reaching an understanding with Roman Catholics, and regard further discussions as futile, pointless and hopeless.[7]

As the Council approached, Protestant emphasis on the importance of the Mariological issues increased.

> A Vatican Council cannot be expected at this time—if ever—to narrow the theological gaps, especially those created or disclosed during the past century, as, for example, by the promulgations of the doctrines of Papal infallibility, the Immaculate Conception, and the Assumption of the Virgin Mary. *But many Catholics are hoping that the Second Vatican Council will not add to them or widen them.* Some hold that it is not so much the doctrines as the cult that has made of Mariology a major obstacle in the path of Christian Unity. There is, also, a different emotional response by Protestants according to whether the Virgin is called "the Mother of God" or "the Mother of Our Lord."[8]

Catholics responded to these critiques.[9] In his letter to the pope about what he hoped the Council would do, American bishop William Brady wrote: "It is not opportune further to define the prerogatives of the Blessed Virgin Mary unless the notion (false but strong) among Protestants is first uprooted that the Catholic Church has the Blessed Virgin Mary for its center and not Christ the Lord."[10]

THE FIRST SESSION

No doubt because nearly a quarter of the bishops who responded to the pope's request for guidance said that they would like to discuss Mary,[11] she became an issue early in the Council debates. Cardinal Ottaviani, a conservative leader, eager to restrain the effects of the ecumenical movement and to discuss an issue that he saw as much safer than schemas on the Church or religious freedom, tried unsuccessfully to get the Council to postpone consideration of *De Ecclesia* (On the Church) and end the First Session by discussing (and hopefully approving) the schema on Mary that had been written by the conservative preparatory commission and handed out to the bishops prior to the beginning of the Council.

Bishops who wanted to improve ecumenical relations questioned the titles and accolades given to Mary in the schema and argued that Mary should not have her own schema but should instead be incorporated into a schema on the Church, because (using savvy political language) "it was not possible to speak of the Church without speaking of Mary."[12] For example, the ecumenical Dutch organization DOC published and disseminated to all of its subscribers a twelve-page paper titled "Some Ideas on the Mariology of Today," which elaborated on the importance of the issue for ecumenical relations. "There is always the danger," it argued, that some terms "suggest some kind of equality or equivalence" with Jesus, and therefore "the very best thing would be to employ terms which are less ambiguous" in whatever conciliar statement was ultimately made on Mary.[13]

A vote was not taken on the conservative preparatory schema, and the First Session closed without any decision. Bishops with ecumenical priorities breathed a small sigh of relief, because as one Catholic theologian observed, if the First Session had ended with the promulgation of a separate schema on Mary, the Council would have been "striking a blow at the ecumenical spirit."[14] DM correspondence between the First and Second Sessions noted that making sure the schema on the Church would include the schema of the Blessed Virgin was a first order of business for the Second Session.[15]

THE SECOND SESSION: THE CLOSEST VOTE OF THE COUNCIL

As the Second Session opened, Council moderators called for a vote on whether Mary should have her own schema or be included within the schema on the Church. Both sides made forceful interventions. Cardinal König, from Vienna, was charged with presenting the progressive view to the assembly just prior to the vote. He told the assembly that the Council should avoid giving the impression that it intended "to create new Marian dogmas" or "encourage false and baseless exaggerations," but then went on to assure the bishops that "The incorporation of the one schema into the other did not imply any lessening of veneration of the Virgin or any concealment of teaching about her, but rather an explanation of her place that would be consistent with the purposes of Vatican II."[16]

Those in favor of a separate schema on Mary argued that "In view of the special dignity of the Blessed Virgin Mary and her singular place in the Church, the Council should treat her in a special schema, which should nonetheless be intimately connected with the schema on the Church, to emphasize her special dignity and pre-eminence" as the Philippine Rufino Cardinal Santos argued in his intervention.[17] Conservatives also engaged in what Rynne called an "extraordinary and intensive propaganda barrage" to convince the bishops that Mary deserved her own separate schema.[18] Father Carlo Balič, a Yugoslavian Mariologist (who composed the separate schema), pamphleteered the bishops as they entered St. Peter's with a statement printed by the Vatican Press office about the importance of a separate schema.[19] Pamphlets also arrived in the bishops' mail, and the conservative press ran reports on the issue which, in the words of one Anglican observer, implied "that anyone voting against the idea of a separate Schema would be guilty of insulting the Virgin Mother."[20]

Conservatives were well aware of how important the issue was to ecumenical relations. In an intervention, one asserted that "the entirety of Catholic doctrine and its dogmas ought to be explained without reservations to the faithful and to the separated brethren."[21] CIP leader Bishop Carli complained that the focus on ecumenism limited his ability to speak freely:

> So many insist that we say nothing about those doctrines of ours that could possibly offend Protestants. Thus it seems that we cannot speak of the Blessed Virgin Mary. . . . [and] the Council is slowly petering out before a series of taboos.[22]

Another supporter of the separate schema suggested to Sigaud that the individuals who wanted to tone down the focus on Mary had an inadequate training in Catholic theology. "Such unhappy figures these priests that live in fear that Our Lord Jesus could lose devotion because of the cult of Our Lady. This is proof that they did not study theology very well, and do not understand anything about Mariology, and I even think [that they] lack spiritual life."[23]

Some conservatives tried to minimize the importance of the status of Mary for ecumenical relations by arguing that Luther himself had venerated her and thus, "The good Lutheran adores Mary as the Mother of Jesus."[24] Archbishop Jozef Gawlina of Poland told the assembly that "the cult of the Virgin" should not "constitute an obstacle to ecumenism" because Luther believed that "Mary does not lead herself but to God."[25] And when Ottaviani tried to get the Council to discuss the separate schema before *De Ecclesia*, he argued: "We have many points in common with our separated brethren. We are united in love for her. After discussing various points of difference, it is well for us to remember that she can serve to unite us."[26]

Once progressives and conservatives were done attempting to marshal support for their respective sides, the Council proceeded to vote on whether Mary should have her own schema. It was the closest vote of the Council (1,114 to 1,074). The progressives had won by only 40 votes.[27]

Such a close vote was an unpleasant shock to many participants, in no small part because divisiveness on any issue was not seen as desirable by either side. Many tried to tone down the repercussions of such open division.

For example, Italian archbishop Constantino Stela told a reporter that "the split in voting yesterday on the schema of the 'Blessed Virgin, Mother of the Church,' did not indicate discord among Council Fathers on the doctrine and dignity of the Virgin, but was only a sign of disagreement over the method of treatment to be given to the schema."[28]

Speculation abounded about the vote. An American bishop attributed the progressive victory to "a goodly number of Latin American bishops" who "have become frightened by the fact that a great many of the people have little religion left except a distorted form of a cult of the Blessed Mother which in many cases is material, if not formal, idolatry. They want to get the devotion to Our Lady into its proper perspective; hence they supported our point of view."[29] Though we now know that the majority of Latin American bishops voted in favor of the separate schema, unlike their more ecumenically oriented colleagues from Northern Europe and the missionary countries (see tables 2.1–2.5), it was nevertheless true that, given the closeness of the vote, the 44 percent who did vote against it (see table 2.3) were essential to this progressive victory.

This significant minority seems to have been swayed by the same legitimacy concerns as their more ecumenically oriented colleagues, concerns that they had become aware of because of the Council.[30] The DM and CELAM leader Manuel Larraín told Caporale that "We have rethought our theology, as for instance, in the new vision of Mary's function."[31] During the debates of the Second Session, another Latin American, this time a Mexican bishop, argued that including Mary in *De Ecclesia* would help to "demarcate the boundaries of Marian devotion to correct certain tendencies in popular devotion" and thus allow the Church "to explain the matter better to non-Catholics who sometimes had wrong notions about the Church because of these excesses." He closed by admitting that "Devotion to Mary and the saints, especially in our countries, at times obscures devotion to Christ."[32] In his careful description of the problem in Brazil, a country with an intense devotion to Mary, Bishop Câmara provides a good example of the position in which many Latin American progressives found themselves. As a very progressive bishop with conflicting ecumenical and pastoral interests, he told Caporale:

> We have developed our ecumenical sense of respect to all. . . . We have a profound respect for Cardinal Bea. In our Hiberic tradition we have a great esteem and love for Our Lady, but we intend to represent her in the framework which is more human. . . . It is a question [of] avoid[ing] . . . scandal[izing] our faithful, while giving Mary the right place.[33]

However, though these more ecumenically oriented Latin Americans were essential to the outcome of this first vote, given the closeness of the vote, the progressive victory was also due to a significant amount of work among other episcopates, particularly those who were divided on the issue of Mary. For example, the day before the vote took place, four theologians addressed the American bishops at their regular weekly meeting.[34] At least one American bishop was convinced that outreach efforts such as these on the part of progressives were the deciding factor in their narrow victory:

> Another factor in the successful vote was the excellent job done by the panel at the meeting of the United States bishops yesterday afternoon. I am convinced that a number of the United States bishops would have voted with the conservatives if they had not had the benefit of the presentation made by this panel on the subject of Mariology. A switch of only twenty votes would have defeated the project. I feel quite sure that at least twenty votes of the United States were switched as a result of that meeting.[35]

This assessment seems plausible. Prior to the Council, more than twenty Americans (more than half of those who wrote about her at all) requested that Mary be granted new and more exalted titles,[36] but ultimately, almost 80 percent of Americans voted against the separate schema.

The American conference was far from the only reported meeting on the issue. Prominent Catholic ecumenists contacted the Belgian, Dutch, and German episcopates and got their acceptance for the proposal to include the Marian schema in *De Ecclesia*, and "some experts were meeting elsewhere" with other prominent bishops and theologians.[37] Cardinal Bea campaigned against the separate schema with his pen, writing an article, "Marian Doctrine and Marian Devotion in Harmony with the Ecumenical Spirit," in French, which was "reprinted in a number of languages in various journals."[38]

Ironically, as much as these varied efforts may have helped progressives, their victory seem to have been due at least as much to conservative organizational weaknesses. As the Council was voting on Mary, CIP leaders were just beginning to correspond and had not yet formed their organization in earnest. In fact, their defeat on the Marian schema, combined with the "disastrous" votes on collegiality the following day, is what probably spurred conservatives to organize.

Thus, though Balič and other Mariologists attempted to marshal supporters by pamphleteering the bishops as they entered the hall, and through strong interventions, their campaign lacked a systematic plan and, most importantly, effective communication with their supporters. Evidence suggests that they could have done much better in regard to the Marian schema had they organized a bit more effectively earlier in the Council.

This evidence comes from the fact that after the vote, the CIP petitioned Paul VI to consecrate the world to Mary.[39] I obtained this petition from

TABLE 5.1
The First Vote Concerning Mary Compared with Support
for the CIP Petition Concerning Mary

CIP Petition Concerning Mary[a]	First Vote Concerning Mary[b]					
	Progressive		Conservative		Total	
	Number	Percent	Number	Percent	Number	Percent
Signed	103	32	253	68	326	100
Did Not Sign	1,012	54	852	46	1,864	100
Total	1,115	51	1,075	49	2,190	100

[a] FSig 2.8.
[b] Second Session, October 29, 1963, *Suffragationes*, vol. 19, no. 97.

the collection of Sigaud's papers at the Instituto per le Scienze Religiose—Giovanni XXIII in Bologna, Italy. In combination with the voting data, the petition provides three indications that the CIP failed to mobilize all of their sympathizers. First, the highest estimates report that only 510 bishops signed it,[40] less than half of the bishops who voted conservatively on the question of the Marian schema. In fact, table 5.1 demonstrates that the CIP did even worse than these initial numbers indicate; more than 800 of the bishops who voted for a separate schema did not sign the subsequent petition to the pope, despite the fact that both are indications of essentially the same sentiment: that the Church and Council should emphasize, rather than de-emphasize, Mary's importance.[41]

Second, and even more importantly, table 5.1 indicates that conservatives could have easily won the first vote on Mary. More than one hundred bishops who signed the petition on Mary voted against the separate schema.

Finally, one more point arises from the comparison of the signers of the CIP petition on Mary and the bishops' votes on the Marian schema. Twenty-seven bishops who signed the petition did not lodge a vote on the schema at all, though they did cast a vote before and after this one (and thus were definitely eligible to vote on the Marian schema).

Together, these findings suggest that conservatives were even closer to winning than the official vote demonstrated, and that if the CIP had been in tune with the assembly, as the DM was, they could have gained a relatively easy victory on this very contentious vote. The key problem for the CIP, it seems, was not a lack of sympathizers, but their lack of knowledge about who their sympathizers were and how to communicate with them.

Protestants were clearly relieved at the outcome of the vote, no doubt because it meant that the schema on Mary would not be a stand-alone statement but rather a small piece of the schema on the entire church, a preference which they had openly indicated. Before the vote, the prominent Protestant observer Robert McAfee Brown had "suggested that the ecumenical dialogue would be helped if Mary were included within the schema on the church."[42] After the decision, a Dutch Protestant observer wrote approvingly that, "there has been a noticeable effort on the part of Catholic theologians to remove the foreign quality that non-Catholics sense about Marian doctrine,"[43] no doubt because ecumenically minded Catholic leaders wanted to "moderate slightly the exuberance which the veneration of Our Lady has often found."[44]

This first vote however, did not determine what, in the end, was said about Mary's place in the Church, and thus exactly how close Catholic and Protestant views of Mary would come. As Brown continued to stress after the Second Session, "Next to Papacy, Mariology is the area of greatest theological division between Catholics and Protestants."[45] Mediating this theological division would take a longer and more detailed period of negotiation between progressives and conservatives at the Council, and yet another vote which would center around the terminology used in any conciliar statement on Mary. Furthermore, everyone was aware, as an Anglican observer wrote after the Second Session, that while a simple majority had been enough on the first vote, since it was only "procedural," the final approval of any document on Mary presented an "extremely serious problem," because the final vote on Mary would require a two-thirds majority.[46]

The Third Session and More Controversy

Once the schema on Mary had been incorporated into *De Ecclesia*, its drafters had to revise the document in a way that would both mollify conservatives and satisfy ecumenical interests.[47] Terminology became the primary issue, as the experts on both sides parried drafts back and forth directly after the vote and for over six months between the Second and Third Sessions.

Two titles were of particular concern "coredemptrix," which means literally that "Mary merited our salvation" or is one of the redeemers of humankind (the other being Jesus Christ), and "mediatrix,"[48] which means that Mary can obtain grace for sinners by acting as a mediator between them and God.[49] As a Dutch Protestant observer wrote before the Third Session, "Protestant criticism of Catholic Mariology tends to see the notion of co-redemptrix as the inevitable and intended climax of the whole doctrine of Mary."[50]

The DM attempted to disseminate the final compromise schema "to the episcopal conferences," to ensure "that the schema would be voted on without being publicly discussed in order to avoid another flaring up of passions." However, despite these efforts, "passions did arise. It was impossible to come to any agreement on the main points of the new version."[51] As the Third Session opened, vigorous debate ensued on the exact terminology which would be used in the schema.

Protestants reacted vehemently to the conservative emphasis on Mary's importance, especially to the terms they used continually in their interventions. A Lutheran observer said that, "These are the darkest days of the Council. I never felt so far from Rome as I do now."[52] Another Protestant observer, Douglas Horton, elaborated on the Protestant view of the debates in his published diary:

> One of the fathers asked that Mary's vow of virginity be mentioned. This I had never heard of before. I had taken it for granted that the "brothers" mentioned in the seventh chapter of John were the sons of Joseph and Mary—but I have since learned that devotional literature has eclipsed the Bible at this point and that Mary's vow is thought to have been taken in her girlhood. . . . No end of praises were thrown, like garlands, before Mary's feet. . . . It seemed that for a great many of the council fathers no superlative of excellence was too brilliant to add to Mary's crown. . . . This will undoubtedly be a major item on the docket of Roman Catholic–Protestant conversations.[53]

A final vote was called during the Third Session on the precise wording to be used to describe Mary in the schema on the Church. In the end, though the document was certainly a compromise, progressives succeeded in keeping the majority of the problematic terms out of it. After this, Horton approvingly wrote:

> Instead of calling Mary either "The Mother of the Church" or "The Mother of our Lord," which have come to be slogans of two differing groups within the church, the schema now speaks of Mary as "a most-loved mother." Some had objected to describing Mary as "Mediatrix." Instead of deleting this word, which would have offended one part of the church, the word had been softened by adding the loose appositives, "Advocate," and "Helper."[54]

The changes Horton refers to seem to have pleased the majority, but far from all, of the bishops. The final schema was approved midway through the Third Session by almost three-quarters of the voters. However, a substantial minority of the voters, almost a quarter of them, submitted modi. Given their first votes on the issue of Mary, it seems likely that approximately two-thirds of these modi were conservative in orientation. The rest were likely authored by progressives who asked their supporters to submit them if they felt "that, in spite of the explanation given [in the

TABLE 5.2
Inconsistency in Stances on the Blessed Virgin Mary[a]

	Final Vote Concerning Mary[c]							
	Conservative		Progressive		Modi		Total	
	Number	Percent	Number	Percent	Number	Percent	Number	Percent
First Vote Concerning Mary[b]								
Conservative	8	1	565	65	293	34	866	100
Progressive	2	0	743	83	147	17	892	100
Total	10	1	1,308	74	440	25	1,758	100
CIP Petition Concerning Mary[d]								
Signed	1	0	208	65	109	34	318	100
Did Not Sign	9	1	1,351	76	412	23	1,772	100
Total	10	0	1,559	75	521	25	2,090	100

[a] Figures are restricted to bishops who voted on both votes concerning Mary.
[b] Second Session, October 29, 1963, *Suffragationes*, vol. 19, no. 97.
[c] Third Session, October 29, 1964, *Suffragationes*, vol. 42, no. 215.
[d] FSig 2.8.

schema] . . . the word Mediatrix itself is a stumbling block in ecumenical dialogue with non-Catholics."[55]

Table 5.2 presents these findings and demonstrates that conservatives, *even once they had a full-fledged organization actively working to elevate Mary's status*, fared worse on the second vote than they had on the first. Of the 866 bishops who originally supported the conservative position on Mary (and were present for the second vote), only about 300 remained conservative by either voting to reject the schema or by submitting modi on the final vote. In other words, conservatives were able to hold onto only 35 percent of their original sentiment pool. Fully 65 percent of those who voted conservatively the first time had swung over to the progressive side by the time the second vote on Mary was taken. In contrast, progressives lost only 2 out of the 858 bishops who voted progressively the first time around.

Table 5.2 also demonstrates that this happened not just among the bishops who voted conservatively the first time around but also among those who were motivated enough to sign the CIP's petition on Mary, almost two-thirds of whom simply accepted the progressive final document.

Despite the strong progressive victory in the second vote on Mary, the story of the schema did not end there. In what many took to be an effort to mollify conservatives,[56] Pope Paul gave a speech at the close of the Third Session which referred to Mary in some of the problematic terms that alienated Protestants. Ecumenical leaders, both Catholic and non-Catholic, were upset at Paul's speech.[57] For example, the prominent Protestant commentator Robert MacAfee Brown wrote:

> The Pope, in his closing speech, gave to Mary the title, "Mother of the Church," even though the bishops in their earlier debate had decided that the title was inappropriate. It seemed for a while as though either the conservatives had gotten through to Paul, convinced him that the council was getting out of hand, and persuaded him to recapture control after the fashion of pre-Vatican II Popes, or that Paul himself had reached a similar decision. The resulting gloom lasted many months, and there were those who, seeing this as a portent of things to come, predicted that the final session would end in disaster.[58]

Another Protestant observer wrote: "While the third session did not add anything doctrinally objectionable in this area, it closed with emphases on Marian devotion which Protestants consider a deviation from true Christian piety."[59]

However, the pope's speech aside, Protestants were overall quite happy with the outcome of the Third Session. One wrote, "the fact that chapter 8 on the Blessed Virgin is firmly set in a decree on the *Church* preserves the possibility" of furthering ecumenical dialogue even if "unhappily," the pope proclaimed Mary to be "Mother of the Church."[60] And indicating that, for Protestants, Council decisions were ultimately what mattered, Brown ended his discussion of the Council's pronouncements on Mary with this positive assessment:

> A further item of ecumenical importance is the inclusion within the constitution of a chapter on Mary. . . . By a very close vote, the council decided to include the Marian material within the context of the material on the church, rather than seeming to encourage Marian theology to continue developing in isolation from the rest of Catholic thought. The resulting chapter, while still fully a "Catholic" statement, has been rewritten with the ecumenical intent of describing Mary as much as possible in Biblical terms, so that an avenue of possible ecumenical discussion may be opened up.[61]

If ecumenical leaders like Brown were satisfied with the Council's statements on Mary, CIP leaders were resigned to them, if perhaps mollified by Paul's speech.[62] As the Fourth Session was beginning, Sigaud wrote:

> Unfortunately, the Council will end without the world's consecration to the Immaculate Heart of Mary. . . . After presenting our request, and having done everything possible in this sense, I feel that the homage that Our Lady requires of us at this moment is to faithfully accept the decision of the Holy Father.[63]

After losing (though by only forty votes) on the issue of the Marian schema, and then a facing a second, and much more decisive, defeat in the Third Session, conservatives were out of options, especially after Paul's qualifying speech. The pope, whose personal devotion to Mary was well known, would do no more for their cause. He told Sigaud that though he would not declare the world to be consecrated to Mary, "nothing forbids the Diocese or religious institutions from carrying out their own consecrations."[64]

CONCLUSION: MARY'S DEACCENTUATION

In the end, the Council would result in an overall deaccentuation of Mary that provides evidence for three important points made in part 1 of this book. First, though Mariological issues were not prominent during the First Session, the events of the First Session were important to how the Council would ultimately treat them. Had conservatives remained in complete control of the agenda, Ottaviani might have been successful in bringing the separate schema on Mary up for discussion before other schemas, and thereby in keeping it a separate document. Had the elections proceeded according to the conservative plan during the First Session, and the drafting committees not been as diverse as they ultimately were, the final schema on Mary would likely have used many of the terms Protestants criticized and progressives thus fought against.

Second, the intense mobilization around the issue of Mary on the part of both progressives and conservatives again provides evidence that progressives, through the DM, had a much more effective organizational structure and strategies than conservatives in the CIP, who often seemed simply inept when it came to communicating with their sympathizers.

Finally, the split over Mariological issues at the Council also demonstrates how important legitimacy concerns are for directing the organizational strategies of religious leaders in some environments. Because Protestants questioned the legitimacy of Catholic devotion to Mary, bishops from countries with a strong ecumenical movement fought against any statements which would be seen as further promoting or even emphasizing this aspect of Catholic spirituality.

However, though I argue that legitimacy concerns determined whether progressives from Northern Europe and North America fought for or against certain reforms, and thus, which reforms passed or failed, the story is, as of right now, incomplete. We have not yet examined what happened to issues that *were not* important for the Church's legitimacy within the ecumenical movement but *were* important to the laity in Northern Europe and North America. As we will see in the next chapter, which deals with the issue of birth control, legitimacy concerns also determined progressives' priorities. Because birth control was an issue about which the ecumenical movement was then conflicted, Protestants did not emphasize the importance of reform. Consequently, progressives who prioritized ecumenical relations did not mobilize their superior organizational capacities to fight for it, and instead let Paul remove birth control reform from the Council agenda with relatively little protest.

Chapter Six

THE COUNCIL'S FAILURE TO LIBERALIZE

BIRTH CONTROL

LACKLUSTER PROGRESSIVE EFFORT MEETS
A HESITANT POPE

> I am the one surrounded by wild, scrappy, noisy,
> dirty little boys, carrying a runny-nosed baby. Vomiting
> at intervals with my next pregnancy; overwhelmed with
> noise, dirt, spilled foods, overflowing diaper pails,
> broken furniture and unpaid bills.
> —*Catholic mother of twelve, 1964*[1]

IN THE end, the Second Vatican Council was an overwhelmingly progressive event, transforming everything from the language of the Mass to dietary restrictions for the laity, nuns' habits, and the Church's relationship with states. However, it is also true that the Council did not reform everything. One of its most obvious lacunae was in its failure to liberalize the Church's stance on birth control. The circumstances surrounding this failed reform are the focus of this chapter.

Birth control is different from the majority of other issues discussed by the Council not only because it represents a complete failure on the part of the progressive faction but because it went through a different process than most other attempts at reform. In a powerful and rare demonstration of his veto authority (the only other issue he removed from the Council's agenda was priestly celibacy, which he did during the Fourth Session), Pope Paul pulled it from the Council agenda prior to the Third Session. However, though his decision ensured that the Council would not liberalize birth control policy, there is still much we can learn from a closer analysis of the way in which the issue played out in the Council, especially in regards to the factors that explain why Paul felt comfortable pulling it from the agenda (progressives had certainly not emphasized its importance) and why there was little protest when he did.

In contrast to their determined mobilization around the issues of religious freedom and the status of Mary, progressives from Northern Europe and North America simply gave up the fight on birth control, not only making it possible for the pope to remove the issue from the Council agenda but making it easy. Protestant indifference seems to have been the key factor: surprisingly, though sexual politics (birth control, abortion, feminism, and even homosexuality) deeply divide mainline Protestants and Catholics today, at the time of the Council, Protestants did not put any pressure on the Church to reform its teachings on birth control. Instead, pressures for reform came largely from other quarters: from practicing Catholics in industrialized countries who wanted to use birth control and professionals at the United Nations and in governments who were worried about the population explosion. Thus, while the UN created some legitimacy concerns for the Church, particularly in missionary countries in Africa and Asia, bishops from stable fields, whose own constituents offered the most vocal requests for birth control reform, were able to largely ignore the issue because the ecumenical movement was not involved (and indeed had its own problems with birth control policy at the time). As a result, they did not emphasize the issue during the first two Council sessions, they did not protest collectively when the Pope removed it from the agenda, and ultimately, Vatican II did not change the Catholic Church's stance on birth control.

CHRISTIANITY'S VARIED STANCES ON BIRTH CONTROL

The Roman Catholic Church condemned "artificial means" of birth control in 1930, the same year that the Anglicans announced that they had approved the use of contraceptives.[2] The focus on "artificial means" was a result of the Church's relatively unique conclusion that a couple could, without sin, attempt to avoid pregnancy by having intercourse only when the woman was in an infertile stage in her menstrual cycle—something popularly referred to as the "rhythm method." This view was different from that of the majority of mainline Protestants, who did not distinguish between artificial and natural methods of contraception.

However, though Protestant and Catholic views on birth control diverged early, their differences were not a serious issue for the ecumenical movement. Prior to John's announcement of the Council and during Council preparations, there was some discussion in the *Ecumenical Review* of the population explosion[3] but very little mention of Roman Catholic views on birth control, and those articles which did discuss Catholic views of birth control were not critical in tone. This lack of attention to birth control seems to have resulted from the fact that the churches participating in the ecumenical movement, or, more specifically, the churches they wished to draw into it, did not agree on the issue themselves, as an article in the *Ecumenical Review* acknowledged in 1959. After reporting increasing consensus, the author noted,

> [W]e are also mindful of the partial character of the evidence so far received. Our information is incomplete and the known silence of important Christian bodies may have diverse meanings. We have in mind in this connection the Orthodox Church, the churches and councils in many parts of Asia, Africa and Latin America, churches in communist countries, as well as some of the churches of the west.[4]

Long a target of the ecumenical movement, the Orthodox Church had been reluctant to join the World Council of Churches, even refusing their invitation to attend the WCC conference in Amsterdam in 1948.[5] Leaders of the movement, however, continued to believe that "The full participation of the Orthodox Churches is a matter of great moment to the World Council of Churches,"[6] mainly because Orthodox participation in the WCC would help to eliminate the (fairly accurate) impression that it was largely a Protestant organization. As one movement leader wrote in 1954:

> On no account ought the World Council to be allowed to give the impression of being either an organization of Protestant Churches, or largely a Western, and more specifically, an Anglo-Saxon organization, which identifies itself, consciously or unconsciously, with the concerns and interests of Western nations.[7]

As the movement worked throughout the 1950s, with some success, to improve its relations with the Orthodox Church, birth control became a particularly problematic issue, because the Orthodox insisted that abstinence was the only legitimate form of birth control. Thus, for the most part, the ecumenical movement largely avoided the matter of birth control,[8] and was thus not inclined to challenge the Roman Catholic Church on this subject because, in contrast to the Orthodox position, the Roman Catholic position seemed almost progressive. For example, after observing that the Roman Catholic Church "seems to be in a somewhat experimental mood at the moment," because it allowed "the so-called rhythm method,"[9] on a principle which could plausibly be extended to use of the pill, one author explained:

> I think fruitful ecumenical dialogue may be opened [on birth control]. . . . [O]fficial Orthodox [Christian] thought tends to be most conservative, regarding abstinence as the only permissible method. Roman Catholic doctrine has officially endorsed the use of periods of sterility as well—indeed, informally at least, Pope Pius XII lent encouragement to this means when he said, "one may even hope . . . that science will succeed in providing this licit method with a sufficiently secure basis, and the most recent information seems to secure such a hope."[10]

As a result, Protestants at the Council generally avoided the issue of birth control.[11] For example, during the Fourth Session, American observer Douglas Horton wrote that birth control was an "intricate question which a council of this size and composition is not designed to discuss successfully."[12] Robert McAfee Brown wrote after the Council's close that birth control was about "the internal life of Roman Catholicism, and the non-Catholic has no right to interfere in what the Church demands of its own constituents."[13]

It seems likely that these Protestants were willing to let the RCC off the hook in relation to birth control, not only because they did not have consensus within the ecumenical movement, but also because they expected that "further clarification of the position is one of the issues in the present *aggiornamento* of the Roman Church," as an author wrote in the *Ecumenical Review* in October 1965, as the Fourth Session of the Council opened.[14]

However, pressures were mounting on the Church to reform its position on birth control—pressures that came not from Protestants but from a number of other sources.

PRESSURE TO CHANGE

By the time of the Council, reports that the laity were having great difficulty with the Church's ban on birth control were appearing in Catholic periodicals, and doctors and theologians in many countries were arguing in favor of the pill.[15] During Council preparations, Roman Catholic periodicals began publishing pro-change statements by theologians and other experts.[16]

There is also evidence that the bishops were getting some direct pressure from the laity. As he prepared for the beginning of the Council, an American Catholic laywoman wrote Bishop Primeau:

> Although it appears that the greatest leakage from the Church is due to birth control, it seems that there has not been a concurrent increase in the Church's study of the problem. Although I am certainly not advocating "birth control," it seems that the problem deserves much greater study and research by those competent to do so, and hopefully, an attempt to provide a more understandable (both to Catholics and non-Catholics) "answer."[17]

The pressure to reform the Church's stance on birth control continued to mount, both directly and indirectly. Indirectly, the issue became more prominent in 1963, as the bishops were gearing up for the Second Session, when Dr. John Rock, a Catholic professor at Harvard who had helped develop the pill, published a book titled *The Time Has Come: A Catholic*

Doctor's Proposals to End the Battle over Birth Control. In it he argued that the pill should be acceptable to Catholics because it was a "morally permissible variant of the rhythm method."[18]

In terms of direct pressure, during the Third Session more than 150 "Catholic laymen" from eleven countries petitioned the pope for a liberalization of the Church's position on birth control.[19] Citing "great difficulties" with the current situation and scientific information about the nature of spermatogenesis (that it is "continuous and dynamic") and conception (that most sexual acts do not result in conception), the petition asked that the Church allow couples to use artificial means.[20] As the Council was drawing to a close, Patrick and Patty Crowley, a lay couple from Chicago who had led the Catholic Family Movement[21] and been appointed to the Pope's Birth Control Commission, reported after visiting thirty-six nations that the majority of Catholic families they spoke with indicated that they would like to see the Church allow modern birth control methods.[22]

Reports of Increasing Use

Although the professionals and laity urging reform were an important source of pressure for change, even more important was the mounting evidence that many Catholics were simply disregarding the Church's ban on birth control. By the 1950s, studies were indicating that about half of the American Catholics practicing some form of birth control were using methods prohibited by the Church, and there was little reason to think similar trends were not occurring in other industrialized countries.[23] Average family sizes had been decreasing in all industrialized countries, including France, Italy, and Spain, which were predominantly Catholic, and there was evidence that this decrease should not be ascribed to the rhythm method.

> In France . . . a survey showed that . . . 69 percent of the women questioned had used contraceptive methods at some stage in their lives . . . among those 37 years or older there were none who had not used such methods. In the United States these methods were used on a much wider scale. . . . Both in the United States and France surveys had shown that a large to very large proportion of Roman Catholic women used methods forbidden by the Church. In Italy . . . there was ample evidence that the pattern was the same.[24]

The Population Explosion

Finally, concerns about the world population explosion were growing at the time of the Council. The UN and many governments had begun promoting birth control and urging the Roman Catholic Church to do the same.[25]

For example, in November 1964, Dr. B. R. Sen, director-general of the Food and Agriculture Organization of the UN, addressed a group of Christian churches in Bombay, India. His statements provide a good indication of the international pressures the Church was facing on this issue:

> The world today faces a situation such has never been known before. The unprecedented rise in population growth, especially since the beginning of this century, has been a factor the implications of which for the future of the human race are only now being gradually understood. . . . Can we anymore turn our faces away from the concept of family planning when the alternative is starvation and death? *This is a question on which we await guidance from the great moral and spiritual leaders of the world.* . . . In this great task of achieving freedom from hunger, the religious bodies can act as powerful allies of the secular organizations.[26]

The United Nations and the World Health Organization announced that "the first ever conference on world population problems" would be held in 1964. Until that time, according to one scholar, the Vatican had been able to avoid such a public discussion of the issue through a "symbiotic alliance" with communist countries, which "contended that a Marxist economic system could support unlimited growth; the Third World nations, which saw population control as part of a Western plot to hold them in subjection; and predominantly Catholic nations, which objected to most forms of birth control on moral grounds."[27]

Thus, by the Council's Third Session, Catholics in most industrialized countries were either already using birth control or were expecting the Church to allow them to do so soon, and more and more people, both Catholic and non-Catholic, were viewing the world population explosion as a problem—one for which the Catholic Church was partly responsible.[28] It is no surprise, then, that many began to acknowledge as did a writer in *Catholic Mind* in January 1964, that "speculation about [birth control] is in the air."[29]

DELIBERATIONS ON BIRTH CONTROL DURING THE COUNCIL

Though Pope John, shortly before his death between the First and Second Sessions of the Council, appointed a committee to study the issue, and though the Dutch bishops petitioned his successor, Paul, asking that it be addressed prior to the Second Session,[30] nothing of note transpired in relation to birth control during the first two sessions. Just before the Third Session opened, Paul announced that he was removing the topic of birth control from the Council discussions.[31]

Despite this, and though Cardinal Agagianian, as a Council moderator, reminded the assembly that "certain points" would not be discussed on the Council floor,[32] a number of bishops did indicate a desire to see the Church reform its doctrine on birth control during the Third Session. The majority of the bishops who mentioned birth control did so in their interventions on the schema titled The Church in the Modern World in relation to the chapter "The Sacrament of Matrimony." Though silent as to means, the draft of the schema promulgated during the Third Session did state that it was a couple's right to decide the number of children they could adequately provide for, a stance that seems to have mollified neither proponents or opponents[33] of artificial birth control.

Since there was no vote on birth control, we are left only with what was said in the Council hall, and by whom, to analyze, and unfortunately, there is not all that much. However, what there is, is illuminating. Given the importance of the issue to their constituents, it is not surprising that those who mentioned it focused on the difficulties the current Church ban on birth control created for married couples. Bishop Alfrink's intervention during the Third Session is a good example.

> Two essential values must be safeguarded in marriage: procreation, and the Christian and human education of children. They cannot be separated, for they form a whole. In reality, a conflict between these two values can arise within conjugal intimacy. The human and Christian education of children is possible only when genuine conjugal love exists, a love that is normally nourished by sexual intercourse. When there is a conflict, the only solution is to make the sex act possible without procreation. . . . Is complete or periodic continence the only efficacious solution for the conflicts of married life from all moral and Christian standpoints?[34]

In general, these progressive interventions indicated that the bishops were aware that many Catholics were not adhering to Church teaching as Patriarch Maximos IV told the Council, "[T]he immense majority of Christians, in practice, are living contrary to the official teaching of the Church . . . [birth control] is at the basis of a grave crisis afflicting the Christian conscience."[35]

However, while a few bishops from stable fields, like Alfrink, did mention birth control in their interventions, most did not make much of a fuss about it during the Council, despite the fact that the laity in stable fields were the most interested in, and actively lobbying for, reform.[36] The progressive organizations that were so active in regard to religious freedom were strangely silent on this issue.[37] There were no conferences on birth control at the Domus Mariae, no petitions from groups of concerned bishops, no serious mobilization to get the issue to the Council floor quickly during the first two sessions,[38] or to pressure the pope to restore it to the

agenda during the third discussion.[39] In fact, the DM minutes from the
Third Session reflect their acquiescent attitude:

> N.B.—Because of the negative consequences on people's conscience and on
> politics, many fear a public debate on birth control . . . [thus] it may be with-
> drawn from public debate and treated in written form in a way that would be
> helpful . . . while awaiting results.[40]

The DM was content to allow the issue to drop. This seems to be not
only because Paul removed it from the agenda but also because the ecumenically inclined bishops from Northern Europe and North America
were not under the same pressures for reform that motivated them to prioritize religious freedom and play down the role of Mary in the Church,
and because the second group of progressive bishops represented at the
DM, the Latin Americans, were primarily interested in reforms that they
thought would give them a competitive edge over the Protestant churches
invading their former monopoly.

The Latin American laity had little access to birth control and were distant from the lay movements in industrialized countries which were push-
ing for change at the time of the Council. It seemed unlikely that reforming birth control would give the Latin American church a competitive
advantage vis-à-vis Protestants, when the vast majority of their constituents would not have access to it. It made much more sense for Latin
Americans to prioritize other reforms that would allow them to more effectively minister to their constituents and alleviate poverty.

Thus, birth control reform was a low priority for two of the three
progressively inclined groups of bishops at the Council. The only exception was the bishops from missionary countries.[41] As Indian bishop Fran
Simons's intervention demonstrates, missionary bishops were dealing with
a legitimacy problem: in the very countries most affected by the population explosion, they were trying to promote a Church which banned birth
control.

> The demographic explosion is an undeniable fact. Hence, there arises a grave
> obligation to arrest this growth in population. It is wrong to say that the
> riches of the world have not yet been completely tapped and that they are in-
> exhaustible. The means used to bring about this check in population growth
> will depend for their moral aspect upon their effects. Laws, even the natural
> law, are for men, not men for the laws. Thus, the conclusions of many theolo-
> gians need to be re-thought. The traditional arguments against birth control
> based on the frustration of nature are not at all convincing.[42]

Thus, even though very little agitation for birth control was coming
from their constituents, missionary bishops were some of the most active

proponents of reform. They believed, as Archbishop D'Souza, a prominent Indian progressive, told Caporale, that "Merely condemning [birth control] does not get us anywhere. There is a feeling that this issue should be raised and that we should face it."[43] Bishop Roberts (who would later be censured for discussing with the press his opinion that the Church needed to allow artificial means of birth control)[44] told Caporale early in the Council that the Indian bishops should be "on the forefront of birth control reform, "especially with the population explosion very much of a problem."[45]

However, the significant interest missionary bishops showed in birth control reform was not enough to mobilize the rest of the progressive leadership, which made almost no effort to restore it to the agenda after Paul removed it. As a result, the Council did not make any official pronouncement on birth control, and the matter remained unsettled until 1968, three years after the Council's close, when Pope Paul VI issued the encyclical *Humanae vitae*. The encyclical reiterated that the Church did not allow the use of artificial means of birth control and warned Catholics that the use of contraceptives was a serious sin against nature, and therefore against God.[46]

CONCLUSION: THE COST TO RELIGIOUS AUTHORITY

Humanae Vitae immediately met a storm of criticism from within the Church.[47] Statements disagreeing with or "qualifying" the encyclical came from all quarters for the next two years. The controversy was fed in part by the *National Catholic Reporter's* report that the papal birth control commission had adjourned with a majority of the members favoring a more permissive stance on birth control, and the pope's refusal to do so was thus a shock and disappointment to many.[48]

Presently, the vast majority of married American Catholics use forms of birth control banned by the Church,[49] and sociologists Michael Hout and Andrew Greeley have demonstrated that *Humanae Vitae* sparked a disaffection from the Church which reduced attendance and damaged papal authority among American Catholics.[50]

The story of why the Council failed to reform the Church's stance on birth control, despite its obvious importance to the laity, would not be predicted by supply-side theory, which argues that religious leaders in competitive environments would be more likely to prioritize their constituents' concerns than those in less competitive environments. This case study demonstrates that the bishops from the prototypical competitive environments, namely, the United States (but others, such as Germany and the Netherlands as well), whose laity were very interested in birth control reform, did not prioritize it. Instead they focused on reforms that would better ecumenical relations and address legitimacy concerns raised by the leaders of other religions prominent in their organizational field. Furthermore, the one group of bishops who did push the Council to reform birth control, those from missionary countries (arguably a very competitive religious economy as well), were reacting to legitimacy concerns about overpopulation, not lay pressure.

These findings simply cannot be explained within current theories in the sociology of religion. This is because the sociology of religion needs to incorporate an understanding of the way in which the broader organizational field affects religious leaders, and thus an understanding of why, particularly in stable fields, legitimacy concerns often become paramount.

RETHINKING THE COUNCIL

In future relations with the Roman Catholic Church we
will be compelled to go deeper, because it is a new
Church we are facing and work with her will be more
useful and fruitful. Every theology from now on will be,
by necessity, ecumenical. We must bring in the other,
always, and we should try to go together into the
world, because the separation between churches is
of far less gravity than the confrontation [and
separation of] the Church and the World. Let
us face the world together.
—*Professor Skydsgaard, Lutheran theologian*[1]

SKYDSGAARD gave Caporale this confident assessment of the Council
more than two years before its overwhelmingly progressive and ecumenical outcome was certain. He was able to do so partly because the First Session demonstrated that the Curia was no longer in control of the Council,
that it could be an event which would bring about real changes, and because by then it was clear that ecumenically oriented reforms would be the
priority of bishops from Northern Europe and North America.

Ecumenically oriented bishops achieved their goals for the Council because they developed a much more effective organizational structure than
conservatives did, one that was better suited to the Council environment.
They were thus able to achieve reforms that even their progressive allies
from Latin America had difficulty supporting, such as the Declaration on
Religious Freedom, and to defeat conservative schemas that the majority
of Latin Americans initially supported, such as those pertaining to Mary.
They were able to do so largely because, even though their priorities were
sometimes at odds, Latin American and ecumenically oriented bishops
shared an important belief in the doctrine of collegiality and thus worked
toward communicating with each other, and with the rest of the voting
bishops, throughout the course of the Council. Thus, even though bishops
from both groups reported having "wrong ideas of each other," because
"we did not know each other,"[2] at the beginning of the Council, by the
close of the First Session, they had "a new sense of strength and better understanding"[3] of the problems their colleagues from different parts of the
worlds faced. They were thus able to develop compromise solutions that
garnered enough support from Latin American bishops to achieve victory
on ecumenically important issues such as Mary.

However, while the ecumenical priorities of the bishops from stable fields and the organizational advantages the DM provided them explain a great deal about why certain issues, like the Church's stance on religious freedom, were reformed and others, like birth control, were not, there are other important aspects of the Council that the analysis presented here has not been able to touch on. One is the special role of the Latin American delegates.

Largely because of the overwhelmingly ecumenical bent of most Council documents, most analysts have concluded that, "what the Latin Americans contributed to the Council—which was relatively little, since it was dominated by European interests—was not nearly as important as what they took away from it."[4] I hope this analysis helps to correct this impression. The Latin American bishops brought to the Council their profound beliefs in collegiality and social justice and the preexisting organizational form of CELAM, which was mimicked by many other ECs. It was their idea to form the DM, and they made up fully a quarter (600) of the voting bishops. It is safe to say that the Council would not have had the progressive, nor even, rather ironically, the ecumenical, outcome it had were it not for Latin America.

Furthermore, because Latin Americans were central to their group, the DM worked throughout the four sessions to have the Council address the issue of poverty. Researchers have noted that the DM's emphasis on the Church of the Poor "contrasts with the lack of interest that the 'Northern Europeans,' with few exceptions, have generally showed for this set of problems at Vatican II."[5] Thus, in both form and substance, Latin American bishops were crucial to the outcome of the Council. As a result the Council represents a "durable transformation of structures,"[6] not only for Latin America but for the entire Church, in both the concrete reforms that it passed and the theological resources it provided.

However, I would be remiss to conclude this book without acknowledging that while some hierarchies took the reforms of the Council home and applied them in very radical ways, the Church, particularly the Vatican, has also gone in a very conservative direction since the Council, especially in regard to issues of sexuality.

Gene Burns argues that the sexual conservativism apparent in the Council's failure to liberalize the Church's stance on birth control arose because "sexuality is one of the few areas of doctrine where Rome can pursue a strategy of centralized institutional authority."[7] While this may indeed be part of the story, particularly for the Church's stances on other issues connected to sexuality which arose after Vatican II, this analysis demonstrates that initially, birth control was not reformed because it was not the focus of legitimacy critiques at the time of the Council. Had Vatican II occurred a few years later, when the women's movement had more influence, it is possible that birth control would have been reformed, particularly if the women's movement had influenced Protestant leaders, and birth control had thus become an issue for bettering Roman Catholic relations with the ecumenical movement.

Today things have changed, and the Church is experiencing strong critiques related to issues of sexuality in many parts of the world. Sexual abuse scandals in the United States have brought priestly celibacy into question. The Church's prohibition against condoms has been heavily criticized in relation to the AIDS crisis in Africa. And, of course, the Church's stand on abortion has long been criticized by feminist groups.

This analysis suggests that if the Church eventually changes its stance on any of these issues, it will do so when Catholic religious leaders begin to feel that they pose a real legitimacy problem for the Church, a conclusion Catholic leaders will be more likely to reach when prominent non-Catholic religious leaders prioritize them in their relations with the Church. And, I daresay, any such changes will take a Council.

Appendix A

ABBREVIATIONS OF PRIMARY SOURCES

Caporale's Materials

CIC   Caporale interview card. The majority of his interviews were transcribed onto note cards, numbered by category.

CHT   Caporale handwritten transcript. Material not transcribed onto note cards.

CT   Caporale typed transcript. Material not transcribed onto the note cards.

Archival Materials

DOH   Daniel O'Hanlon Collection from the Graduate Theological Union, Flora Lamson Hewlett Library, Berkeley, CA. DOH 3(10), for example, denotes box 3, file folder 10, of this collection. O'Hanlon was the interpreter for the English-speaking observers at the Council. As a result, his archive contains a great deal of useful information about the activities of the observers and the SCU. The materials are in English, French, and Latin as well as German and Dutch.

EA   Etchegary Archive of the Instituto per le Scienze Religiose—Giovanni XXIII, Via San Vitale 114, Bologna, Italy (ISR). EA 5.4, for example, denotes box 5, file 4, of this collection. French peritus Roger Etchegary was the DM secretary for the four Council sessions. His archive has valuable materials on the DM, the majority of which are in French or Latin and have been translated into Italian.

FCrl   Fondo Carli, or Carli Archive, ISR. FCrl 1.2, for example, denotes box 1, file 2, of this collection. Italian bishop Luigi Carli was one of the three founding members of the CIP. His archive consists mainly of personal correspondence with Berto, his theologian, and CIP co-founder Superior General Marcel Lefebvre, the majority of which is in Italian and French.

FSig   Fondo Sig, or Sigaud Archive, ISR. FSig 1.84, for example, denotes box 1, file 84, of this collection. Brazilian archbishop Geraldo de Proença Sigaud was one of the three founding members of the CIP. His archive consists mainly of correspondence with Lefebvre, the majority of which are in Latin, Portuguese, or French.

PC   Primeau Collection, Vatican II Archive, Catholic University of America, Washington, DC. PC 21(7), for example, denotes box 21, file 7, of this collection. Bishop Ernest Primeau was the American representative to the DM as well as a member of the SCU, and thus his archive has

valuable documents pertinent to each organization. The majority of
DM minutes cited in this book are available in the Primeau collection,
in Latin or French. "Minutes of the x meeting at the Domus Mariae
during the y Session" are abbreviated "DM Minutes x:y," followed by
the date. "Report to the U.S. Hierarchy of the Meeting of the International Committee, September 18, 1964—*Domus Mariae*," is abbreviated
as "Report to the U.S. Hierarchy of the DM, September 18, 1964."

Appendix B

METHODOLOGICAL INFORMATION

Votes from the Second Vatican Council

My research assistants entered the Council votes into Microsoft Access from photocopies of the original vote tallies obtained from the Vatican Secret Archive (Archivio Segreto Vaticano, Cortile del Belvedere, 00120 Vatican City). The copies of the vote tallies that I received gave each bishop's name, diocese, title, and vote, all of which were entered twice by two different assistants. The two entries of each vote tally were compared and discrepancies corrected; the final version was then checked a third time. Each of the votes as tallied by my team matches the official totals provided by the Vatican at the time of the Council, unless a discrepancy is noted. The four votes analyzed in this book are described in chronological order below.

1. The Vote on the Sources of Revelation (First Session, November 20, 1962, *Suffragationes*, vol, 1, no. 5) was one of the first votes taken at the Council (see chapter 1). The issue concerned whether the conservative preparatory schema needed revision. The draft of the schema being voted on upheld the inerrancy of the Bible, refuted the validity of historical or anthropological research into the Bible, and asserted that there were two sources of revelation: scripture and tradition (tradition meaning Church interpretation or doctrine). Ecumenists wanted to tone down the focus on the two sources, because Protestants had long argued that the only valid source of revelation was scripture. Other progressives supported historical and anthropological investigation into the bible.[1] The progressive position, that the conservative schema needed revision, won, with 1,368 placets (accept), 822 non-placets (reject).

2. The First Vote on the Blessed Virgin Mary (Second Session, October 29, 1963, *Suffragationes*, vol. 19, no. 97) was the most divisive of all those taken during the Council, with 1,115 voting to include Mary in the schema on the Church (the progressive position, because it deemphasized Catholic devotion to Mary in order to be more compatible with Protestant views) and 1,075 voting to give her a separate schema.[2]

3. The Vote on the Fourth Point on Collegiality (Second Session, October 30, 1963, *Suffragationes*, vol. 20, no. 104) questioned whether the Council would approve the most progressive statement on collegiality, which essentially stated that when acting together with the pope, the bishops also have, by divine right, ultimate teaching authority. It passed with majority support: 1,717 placets to 408 non-placets.[3]

4. The Final Vote on the Blessed Virgin Mary (Third Session, October 29, 1964, *Suffragationes*, vol. 42, no. 215) sought approval of the final Council

document on Mary. More than the necessary two-thirds majority voted for unqualified approval with 10 non-placets (the most conservative position), 1,559 placets (the moderate position), and 521 modi.

After the voting data was entered, I then entered a number of other variables about both the individual bishops (such as date and place of birth and whether they signed either of the two CIP petitions I obtained from the archives) and their countries (the percent of the population that was Catholic, the relationship between the Church and the state, etc.). I relied primarily on the 1965 *Annuario Pontificio* (*AP*) to obtain country of service and other biographical information. If information was not available for a bishop in the 1965 *AP*, his information was obtained from the most recent issue of the *AP* that listed him. Though this method worked for the majority of the 2,929 bishops who voted on these isssues, the time of the Council was a tumultuous political one for many areas of the world, particularly Africa. Many countries at this time were gaining independence, or would soon, and as a result, many of the often arbitrary colonial borders underwent significant changes: some regions which had been divided between two or more colonial powers combined into one nation, while others, unified under colonial rule, split into two or more independent nations once the colonial power had vacated.

Needless to say, such flux in borders, governments, and national names made assigning country-of-service characteristics particularly difficult for some of the bishops in the database. For reasons of its own, the Church did not recognize some countries and thus the *AP* did not differentiate between East and West Germany, North and South Korea, North and South Vietnam, Ireland and Northern Ireland, or the Democratic Republic of Congo and the Republic of Congo, nor did it differentiate between many African countries but referred to them instead by general geographic terms such as "Equatorial Africa" or "Occidental Africa." If I was uncertain how to designate a bishop's country of service, an assistant looked up his city (usually given under the diocese address in the *AP*) in a gazetteer from 1965.[4] Doing so allowed me to obtain country information for more than 95 percent of the bishops who voted at the Council.[5]

Obtaining systematic data on the relationship between the Church and the state in each country at the time of the Council was also complicated, primarily because of the Declaration on Religious Freedom. Among other problems, I found that the 1965 *National Catholic Almanac* (*NCA*) did not mention the legal situation of the Church in eight of the nine countries where Catholicism was noted as the state religion in 1955.[6] I therefore used the 1955 *NCA*, which represents the Church's relationship with the state three years before John's announcement of the Council, for my measure of whether Roman Catholicism was the state religion or given any kind of special status in a particular country.

CAPORALE'S SAMPLE

For his dissertation research in sociology at Columbia University in 1964, Rocco Caporale interviewed more than eighty of the most important bishops and theologians at the Council in nine languages. In order to obtain a sample of leaders,

Caporale asked his respondents to identify five of the most important people at the Council and stopped when no new names were being volunteered. Caporale's interviews were completed by the second of the four Council sessions, so they provide an important picture of leaders' reactions to the Council, and the issues it would address, before its outcome was certain.

I obtained Caporale's transcripts with the help of Joseph Komonchak, who also deserves thanks for alerting me to Caporale's study. When asked, Caporale readily agreed to allow me access to the transcripts, the originals of which are now publicly available at Catholic University of America's Vatican II Archive.

Tables B.1 provides a detailed list of the bishops and table B.2 a list of the periti and non-Catholic observers he interviewed, as well as pertinent biographical information when it was available. I use Caporale's original coding scheme when identifying liberal, moderate, or conservative bishops from his sample.

Using the voting data, I compared Caporale's sample to the bishops at the Council as a whole. I found that while his sample is an accurate representation of the proportion of the bishops who were conservative, there is almost double the proportion of progressives in his sample as there was in the assembly as a whole and only half the proportion of moderates.

His oversampling of progressive leaders is an understandable result of the time at which he conducted his interviews, when the possibilities for change had just recently become clear. That he interviewed a largely representative portion of conservatives is impressive, given the overall eventfulness of the Council during the first two sessions. That he interviewed someone who would later become a key leader of the CIP is remarkable, since the CIP had not yet been formed when he conducted most of his interviews.

Thirteen of the twenty-two DM members (noted by an asterisk on table B.1) were interviewed by Caporale, and an even larger number (19) made it into the general pool of leaders recommended as potential interviewees. The DM's presence in Caporale's sample does not seem to be simply an artifact of his sampling technique. The number of DM members recommended to Caporale as respondents remains constant even if we count only recommendations by bishops who were not themselves DM members, and only one-third of those whom DM members recommended were also DM members.

Members of the Domus Mariae

The DM was also called the "Conference of Twenty-Two" and the "Inter-Conference."[7] Table B.3 presents the bishops whom I have identified as core leaders of the DM and the primary episcopal conference to which each member belonged.[8]

CELAM Membership

I have treated Central American bishops as members of CELAM for all of the calculations in this study because there seems to have been enough overlap between all Latin American bishops so that communication flowed readily between them and to and from the DM. This is supported by what bishops from Central America

TABLE B.1
Caporale's Sample of Bishops and Cardinals (n = 73)

Europe (Monopolistic)	Europe (Non-Monopolistic) and North America	Latin America	Africa and Asia	Communist
Benjamín de Arriba y Castro (Spain)	George Beck (England)	Ramón Bogarín (Paraguay)	Joseph Blomjous (Tanganyika)	Frane Franic (Yugoslavia)
Michael Browne (Ireland)	Warren Boudreaux (USA)	Helder Pessoa Câmara (Brazil)	Joseph Cordeiro (Pakistan)	Endre Hamvas (Hungary)
Raffaele Calabria (Italy)	Alexander Carter (Canada)	Orlando Chaves (Brazil)	Marcel Daubechies (Zambia)	Michal Klepacz (Poland)
Luigi Carli (Italy)	Charles De Provenchères (France)	Pablo Correa León (Colombia)	Eugene D'Souza (India)	Josip Lach (Yugoslavia)
Guiseppe Carraro (Italy)	Emile De Smedt (Belgium)	Eugênio de Araújo Sales (Brazil)	Angelo Fernandes (India)	Paul Yü-Pin (China)
José Cirarda Lachiondo (Spain)	Léon Elchinger (France)	Alberto Devoto (Argentina)	Adam Kozlowiecki (Rhodesia)	
William Conway (Ireland)	Emile Maurice Guerry (France)	José Armando Gutiérrez Granier (Bolivia)	Owen McCann (South Africa)	
Armando Fares (Italy)	Paul Hallinan (United States)	Jorge Kémérer (Argentina)	Laurentius Nagae (Japan)	
Manuel Fernández-Conde (Spain)	Franz Hengsbach (Germany)	Manuel Larraín Errazuriz (Chile)	Simon Hoa Nguyên-Van Hien (Vietnam)	
Ermenegildo Florit (Italy)	Josef Höffner (Germany)	Marcos McGrath (Panama)	Alejandro Olalia (Philippines)	
António Ferreira Gomes (Portugal)	François Marty (France)	Miguel Miranda y Gómez (Mexico)	Gilbert Ramanantoanina (Madagascar)	
Emilio Guano (Italy)	Georges Pelletier (Canada)	Leonidas ProañoVillalba (Ecuador)	Leonard Joseph Raymond (India)	
Casimiro Morcillo González (Spain)	Ernest Primeau (United States)	José Rafael Pulido Méndez (Venezuela)	Thomas Roberts (India)	
Enrico Nicodemo (Italy)	Leo Josef Suenens (Belgium)	José Vincente Távora (Brazil)	Maximos Saigh IV (Syria)	
Luigi Rinaldi (Italy)	Robert E. Tracy (United States)	Fidel Mario Tubino Mongilardi (Peru)	Félix Scalais (Dem. Rep. of Congo)	
Ernesto Ruffini (Italy)	John Joseph Wright (United States)		Seige* (Indonesia)	
Giuseppe Siri (Italy)	Guilford Young (Australia)		Tikka* (India)	
Domenico Valerii (Italy)			Jean Baptiste Zoa (Cameroon)	
Total 18	17	15	18	5

* Additional information is unavailable.

TABLE B.2
Caporale's Other Interviewees

Roman Catholic Periti	Protestant and Orthodox Observers
Henri DeLubac • French Jesuit theologian	Vitaly Borovoy • Archpriest of the Russian Orthodox Church, associate director of the WCC Secretariat on Faith and Order
Roger Etchegaray • Deputy director of the French EC and DM secretary	
P. Guglielmi* • Peritus of the Brazilian episcopate	Douglas Horton • American delegate to the WCC for the Congregational Church, dean of the Harvard Divinity School
Bernard Haring • German professor of moral theology at the Alfonsian Academy in Rome	
	Z. K. Matthews • South African anti-apartheid activist, secretary of the Africa division of the WCC
Fred McManus • American theologian and professor of law at the Catholic University of America	Edmund Schlink • German Lutheran Theologian, professor of dogmatic and ecumenical theology at the University of Heidelberg, director of the WCC Secretariat on Faith and Order
Joseph Neuner • Jesuit theologian in India	
Jean Sainsaulier • French theologian, peritus for Bishop Marty of Reims	
P. Tavare*	Kristen Skydsgaard • Danish Lutheran theologian, professor at the People's University in Copenhagen
Yves Tourigny • Secretary and peritus for the African bishops	
Gustave Weigel • American Jesuit, professor of Sacred Theology at Woodstock College	Lukas Vischer • Swiss minister of the Reformed Church, member of the WCC Secretariat on Faith and Order
Total 10	6

* Additional information is unavailable.

(Chile, Colombia, Venezuela, Panama, Paraguay, and Uruguay) told Caporale. For example, Bishop Bogarín of Paraguay said. "Usually we support and give our name to a representative speaker from other countries. . . . We participate at the Americana [Hotel, where] . . . there is a great spirit of collaboration [and freedom]. The Cardinal of Santiago [Cardinal Larraín, vice-president of CELAM and founder of the DM] is always present." Bogarin went on to note that the

TABLE B.3
Members of the Domus Mariae

Africa	Asia	Europe	North America	CELAM	Oceania
Joseph Blomjous* (Tanganyika) Jean B. Zoa* (Cameroon)	Victor Bazin (Burma) Thomas B. Cooray (Ceyloan) Michael Doumith (Lebanon) Néophytos Edelby (Syria) Angelo Fernandes* (India) Alejandro Olalia* (Philippines) Laurentius Nagae* (Japan) Pierre Ngô-dihn-Thuc (Vietnam)	George Beck* (England) Pedro Cantero Cuadrado (Spain) Josef Höffner* (Germany) I. Marijan Oblak (Yugoslavia) Pierre Veuillot (France)	Maurice Baudoux (Canada) Ernest Primeau* (United States)	Helder Pessoa Câmara* (Brazil) Manuel Larraín* Errazuriz (Chile) Marcos McGrath* (Panama) Miguel Miranda y Gómez* (Mexico)	Victor Foley (Fiji Islands)

* Caporale's respondents.

Americana group met frequently, on "Mondays and Wednesdays," and that the "meetings have a serious influence on all [of the] bishops, even those who don't go there."[9]

FACE Membership

FACE membership was difficult to pin down. FACE was the largest of a plethora of African organizations and suborganizations, including one for French-speaking Africa, or West Africa, and one for English-speaking, or East Africa (Inter-Territorial Episcopal Board of East Africa, or ITEBEA). Caporale's respondents told him that between twelve and fifteen countries participated in the African episcopal conferences, which seem to have had some overlap in membership. I have been able to verify that most African countries were somehow connected to the DM.[10]

The Dutch Documentation Center (DOC)

A key organizational location for the dissemination of the progressives' "new theology" (particularly regarding ecumenically important issues) was the Dutch Documentation Center, or DOC. For a twenty-dollar annual fee, DOC provided

TABLE B.4
DOC Theologians

National or Organizational Affiliation	Number of Theologians	Percent of All Theologians	Number of Documents	Percent of All Documents
Holland	27	29	52	34
Belgium	10	11	15	10
France	7	7	15	10
Vatican ("Rome")	10	11	13	9
Protestant	8	9	11	7
Spain	4	4	11	7
Palestine/Lebanon	7	7	8	5
Germany/Austria	5	5	8	5
United States	6	6	7	5
Latin America	5	5	5	3
Denmark	2	2	3	2
Africa and Asia	3	3	3	2
Total	94	100	151	100

"at least one document a week" (as well as additional "urgent" material) in the subscriber's language of choice: Dutch, French, Spanish, English, German or Italian.[11] In each of the last three sessions of the Council, DOC published a series of 45 to 50 **"documents of outstanding theological, historical, sociological value** written by theologians such as Prof. Schillebeekx, Prof. Congar, J. Courtney Murray, R. Laurentin, etc."[12] Even those bishops who were not subscribers benefited from the service, because DOC provided those documents it considered essential to all the bishops free of charge and sponsored and taped lectures by prominent theologians.[13] Table B.4 presents a brief synopsis of DOC theologians, the majority of whom where from stable organizational fields in Northern Europe.

ANALYSIS OF THE *ECUMENICAL REVIEW*

In addition to the archival materials, the *Ecumenical Review* provided an important source of data for this project. I gathered, coded, and analyzed all articles pertaining to the Roman Catholic Church from the journal's inception, in 1948, until the close of the Council.

COMMUNISM AND THE COUNCIL

Communism was an important issue at the Council. As the CIP's petition analyzed in chapter 3 suggests, many conservatives were quite invested in getting the Council to condemn it. However, for a variety of reasons, progressives generally avoided the issue,[14] and no condemnation of communism came from the Council.

TABLE B.5
Voting Patterns among Bishops from Communist Countries

Country[a]	Number of Bishops	Percent of All Bishops (n = 2,594)	Percent Voting Progressively on Revelation[b]	Percent Voting Progressively on the First Vote on Mary[c]	Percent Voting Progressively on the Fourth Point on Collegiality[d]
Formerly Catholic					
Poland	51	2.0	78	52	88
Subtotal for Formerly Catholic Countries	75	3.0	75	50	88
Formerly Non-Catholic					
China	116	4.0	62	40	74
Yugoslavia	28	1.0	76	25	89
Rumania	4	0.2	NA	NA	NA
Albania	3	0.1	NA	NA	NA
Subtotal for Formerly Non-Catholic Countries	173	6.0	69	43	91
Total[e]	248	10.0	70	45	84

[a] Country designations and the number of bishops in each country reflect the Church's categorization in the *Acta* (1960–61), and thus represent the total number of bishops serving in a given country at the beginning of the Council, not necessarily the number who went to the Council or who voted on any particular issue.

[b] n = 102. First Session, November 20, 1962, *Suffragationes*, vol. 1, no. 5.

[c] n = 108. Second Session, October 29, 1963, *Suffragationes*, vol. 19, no. 97.

[d] n = 109. Second Session, October 30, 1963, *Suffragationes*, vol. 20, no. 104.

[e] To protect the bishops' anonymity (as per my agreement with the Vatican Secret Archive), all countries where 100 percent of the bishops voted one way (whether conservatively or progressively) on any vote were removed from the table, but these bishops and their votes were included in the subtotals and totals. On this table, the totaled figures thus include 46 bishops from Bulgaria, Cuba, Czechoslovakia, Hungary, and Russia.

It is also exceedingly difficult to draw any conclusions about the effect of communism on the bishops at the Council. The Church was either entirely outlawed, or heavily censored,[15] in almost all communist countries during the early sixties, and many bishops were either already exiled from their countries or, if still resident, forbidden from participating in the Council. Table B.5 presents the number of bishops serving in communist countries at the time of the Council and the votes of those permitted to attend.

Given the spotty nature of the data, any conclusions drawn about the voting patterns of bishops from communist countries are merely speculative, but the data presented in table B.5 indicates that they voted very similarly to the bishops from Latin America: progressively on revelation and collegiality, conservatively on Mary. This suggests that the bishops from communist countries interpreted their political repression similarly to the way in which the Latin Americans interpreted the decline in their church—as a crisis.

Because reliable statistics about religious affiliation are not available for most communist countries at, or even close to, the time of the Council, it is difficult to assess how this is related to the religious diversity in each country. It is possible, however, to roughly categorize each of the communist countries according to whether the Roman Catholic Church dominated prior to the communist takeover. I have done this in table B.5, which demonstrates that bishops from formerly Catholic countries such as Cuba, Hungary, and Poland voted slightly more progressively than the bishops from communist countries which were not predominantly Catholic. This suggests that bishops from formerly Catholic countries may have been more likely to interpret the communist takeover as a crisis than bishops from countries that were not former Catholic monopolies.

Appendix C

TIMELINE OF THE SECOND VATICAN COUNCIL[1]

PREPARING FOR THE COUNCIL, 1958–61

1958 Oct. 9   Pius XII dies.

          Oct. 28 John XXIII is elected pope.

1959 Jan. 25 John XXIII calls for a Council.

          May 17   John XXIII appoints an Ante-Preparatory Commission, headed by Cardinal Tardini, to consult bishops about the agenda.

1960 June 4   John XXIII issues a motu proprio (administrative document) establishing eleven commissions and two secretariats for Vatican II, which begin drafting the preparatory schemas.

1961 June   Holy Office (Cardinal Ottaviani) suspends Stanislas Lyonnet, SJ, and Maximilian Zerwick, SJ (important theologians of religious freedom) from teaching.

THE FIRST SESSION, 1962–63

1962 Oct. 11 Solemn opening of the Council.

          Oct. 13 Motion for free elections.

          Nov. 11 First official meeting of the DM.

          Nov. 14 Schema on the Liturgy is adopted.

          Nov. 20 Conservative Schema on the Sources of Revelation is rejected.

          Dec. 8   Solemn closing of the first session.

1963 June 3   John XXIII dies of cancer at age 81.

          June 21 Paul VI is elected pope and announces that the Council will reconvene.

THE SECOND SESSION, 1963–64

          Sept. 21 Paul VI announces reform of Curia.

          Sept. 29 Vatican II reconvenes.

          Oct. 29 First vote on the schema pertaining to the Blessed Virgin Mary. Progressives win, with forty more bishops voting to include a statement on her in *De Ecclesia* than those voting for the statement to appear in a separate schema.

          Oct. 30 The four points on collegiality are approved with more than two-thirds support.

	Nov. 6	CIP leaders begin corresponding with increasing concern about the number and pace of progressive victories.
	Nov. 19	The first draft of the Declaration on Religious Freedom is introduced as chapter 5 of the Schema on Ecumenism.
	Dec. 2	A vote is called on chapters 1–3 of the Schema on Ecumenism and chapters 4 (On the Jews) and 5 are tabled until the Third Session.
	Dec. 4	End of Second Session.
1964	Jan. 4–6	Paul VI's visit to the Holy Land.
	June 23	Paul VI removes birth control from the Council agenda, appoints a special commission.

THE THIRD SESSION, 1964–65

	Sept. 14	Vatican II reconvenes.
	Oct. 29	The chapter on Mary in *De Ecclesia* is approved by the necessary two-thirds majority despite CIP efforts with the modi.
	Nov.	Council discusses the Declaration on Religious Freedom.
	Nov. 21	End of Third Session. Paul VI proclaims Mary "Mother of the Church."
1965	Feb. 18	Cardinal Bea visits World Council of Churches.

THE FOURTH SESSION, 1965

	Sept. 14	Vatican II reconvenes.
	Sept. 21	Ninety percent of the bishops approve the Declaration on Religious Freedom.
	Oct. 4	Paul VI visits the United Nations.
	Oct. 11	Paul VI removes clerical celibacy from Council discussion.
	Nov. 11	The Schema on the Missions is approved, but thanks to DM effort, the fifth chapter receives 712 modi, and thus has to be revised.
	Nov. 19	Council approves the final draft of the Declaration on Religious Freedom.
	Dec. 8	Conclusion of Vatican II.

NOTES

Introduction

1. Dugan, "U.S. Catholics Begin Reforms in the Mass," 1.

2. Hereafter I will refer to the Roman Catholic Church, and only it, as the "Church."

3. Smith, *The Emergence of Liberation Theology*; Dillon, *Catholic Identity*; Burns, "The Politics of Ideology," and "Commitments and Non-Commitments"; Casanova, *Public Religions in the Modern World*; Greeley, *The Catholic Revolution*.

4. Some researchers in the sociology of religion (e.g., Finke and Stark, *Churching of America*) see these reforms as a quintessential example of religious accommodation to the detriment of the institution. I believe the verdict is still out on the overall effects of the Council, a question which is unfortunately too complex for, and far beyond the scope of, this book.

5. The only other sociological study of the Council (Caporale, *Vatican II*), which was a crucial data source for me, does not examine the causes of the Council's outcome because the events were still unfolding at the time when it was conducted.

6. See Rynne, *Vatican Council II*; Alberigo and Komonchak, *History of Vatican II*, vols. 1–4.

7. Max Weber, *Economy and Society* and *Ancient Judaism*; Émile Durkheim, *The Elementary Forms of Religious Life*.

8. E.g., Chaves, *Ordaining Women*; Eisenstadt, "Social Change, Differentiation and Evolution"; Finke, "Innovative Returns to Tradition"; Kurtz, *The Politics of Heresy*; Seidler and Meyer, *Conflict and Change in the Catholic Church*; Smith, *Liberation Theology*; Wallace, "Revitalization Movements"; Wuthnow, *The Restructuring of American Religion* and *Communities of Discourse*; Zaret, *The Heavenly Contract*.

9. E.g., Sewell, "Three Temporalities" and "Historical Events as Transformations of Structures"; DiMaggio and Powell, "The Iron Cage Revisited"; Fligstein, "Markets as Politics"; March and Olsen, *Rediscovering Institutions*; Meyer and Rowan, "Institutionalized Organizations"; Meyer et al., "World Society and the Nation-State"; Rao, Morrill, and Zald, "Power Plays"; Scott et al., *Institutional Change and Healthcare Organizations*; Stryker, "A Political Approach to Organizations and Institutions"; Armstrong, *Forging Gay Identities* and "Crisis, Collective Creativity, and the Generation of New Organizational Forms"; Binder, *Contentious Curricula*; Clemens, *The People's Lobby*; Clemens and Cook, "Politics and Institutionalism"; Meyer and Minkoff, "Conceptualizing Political Opportunity"; Swidler, "Culture in Action," "Cultural Power and Social Movements," and *Talk of Love*; Turner, *The Ritual Process*; Banaszak, *Why Movements Suceed or Fail*; Clemens, "Organizational Repertoires and Institutional Change"; Ganz, "Resources and Resourcefulness"; Katzenstein, *Faithful and Fearless*; Polletta,

Freedom Is an Endless Meeting; Smith, *Liberation Theology*, *Disruptive Religion*, and *Resisting Reagan*; Snow et al., "Frame Alignment Processes, Micromobilization and Movement Participation"; Snow and Benford, "Master Frames and Cycles of Protest"; Stevens, *Kingdom of Children*; Wood, *Faith in Action*; Wuthnow, "World Order and Religious Movements"; Young, "Confessional Protest."

10. Bellitto, *The General Councils*.

11. January 4, 1963.

12. See Komonchak, "Convening Vatican II: John XXIII Calls for a Council," 10–11.

13. See Goodwin and Jasper, "Caught in a Winding, Snarling Vine"; Meyer and Minkoff, "Conceptualizing Political Opportunity"; McAdam, Tarrow, and Tilly, *Dynamics of Contention*; Tarrow, *Power in Movement*; McAdam, *Political Process and the Development of Black Insurgence*; Tilly, *Popular Contention in Great Britain*; Piven and Cloward, *Poor People's Movements*.

14. Furthermore, the extensive focus on John XXIII as an individual overlooks the fact that previous popes had spoken of a council and John himself reportedly mentioned the need for one prior to his election, and thus in time for those electing him to be aware of his predispositions toward one. See Komonchak, "Popes Pius XI and Pius XII and the Idea of an Ecumenical Council."

15. Accused of having a "Hamlet-like complex" (*Time*, December 6, 1963) and named the "Pope of buts" by the press, Paul VI was generally "more timorous and cautious" than John XIII (Rynne, *Vatican Council II*, 430 and 287).

16. There are three ways in which a pope can direct the course of a council. At any point, he can mandate that an issue be discussed or removed from discussion. Paul used this option twice by removing birth control and priestly celibacy from the Council's agenda, despite many progressive bishops' stated desires to reform the Church's laws on these matters. Once a document has been approved by the Council, the pope has "veto" authority and can mandate that the drafting committee amend it. Paul did this most notably during the Third Session, when he qualified the Council's statement on collegiality, which he felt was too progressive. Finally, the pope can simply draft his own statements or encyclicals on any matter on which he disagrees with the Council. Paul used this option in his speech which closed the Third Session, when he referred to the Virgin Mary in terms progressive bishops had successfully kept out of Council documents (Rynne, *Vatican Council II*, 406, 425, and 444; Alberigo and Komonchak, *Vatican II*, 3:332).

17. Throughout the book I use the terms "progressive" and "conservative" as shorthand for openness or resistance to accommodating the Church to societal change. Many have noted that such categorization of the episcopate is problematic because positions were not always consistent (e.g., Komonchak 1999e, 13). For example, as my own analysis in chapter 5 demonstrates, many progressively inclined bishops voted conservatively on the issue of Mary. For this reason, I use these terms as shorthand while keeping the variation *within* each group in mind, much of which is the focus of chapter 2. When referring to Caporale's respondents, I use his original coding scheme, which I found to be highly reliable when I cross-checked it with his respondents' votes.

18. Because the archival materials, as well as many secondary sources, were in Latin, French, Italian, English, German, Portuguese or Spanish, I cite secondary sources that can be found in English along with the primary sources I used whenever possible.

CHAPTER ONE

1. CIC 14.

2. Alberigo and Komonchak, *Vatican II*, 1:1.

3. CIC 12.

4. About two-thirds of the progressive bishops Caporale interviewed told him that they had thought of or wished for a Council, or had felt change was needed, prior to John's announcement. For example, French bishop François Marty told Caporale, "We did not think about the Council because it seemed impossible; we thought it was necessary, though" (CIC 12).

5. Tracy, *American Bishop at the Council*, 34.

6. Alberigo and Komonchak, *Vatican II*, 1:336–37.

7. CIC 1.

8. McGrath, "Impressions of the Council," 182.

9. Sewell, "Bastille," 844.

10. Others have also used Sewell's theory to understand the Council, e.g., Greeley, "The Second Vatican Council—Occurrence or Event?" and *The Catholic Revolution*; Komonchak, "Vatican II as an 'Event.'"

11. By durable I do not mean inflexible or even permanent. Many researchers have noted a "backlash" of conservatism that began as soon as the Council ended (see Greeley, *The Catholic Revolution*). However, even if many Council reforms were stalled, watered down, or ignored for a time in certain areas of the world, many were implemented and have had a lasting effect on the Church.

12. Sewell uses the term "schemas" instead of Gidden's "rules" (Sewell, "Theory of Structure") to signify the "meaning, motivations, and recipes for social action" individuals have (Sewell, "Bastille"). Because using the term schema in this way would cause undue confusion in the present context, as (Council documents were also called schemas), I substitute "cultural beliefs or repertoires" (Clemens, "Organizational Repertoires"; Swidler, *Talk of Love*), or sometimes simply just "culture" throughout the book.

13. Sewell, "Bastille," 842.

14. Casanova, *Public Religions*, 71; Dillon, *Catholic Identity*, 45–47.

15. Sewell, "Bastille," 842.

16. Ibid.

17. Ibid., 843.

18. Falconi, *Pope John and the Ecumenical Council*, 164.

19. See Alberigo and Komonchak *Vatican II*, 1:95 and 166 for details. Another problem with the process was that the bishop's responses (called *vota*) were far from candid and consisted mostly of declarations of their willingness to take part in the Council (ibid., 108; Komonchak, "U.S. Bishops' Suggestions for Vatican II").

20. Brouwers, "Vatican II: Derniers Préparatifs et Première Session."

21. Alberigo and Komonchak, *Vatican II*, 2:26.

22. At the beginning of the Council two authorities were competing to run its everyday operations: the Council of Presidents and the Secretariat for Extraordinary Affairs. The Council of Presidents consisted of nine of the world's most prominent cardinals, whose responsibility it was to figure out the order and procedures by which the Council was to progress. However, the Council of Presidents often conflicted with the Secretariat for Extraordinary Affairs, for which Felici was the liaison. As another example of the way in which the procedures and power structures of Vatican II were far from solidified at the beginning, the Council of Presidents eventually "disappeared" and the Secretariat became the primary authority determining the agenda and procedures of the Council (Alberigo and Komonchak, *History of Vatican II*, 2:62–63).

23. Alberigo and Komonchak, *Vatican II*, 2:28–31.

24. Since the bishops came from more than thirty countries, and spoke half as many languages, the pope and the Curia decreed that all official Council communications would take place in Latin, the official language of the Church. Though not all of the bishops, and very few of the observers, were fluent in the dead tongue, no simultaneous translation was provided until the Second Session, and then it was provided only for the non-Catholic observers.

25. The two other cardinals were Julius Döpfner of Germany and Franz König of Austria (Komonchak, "The Elections to the Conciliar Comissions"; Alberigo and Komonchak, *Vatican II*, 2:28–31).

26. In this instance, it seems likely that applause was used because it was a ritual which easily aligned "everyone present with the newly posited ultimate source of power"—the Council (Sewell, "Bastille", 869).

27. Sewell, "Bastille," 843.

28. "Of the 160 elected," more than "one hundred had been proposed by the episcopal conferences of Central and Northern Europe" (Brouwers, "Derniers Préparatifs," 356–57). But because they were well known as experts, many members of the Curia and their allies were also elected, and thus still constituted approximately half of the members of the final commissions (Wiltgen 1985, 18).

29. Just as "the acts of the Parisian people [could not] be viewed as a revolution" in 1789 until "it became clear that the taking of the Bastille had forced the king to yield effective power to a different authority in the National Assembly" (Sewell, "Bastille," 853).

30. Robert Dwyer quoted in Komonchak, "Elections," 3.

31. Brouwers notes that the number of ECs almost doubled, from forty to more than seventy, during the course of the Council ("Dernier Préparatifs," 360; cf. Noël, "Gli incontri della conferenze episcopali durante il Concilio," 96).

32. There is ample archival evidence that the ECs, particularly those of "central and northern Europe (Germany, Austria, Belgium, France, the Netherlands, Poland, Switzerland, Yugoslavia and the Scandinavian countries)" (Brouwers, "*Vatican II*," 356–57) undertook this task immediately. See, for example, "American Bishops Nominations for the Commissions," undated document authored by Cardinal Ritter, PC; "Canadian Hierarchy Nominations for the Commissions," October 14, 1962, PC; "Patrum Conciliarium Indices Sicut A Conferentiis

Episcopalibus Exhibiti Sunt As Commissiones S. Concilii Eligendas," PC, as well as lists from various sources dated between October 13 and 15, 1962, in the Primeau Collection.

33. Caporale, *Vatican II*, 51; Noël, "Gli incontri," 95; Grootaers, *Actes et Acteurs*, 134; Komonchak, "Introduction: Episcopal Conferences under Criticism"; Alberigo and Komonchak, *Vatican II*, 3:466–71.

34. Liénart's well-known French colleague Cardinal Lefebvre asked Liénart to speak and provided him with the Latin translation of the motion. Liénart, however, has always denied that there was any advance agreement with Frings that he would second the motion (Alberigo and Komonchak, *Vatican II*, 2:32). Falconi claims that the decision to act was made in concert with the Dutch, German, Austrian, Swiss, and Belgian episcopates (*Pope John and the Ecumenical Council*, 161). See Komonchak, "Elections," for a full account of the variety of groups and plans that had formed in opposition to quick elections.

35. Etchegaray, "Interventi Scritti," 293.

36. In fact, though the DM did not officially form until a few weeks later, those who would become key members were active from the very beginning. During the elections, Brouwers notes that EC secretaries played a great role "by maintaining mutual contacts, providing information on the appropriate candidates and exchanging of provisional lists" and attributed their desire to form an official group to the experience they had and contacts they made with other episcopates during this period ("Derniers Préparatifs," 357 and 361; cf. Grootaers, *Actes et Acteurs*, 134). Six of the eventual twenty-two members of the DM were involved in distributing Dutch theologians' comments on the preparatory schemas at the beginning of the Council (Brouwers, "Derniers Préparatifs," appendix 1, 364–65).

37. Brouwers, "Derniers Préparatifs," 354.

38. Komonchak, "The Constitution on the Liturgy," 2.

39. "Obtaining a vote on the liturgy" was on the agenda of the very first DM meeting ("Secretary of the C.C.C.," November 13, 1963, EA 1.5.5).

40. Caprile, quoted in Komonchak, "Liturgy," 3.

41. Anderson, *Council Daybook: Sessions 1 and 2*, 75. The issue on which the Council voted depended upon the stage of the document. In its early stages the Council could simply vote to accept the document as it was, providing that the responsible commission take into account the concerns raised in the Council hall, or they could vote to reject it entirely and return it to committee.

42. Tikka, India, CIC 7.

43. CIC 7.

44. CIC 1.

45. Verghese, "Aggiornamento and the Unity of All," 379.

46. Mehl, "The Ecumenical Situation," 7.

47. Alberigo and Komonchak, *Vatican II*, 2:234–36.

48. CIC 7.

49. Wiltgen, *Rhine Flows*, 23.

50. DM Minutes 1:1, November 9, 1962, PC, French.

51. Support for a proposal was difficult to gauge through the debates, as not everyone was granted an opportunity to speak. In order to speak or make an intervention, bishops had to submit a request, and a copy of their speech written in

Latin, days in advance. While it seems that progressive and moderate bishops were happy to allow those bishops who were experts on various topics (and usually more fluent in Latin) to do the speaking, conservatives seemed to be more invested in making sure each person was heard. This often resulted in redundancy (about which many bishops in Caporale's sample complained) and a misrepresentation of the proportion of bishops supporting a viewpoint. As the progressive Canadian bishop Alexander Carter noted: "The voting pattern has been surprising at times. While the number of interventions [in support of each side] seems equal, the . . . voting is overwhelmingly uneven. Probably this may be explained by the fact that the men who disagree feel the need to talk the most" (CIC 10).

52. Alberigo and Komonchak, *Vatican II*, 2:263.

53. Ibid., 265

54. Sewell, "Bastille," 875.

55. Grootaers, *Actes et Acteurs*, 142–44; Komonchak, "The Conciliar Discussion on the Sources of Revelation."

56. Though there was no historical precedent for such an argument and council votes had always been binding, this was easy to ignore because councils are such rare events. Henri DeLubac, an important progressive French theologian, voiced frustration over this tactic, telling Caporale that conservatives' position "that the Council has no authority unless approved by the Pope, is contradicted by several councils in the past where the Pope was absent and the approval was discounted as a matter of course (Nicea). This view and position is definitely against traditional thought; otherwise it makes no sense whatsoever. [Why convoke] a Council?" (CT).

57. Primeau to Tirot, February 4, 1966, PC 21(7).

58. Caporale began his interviews during the First Session and completed them before the end of the Second. Thus, while some of his respondents may have been interviewed later than others in the course of the Council, all of them were interviewed while the events of the First Session were unfolding or relatively soon thereafter, and long before the overall outcome of the Council was clear.

59. CIC 7.

60. July 28, 1963, PC.

61. CIC 7.

62. CIC 10.

63. CIC 7.

64. CIC 14, emphasis added.

65. Progressives benefited from these contacts more than conservatives. Whereas almost ninety percent of his non-conservative respondents stated that they got to know many new people through the Council, only half of his conservative respondents said so. For example, Michael Cardinal Brown, a conservative member of the Curia, stated that he "did not have many contacts." Though he had been "invited by various groups of bishops to talk," he had declined because he "did not participate at meetings" outside of the Council hall (CIC 3).

66. CIC 14.

67. See McGrath or Hengsbach, CIC 7.

68. Turner, *Ritual Process*.

69. Durkheim, *Elementary Forms*, 228.

70. *Lettre dal Concilio*, quoted in Alberigo and Komonchak, *Vatican II*, 2:13–14.

71. Sewell, "Bastille," 845.

72. Turner, *Ritual Process*.

73. Sewell "Bastille," 871.

74. CIC 14.

75. Sewell, "Bastille," 861.

76. Other researchers have found similar uses. Matthew Lawson notes that the charismatic Catholics he studied often invoked the Holy Spirit in an attempt to describe a "pattern of social interaction" which reinforces what "Durkheim called a *conscience collective*" ("The Holy Spirit as Conscience Collective," 341).

77. McCarthy, *The Catholic Tradition*, 112.

78. CIC 7.

79. Ibid.

80. Ibid.

81. CIC 7a, emphasis added.

82. Caporale, *Vatican II*, 130–31.

83. CIC 10.

84. Ibid.

85. Komonchak, "Convening Vatican II," 11.

86. American bishop Joseph M. Marling in a speech given in the spring of 1963. Quoted in Komonchak, "Elections," 4.

87. CIC 2.

88. CIC 14.

89. CIC 14a.

90. CIC 4.

91. CT.

92. Alberigo and Komonchak, *Vatican II*, 2:93.

93. CIC 7.

94. Ibid.

95. CIC 14.

96. CIC 10.

97. Sewell, "Bastille," 869.

98. Ibid., 862.

99. Sewell, "A Theory of Structure." See also Beisel and Kay, "Abortion, Race, and Gender in Nineteenth-Century America."

CHAPTER TWO

1. Snow and Benford, "Master Frames"; Snow et al., "Frame Alignment Processes."

2. Because the data are patchy as well as problematic, bishops from communist countries are excluded from the analysis in this chapter. For information on the voting patterns among the bishops from communist countries, please see the methodological appendix.

3. McCarthy, *The Catholic Tradition*, 343.

4. Alberigo and Komonchak, *Vatican II*, 3:98; Fesquet, *The Drama of Vatican II*, 199; Rynne, *Vatican Council II*, 214. After entering the first vote on the Blessed

Virgin Mary into an electronic database, I found that the Vatican's official totals were off by one placet and one non-placet, most likely because two individuals were isolated on the last page of the vote summary and were not included in the totals. See appendix B for more information on how the voting data was entered and analyzed.

5. CIC 9.

6. Seidler and Meyer, *Conflict and Change in the Catholic Church*, 56–57.

7. The Dutch Documentation Center, or DOC, was especially active in disseminating this theology during the Council. See table B.4 for more information on DOC and the theologians who wrote for it.

8. Anderson, *Council Daybook: Vatican II, Sessions 1 and 2*, 286.

9. As a predominantly Catholic country, France, along with Belgium, was different from the majority of the countries on table 2.2. Contrary to what we would expect from majority Catholic countries, both France and Belgium had hierarchies friendly to the ecumenical movement. This fact can be explained by the relatively unique histories of the Church in these two, often interwined, countries. Belgium's uniqueness stems from the fact that it lost political sovereignty to the Netherlands, and the Protestant House of Orange, in 1815. Catholic clergy allied with liberals, and Belgium ended up with a very strong separation of church and state and a significant and powerful Protestant presence (Gould, *Origins of Liberal Dominance*, 28). In 1903 the French government expelled all members of Catholic religious orders, and many of them, particularly those who would be important theologians at the Council, spent their exile in Belgium (Martina 1988, 34).

10. A few countries on table 2.2 stand out as more conservative than the others, particularly Greece and Australia, and to a lesser extent, Switzerland. This is generally consistent with the overall argument presented in this chapter, because neither Greece nor Australia was closely connected to the ecumenical movement. Protestants in geographically more isolated Australia had focused on missionizing the "South-west Pacific" rather than on building better relationships between Protestants in Australia (Rouse and Neill, *History of the Ecumenical Movement*, 375, 400, and 482). Greece was dominated by the Greek Orthodox Church, which was "on the periphery of the World Council of Churches" (Mehl, "The Ecclesiological Significance of the World Council from a Roman Catholic Standpoints," 242).

11. Falconi, *Pope John and the Ecumenical Council*, 343.

12. Peru, Ecuador, Guatemala, the Dominican Republic, and El Salvador were noticeably more conservative than the rest of Latin America, possibly because the majority of their bishops were not natives of those countries (as was generally the case for bishops from Brazil, Chile, Argentina, Mexico, and Venezuela) but of Spain and Italy. For example, 64 percent of the 14 native Peruvians voted progressively on revelation, as compared to only 35 percent of non-native Peruvians. Guatemala, the Dominican Republic, and El Salvador had only two native bishops each who took part in this vote. Ecuador seems to be the only Latin American outlier in this regard, with four of its six native bishops voting conservatively on revelation.

13. CIC 5.

14. "Ecumenism in Africa," 19.

15. Warner, "Work in Progress toward a New Paradigm for the Sociological Study of Religion in the United States."

16. E.g., Finke and Stark, *The Churching of America*; Finke, Guest, and Stark, "Mobilizing Local Religious Markets"; Stark and Iannaccone, "Response to Lechner."

17. Stark and Finke, *Acts of Faith*, 36.

18. It is thought that regulation, in the form of governmental support (through laws, subsidization or tax breaks), creates a "lazy" institution, whereas governmental neglect or sanction contributes to a competitive environment.

19. Finke and Stark, *The Churching of America*, 18–19; Olson, "Religious Pluralism and U.S. Church Membership"; Stark and Finke, *Acts of Faith*, 219.

20. Most empirical tests have focused on the U.S., which has much higher levels of both religious participation and religious pluralism than most other nations, a situation which has made differentiating between these factors difficult. See, for example, Blau, Redding, and Land, "Ethno-cultural Cleavages"; Breault, "New Evidence on Religious Pluralism"; Finke, Guest, and Stark, "Mobilizing Local Religious Markets"; Finke and Iannaccone, "Supply-Side Explanations for Religious Change"; Finke and Stark, *The Churching of America*, "Religious Economies and Sacred Canopies," and "Reply"; Johnson, "Supply-Side and Demand-Side Revivalism?"; Land, Deane, and Blau, "Religious Pluralism and Church Membership"; Olson, "Contemporary U.S. Counties" and "U.S. Church Membership"; and Perl and Olson, "Religious Market Share." By focusing primarily on one country that has formal religious freedom, great pluralism, and no clearly dominant religious institution, researchers have been unable to differentiate among the factors which determine competition, much less incorporate other important factors. Though researchers have begun to apply supply-side theory to other countries, these studies also have limitations. By and large, they examine only a selection of countries, whether that selection is based on perceived outliers (see Hamberg and Pettersson, "The Religious Market"; Olson and Hadaway, "Religious Pluralism and Affiliation"; Stark, "Do Catholic Societies Really Exist?"; Stark, Finke, and Iannaccone, "Pluralism and Piety"; Stark and Iannaccone, "Response to Lechner"; Wilde, "From Excommunication"), industrialized countries for which survey data is available, or one area of the world such as Latin America or Europe (see Chaves and Cann, "Regulation, Pluralism and Market Structure"; Chaves, Schraeder, and Sprindys, "State Regulation of Religion"; Gill, "Government Regulation"; Iannaccone, "The Consequences of Religious Market Structure" and "Religious Markets"; Jelen and Wilcox, "Context and Conscience"; Lechner, "Secularization in the Netherlands"; Stark, "Europe's Receptivity to New Religious Movements"; and Verweij, Ester, and Nauta, "Secularization as an Economic and Cultural Phenomenon").

21. Finke and Stark, *Acts of Faith*, 201, emphasis mine.

22. Finke and Stark, "Religious Economies and Sacred Canopies"; Iannaccone, "The Consequences of Religious Market Structure"; Finke and Stark, *The Churching of America*; Finke and Iannaccone, "Supply-Side Explanations for Religious Change"; Hamberg and Pettersson, "The Religious Market"; Stark, Finke, and Iannaccone, "Pluralism and Piety"; Finke, Guest, and Stark, "Mobilizing Local Religious Markets"; Stark and Iannaccone, "Response to Lechner"; Perl and Olson, "Religious Market Share and Intensity of Church Involvement in Five Denominations."

23. Cf. Gorski, "Historicizing the Secularization Debate," 160; e.g., Breault, "New Evidence on Religious Pluralism, Urbanism, and Religious Participation"; Land, Deane, and Blau, "Religious Pluralism and Church Membership"; Chaves and Cann, "Regulation, Pluralism and Religious Market Structure"; Chaves, Schraeder, and Sprindys, "State Regulation of Religion and Muslim Religious Vitality in the Industrialized West"; Verweij, Ester, and Nauta, "Secularization as an Economic and Cultural Phenomenon"; Olson, "Religious Pluralism in Contemporary U.S. Counties" and "Religious Pluralism and U.S. Church Membership"; Olson and Hadaway, "Religious Pluralism and Affiliation among Canadian Counties and Cities"; Chaves and Gorski, "Religious Pluralism and Religious Participation."

24. Finke and Stark, *The Churching of America*, 19.

25. Smith attributes the emergence of liberation theology to a number of factors which created a growing sense of insecurity within the Latin American church: the successes of both non-Catholic religious groups and "secular working class movements, such as labor unions, socialist organizations, and communist parties," which were making visible headway among the urban poor in many countries by the 1930s (Smith, *Liberation Theology*, 76); the publication of studies by "sociologist-priests which confirmed the weakness of religious commitment among most of the laity" (ibid., 78); and urbanization, which made the Church's failures easily visible (ibid., 71–88); See also Neuhouser, "The Radicalization of the Brazilian Catholic Church in Comparative Perspective." Vallier argues that the Church became more progressive more quickly in Brazil and Chile because these countries had a longer-established separation of church and state (*Catholicism, Social Control, and Modernization in Latin America*, 179).

26. Smith, *Liberation Theology*, 76.

27. "Chilean Cardinal Points Out Great Differences in Protestantism Geographically," November 28, 1963, DWNS, DOH 1(28).

28. CIC 5. This note card was almost illegible. It took careful work, with the help of William John Shepard at CUA, to reconstruct this quote, and thus it is only an approximation.

29. Catholic Action began in France, when the exiled members of the French Church returned from Belgium between 1937 and 1939 to find a largely unreceptive audience, particularly among the working classes, which were heavily involved in Marxist political parties. In response to this situation, leaders of the French church began to develop a theology of social justice, Catholic Action, and by the time of the Council, the French church was one of the most progressive, in terms of both social justice and ecumenism, of all the Roman Catholic churches in Europe (Martina 1988).

30. Schmitt, *The Roman Catholic Church in Modern Latin America*, 18–19.

31. Though Latin American progressivism was in place by the early 1950s, with few exceptions (e.g., Dussel, *A History of the Church in Latin America;* Neuhouser, "The Radicalization of the Brazilian Catholic Church"; Núñez and Taylor, *Crisis in Latin America*; Smith, *Liberation Theology;* Schmitt, *The Roman Catholic Church in Modern Latin America;* Vallier, *Catholicism, Social Control, and Modernization in Latin America* and "Church 'Development' in Latin America"), most investigations of liberation theology focus on its growth after the Council.

32. Though Protestant and Marxist successes varied from country to country, with the Church in Brazil and Chile taking some of the most serious hits (and bringing forth the most progressive leaders, see Vallier, *Catholicism, Social Control, and Modernization*), by and large, the Latin American hierarchy interpreted these losses as regional, not national. They responded by building the largest supranational organization within the Catholic Church outside of the Vatican, the Latin American Episcopal Conference, or Consejo Episcopal LatinoAmericano (CELAM) in 1955, under the guidance of important leaders such as Bishops Manuel Larraín, from Chile, Helder Camâra, from Brazil, and Marcos McGrath, from Panama (Smith, *Emergence of Liberation Theology*, 102).

33. Though supply-side theorists have acknowledged that legitimacy concerns are important to religious institutions, they mainly focus on how incorporating legitimacy concerns can lead to an organization's decline (as with their studies of Methodists or the effects of the Council), or on how churches are more subject to legitimacy concerns than sects. See Finke and Stark, *The Churching of America*; Finke, "The Illusion of Shifting Demand: Supply-Side Interpretations of American Religious History"; Stark and Finke, *Acts of Faith*. What is lacking is a coherent theory of when and why legitimacy concerns become paramount to some religious leaders and not others.

34. DiMaggio and Powell, "Iron Cage," 150.

35. Armstrong, *Forging Gay Identities*, 9.

36. DiMaggio and Powell, "Iron Cage," 148.

37. Researchers typically use the term "structurated." I will use structured throughout the text, in an attempt to be kind to my readers.

38. Supply-siders have also noted that professionalization has important effects on religious leaders, especially the religious leaders of large institutions, and argue that it is one of the two key sources of pressure for accommodation (Finke and Stark, *Churching*, 150; Finke and Dougherty, "The Effects of Professional Training"; Stark and Finke, *Acts*, 164–67). They argue that it encourages clergy to no longer focus on "religious motives" but instead seek to accommodate their institution to the world in order to gain and keep constituents.

39. Fligstein, "Markets as Politics," 657.

40. Ibid.

41. Ibid., 659.

42. Ibid.

43. Bourdieu, "Genesis and Structure of the Religious Field."

44. Cf. Miller, "Competitive Strategies of Religious Organizations."

45. Berger, "A Market Model for the Analysis of Ecumenicity."

46. Fligstein, "Markets as Politics," 663. Fligstein applies the three typologies I use here in reference to markets but acknowledges that his view of markets is "roughly consistent with the idea of organizational fields" (663, note 8). Because I feel that the term "field" is more applicable and generalizable and less confusing (especially because supply-side theorists already use the term "market" in a different way), I refer only to fields in reference to his theory.

47. Fligstein, "Markets as Politics," 664.

48. Ibid.

49. An implication of the findings presented in this chapter is that sociologists need to stop referring to the goals and decisions of religious leaders strictly as "marketing strategies" and instead think about them as *organizational strategies*, of which the decision to market to constituents is but one possibility. My understanding of organizational strategies is roughly consistent with Fligstein's "conceptions of control," which "refer to understandings that structure perceptions of how a market works and that allow actors to interpret their world and to control situations" ("Markets as Politics," 658).

50. Anthony Gill found that only "a relatively modest increase in religious competition (4% to 6%)" was needed to liberalize the Church in the more progressive countries in Latin America (*Rendering into Caesar*, 420).

51. Swidler, "Culture in Action."

52. Fligstein, "Markets as Politics," 669.

53. Here I am describing the process of institutional diffusion, "the spread of normative expectations across the organizations in a field" (DiMaggio, "The Relevance of Organization Theory to the Study of Religion," 14) which theorists call "isomorphism." Organizational theorists identify three types of isomorphism: coercive, normative, and mimetic. Consistent with theorists' predictions, mimetic isomorphism, which occurs when professionals mimic the successful strategies employed by other firms, seems to have been most powerful in fields in crisis. Normative isomorphism, which occurs when the "professional networks that span organizations" diffuse concepts, strategies, tactics, and institutional forms from one organization to another (DiMaggio and Powell, "Iron Cage," 152), was most powerful in stable fields. Coercive isomorphism, which stems from "political influence and the problem of legitimacy," and comes from both "formal and informal pressures" (ibid., 150), was not as common as either of the other two forms. Because of Vatican's unique situation as a religious city-state, the Church had little formal coercive pressures on it at the time of the Council.

54. "Chilean Cardinal Points Out Great Differences in Protestantism Geographically," November 28, 1963, DWNS, DOH 1(28).

55. Vischer, "Report on Second Vatican Council," 58.

56. Chikeka, *Decolonialization Process in Africa*.

57. Wilson, *African Decolonialization*, maps 1 and 2.

58. Cf. Martina, "The Historical Context in Which the Idea of an Ecumenical Council was Born," 6.

59. Gifford and Louis, *Decolonialization and African Independence*, 17.

60. Birmingham, *The Decolonialization of Africa*, 7.

61. Godement, *The New Asian Renaissance*; Berger, *The Battle for Asia*; (Jeffrey, *Asia*, xiv–xv).

62. Godement, *The New Asian Renaissance*, 85.

63. Ibid., 86.

64. Ibid., 84.

65. Fligstein, "Markets as Politics," 668 and 663.

66. Ibid., 657.

67. Ibid., 659.

68. Bilheimer, *Breakthrough*; Lee, *Social Sources of Church Unity*, 78; Berger, "A Market Model for the Analysis of Ecumenicity."

69. Lee, *Social Sources of Church Unity,* 124. Lee argues that World War II cemented the role of the Federal Council of Churches within Protestantism in the United States when the U.S. government used it as the primary organization through which to obtain chaplains for the military. In addition, he argues that decreasing class, racial, regional, ethnic, and cultural disparities among American Protestants in the 1950s as immigrant groups assimilated made ecumenism more likely. Finally, Lee argues that denominational mergers and an interchangeable ministry, caused by the pressures of professionalization connected to seminary training, led to theological and ideological convergence among the larger Protestant denominations, and thus a sense that American Protestants shared more similarities than differences (*Social Sources,* 89–93). Lee's analysis of this process is very similar to the factors Robert Wuthnow argues have led to a "restructuring" of American religion.

70. Gaines, *World Council of Churches,* 17.

71. Bilheimer, *Breakthrough*; Gaines, *World Council of Churches*; Van der Bent, *Historical Dictionary of Ecumenical Christianity*; Visser't Hooft, *The Genesis and Formation of the World Council of Churches*; Zeilstra, *European Unity in Ecumenical Thinking.*

72. See the "Ecumenical Chronicle" section of the *Ecumenical Review.*

73. Todd, *Catholicism and the Ecumenical Movement,* 1.

74. See Hennesy, *American Catholics.*

75. Underwood, *Protestant and Catholic,* xix. See also Ellis, *American Catholicism*; Greeley, *American Catholic*; O'Brien *Public Catholicism*; Orsi, *The Madonna of 115th Street.* Examples of Protestant-Catholic tension in the United States from the 40s and 50s abound. Openly anti-Catholic sentiments appeared in Paul Blanshard's *American Freedom and Catholic Power* and a variety of other publications. For example, sociologist John J. Kane counted forty-two articles, editorials, and letters "critical of Roman Catholicism" in the American Protestant periodical *Christian Century* during the first six months of 1949 (*Catholic-Protestant Conflicts in America,* 6; cf. Underwood, *Protestant and Catholic,* xvii). This anti-Catholic barrage was met by a less extensive, but still quite forceful and substantial, response from Catholics in their periodical *America,* which, according to Kane, published fourteen articles critical of Protestantism during the same period.

76. Orsi, *The Madonna of 115th Street,* 56.

77. Lee, *The Social Sources of Church Unity*; Wuthnow, *Restructuring,* 81.

78. McCarthy, *The Catholic Tradition,* 177–83; Todd, *Catholicism and the Ecumenical Movement.*

79. The fact that tensions began to decrease during the early 1950s is indicated by Kane's finding that both Protestants and Catholics published only a third as many articles critical of each other in 1954 as they had in 1949 (*Protestant-Catholic,* 7), and by the fact that by 1955 a Protestant ecumenist wrote, "There are quite a number of people in the Roman Catholic Church, some of them influential, who are seriously prepared to discuss the subject . . . many Catholics *want* to discuss the matter as representatives of their Church" (Kinder, "*Protestant–Roman Catholic Encounter,*" 339–43).

80. A Roman Catholic journalist's assessment of the 1955 World Council of Churches Assembly in Evanston provides a good indication of both the improving

relations as well as the tensions which remained. After remarking that "The sight of Paul Blanchard's work in the Assembly book-shop naturally offended a Catholic eye, for his books can hardly be classified under 'ecumenical literature,'" and complaining of the presence of anti-Catholic signs and pamphlets and "the distribution of *The Protestant Reporter,* an anti-Catholic periodical," Jung closed by noting the exceptional nature of these instances of hostility amid "the excellent intentions of most officials of the World Council," and by optimistically predicting that "Catholic and Protestant theological thinking are no longer moving along diverging lines, ignoring each other, but along converging lines which eventually will meet ("Roman Catholic Impressions of the Evanston Assembly," 121, 125).

81. As a Catholic journalist noted in his description of the 1955 WCC Assembly: "I believe I can summarize the [Protestant] position [on Roman Catholicism] in this way: much friendliness and courtesy on the part of the delegates to the Assembly and of its staff for individual Catholics—little sympathy, to say no more, towards the Catholic Church as an institution" (Lialine quoted in "Various Voices on Evanston: From the Roman Catholic Church," 278).

82. As a Roman Catholic writer explained the hierarchy's reluctance, "If the Roman Catholic Church agreed to take part in the ecumenical movement, she would be bound to regard herself as one Christian communion among others, seeking the Body of Christ, unaware where and how that Body expresses itself; this would be tantamount to admitting that Christ has deserted His Church, and has denied it the means of recognising and expressing itself as His Body" (Rocquette, quoted in "Some Roman Catholic Voices about the First Assembly," 433–34).

83. Ellis, *American Catholicism*; Greeley, *The American Catholic.*

84. See Stark and Finke, *Acts of Faith,* 242; Coleman, *The Evolution of Dutch Catholicism.*

85. Sengers, "'Although We Are Catholic, We Are Dutch,'" 134.

86. I am grateful to an anonymous reviewer for pointing out that Pius XII first allowed Catholic biblical scholars to use modern methods of scholarship in an encyclical issued in 1943. That encyclical was authored by the Catholic ecumenical leader Augustine Cardinal Bea, who would become a major figure at the Council as the head of the Secretariat for Promoting Christian Unity (Martina, "Historical Context," 15). Though it is difficult, if not impossible, to trace the relationships and institutional affiliations of the Catholics who became active in biblical scholarship, it is conceivable that they too forged an important connection with Protestants in the years leading up the Council, one that was separate from, if often linked to, the network which was growing as a result of the ecumenical movement (see Fogarty 1989).

87. Todd, *Catholicism and the Ecumenical Movement,* 1. See also Sperry, *Religion and Our Divided Denominations* (1945); Skydsgaard, *One in Christ* (1957).

88. For example, in 1955 a Roman Catholic wrote that the world had entered "The Hour of Protestantism," and that Protestantism's "hour to deliver its message to the world would seem to have come at last" (Lambert, quoted in "Various Voices on Evanston: From the Roman Catholic Church," 275). In 1955, the *Ecumenical*

Review published five articles which focused solely on the RCC, more than it published from 1950 to 1954 altogether.

89. Kinder, "Protestant-Roman Catholic Encounter," 339.

90. Ibid., 343.

91. "Ecumenical Chronicle: Notes on Roman Catholic Writings Concerning Ecumenism."

92. "The Ecclesiological Significance of the World Council from a Roman Catholic Standpoint," 240.

93. Between 1959 and 1962, after John's announcement, but before the Council started, the *Ecumenical Review* published twenty-four articles that focused on or gave significant attention to the Roman Catholic Church. The same number had appeared in the previous decade (1948–58).

94. "Ecumenical Chronicle: Report of the Executive Committee to the Central Committee," 78; emphasis added.

95. Hengsbach, CIC 5.

96. CIC 5.

97. Ibid.

98. Ibid.

99. Also see, for example, the personal correspondence between Bishop Ernest Primeau and the prominent American Protestant observer Douglas Horton (Horton to Primeau, February 4, 1963, PC; Horton to Primeau, March 16, 1963, PC; Primeau to Horton, March 14, 1963, PC).

100. CIC 5.

101. Baum, "Montreal: Faith and Order," 510.

102. E.g., Bender, *Heaven's Kitchen*; Chaves, *Ordaining Women*; Demerath et al., *Sacred Companies*; Dillon, *Catholic Identity*; Finke and Stark, *Acts of Faith*, 164; Finke and Dougherty, "The Effects of Professional Training"; Finke, "Innovative Returns to Tradition"; Wuthnow, "World Order."

103. DiMaggio and Powell, "Iron Cage," 148.

104. For example, after unofficially observing the 1949 WCC Assembly in Amsterdam (because the hierarchy would not allow any Catholics to officially attend), Father Charles Boyer (cofounder in 1952 of one of the first Roman Catholic ecumenical organizations, Foyer Unitas [see Koet, Galema, and Van Assendelft, *Hearth of Unity*]) thanked "all those who gave him such a courteous and cordial welcome in Amsterdam," and mentioned "pleasant and valuable discussions" (quoted in "Ecumenical Chronicle: The Roman Catholic Church and the First Assembly of the World Council of Churches," 203). Furthermore, though it is not the focus of the present analysis, it is clear that a reciprocal process also occurred, with many Protestants coming to see Catholic leaders as colleagues. By 1963, Daniel O'Hanlon (the interpreter/guide for the English-speaking Protestant and Orthodox observers at the last three sessions of the Council) wrote that it had become "quite natural to invite a Catholic representative to sit in" on the planning committees for the WCC's Faith and Order Conference in Montreal ("Faith and Order Conference,"138).

105. Fligstein, "Markets as Politics," 667; DiMaggio and Powell, "Iron Cage," 148.

106. de Araujo Sales, Brazil, CIC 5.
107. CIC 5.

Chapter Three

1. E.g., Freeman, "The Tyranny of Structurelessness"; Epstein, *Political Protest and Cultural Revolution*; Stevens, *Kingdom of Children*.

2. This argument is consistent with that made by Rory McVeigh, Daniel Meyers, and David Sikkink in their study of the relationship between structure and framing in social movements: "Mobilizational efforts benefit when movement framing is congruent with local structural conditions" ("Corn, Klansmen, and Coolidge," 653).

3. Perrin, "Il 'Coetus Internationalis Patrum' e la minoranza conciliare," 179–80; Alberigo and Komonchak, *Vatican II*, 2:198.

4. See Alberigo and Komonchak, *Vatican II*, 2:194–221 about other informal groups at the Council. For assessments of the DM, see Alberigo and Komonchak, *Vatican II*, 3:61–62; Caporale, *Vatican II*, 72–73; Grootaers, *Actes et Acteurs*, 133–65; Laurentin, *Bilan du concile*, 43–44; Noël, "Gli incontri"; Wiltgen, *Rhine Flows*, 129. For assessments of the CIP, see Alberigo and Komonchak, *Vatican II*, 3:170–75; Laurentin, *Bilan du concile*, 39–41; Perrin, "Il 'Coetus Internationalis Patrum'"; Wiltgen, *Rhine Flows*, 148–50, 274–78, 235–52.

5. Morris, *The Origins of the Civil Rights Movement*; Zald and McCarthy, "Religious Groups as Crucibles of Social Movements"; Smith, *Disruptive Religion* and *Resisting Reagan*; Patillo-McCoy, "Church Culture as a Strategy of Action in the Black Community"; Wood, "Religious Culture and Political Action" and *Faith in Action*; Young, "Confessional Protest."

6. E.g., Wood and Zald, "Aspects of Racial Integration in the Methodist Church"; Kniss, "Ideas and Symbols as Resources in Intrareligious Conflict."

7. E.g., Katzenstein, *Faithful and Fearless*; Smith, *Liberation Theology*.

8. E.g., Seidler and Meyer, *Conflict and Change*.

9. E.g., Tarrow, *Power in Movement*, 286; Ganz, "Resources and Resourcefulness," 1036.

10. McAdam, Tarrow, and Tilly, *Dynamics of Contention*.

11. Snow et al., "Frame Alignment Processes."

12. Ganz, "Resources and Resourcefulness."

13. Ibid., 1005.

14. Polletta, *Freedom*.

15. Ibid; Swidler, *Talk of Love* and "Culture in Action"; Clemens, "Organizational Repertoires"; Armstrong, *Forging Gay Identities*; Sewell "A Theory of Structure"; Steensland, "Cultural Categories and the American Welfare State"; Weber, *Economy and Society*; Stevens, *Kingdom of Children*.

16. I use culture here to refer to both the religious beliefs held by these religious leaders, as well as to the quite different worldviews and understandings of the Church these implied and supported. To some extent, these map along national lines, according to the progressive and conservative and so also encompass national or regional cultures, divisions examined in chapter 2.

17. In the end, the Council validated collegiality but did so with considerable ambiguity, much of which resulted from qualifications added to the document at the behest of Pope Paul to appease conservatives (cf. Guimarães, *In the Murky Waters*). This occurred long after both of the organizations examined here were created, and thus, long after their disparate views of collegiality had determined their organizational forms, strategies, and tactics.

18. Huebsch, *Vatican II in Plain English*, 215.

19. *The Catholic Encyclopedia*; McCarthy, *The Catholic Tradition*, 120–25.

20. *The Catholic Encyclopedia*.

21. Pottmeyer, *Towards a Papacy in Communion*.

22. United States Bishops Press Panel, "Excerpts from the Address of Archbishop Lawrence J. Shehan of Baltimore," October 23, 1963, DOH 1(22).

23. "Undersecretary of Vatican Council Shows Council's Role in Church Unity," October 8, 1963, DWNS, DOH 1(20).

24. Wenger, *Vatican II*, 1:115–18.

25. Petition on Collegiality, undated, EA 1.5.11, French.

26. DM Minutes 5:2, November 8, 1963, PC, Latin.

27. DM Minutes 3:4, October 1, 1965, PC, Latin.

28. Perrin, "Il 'Coetus Internationalis Patrum,'" 177.

29. CT.

30. CIC 6.

31. Berto to Carli, January 1, 1964, FCrl 15.32; December 9 and November 13, 1963, FCrl 15.31; March 13,1964, FCrl 17.1, Italian.

32. Berto to Carli, November 6, 1963, FCrl 15.3, Italian.

33. Etchegaray, "Interventi Scritti," 293.

34. CT.

35. DM Minutes 2:1, November 20, 1962, PC, Latin.

36. Polletta, *Freedom*.

37. Flyer titled "Meeting of Delegates from ECs," Fourth Session, PC.

38. Alberigo and Komonchak, *Vatican II*, 2:207–9.

39. The method of appointing a DM representative seems to have varied with each EC. Some simply volunteered or were invited because of network connections; others were elected by their conferences.

40. Cf. Grootaers, *Actes et Acteurs*, 136, n. 6; Falconi, *Pope John*, 343.

41. See the appendix B and table B.3 for details.

42. The country designations and the number of bishops in each country presented on figure 3.1 reflect the Church's categorization in the *Acta* (1960–61) and thus represent the total number of bishops serving in a country at the beginning of the Council, not necessarily the number who went to the Council or who voted on any particular issue. The countries shown as members of CELAM or FACE on figure 3.1 are only those mentioned by Caporale's respondents as key participants. However, the total number of bishops counted as members of CELAM and FACE represents the number of bishops serving in Latin America and Africa (see tables 2.3 and 2.4 for details), not just the members of those countries shown. This seemed like a reasonable decision because the active meetings, collegial outlook, and degree of consensus within CELAM and FACE

suggest that communication flowed readily from the bishops who belonged to more active member ECs to those who did not.

43. I included countries even if I could not find definitive information about their EC as long as it had some sort of likely communication with a DM representative, because the DM did not rely unilaterally on the EC structure. During their second meeting of the Second Session, they noted that because they "very much desired" to "feel connected with other conferences, which are not represented," or which "do not have a 'continental' structure," a subcommittee of DM members was going to meet to consider the best way to communicate with unrepresented bishops (DM Minutes 2:2, October 11, 1963; PC, Latin). Similarly, all bishops from countries represented by the Eastern Orthodox Catholic Church are included under the Eastern Orthodox category on figure 3.1, because, despite the rather small number of Eastern Orthodox bishops at the Council, they had two core representatives at the DM during all four sessions. The Eastern Orthodox group includes 2 bishops from the Arabian peninsula, 4 from Iran, 12 from Iraq, 1 from Jordan, 26 from Lebanon, 10 from Pakistan, 4 from Palestine, 15 from Syria, and 1 from Turkey.

44. The DM's efficiency was noted by others. Laurentin refers to it as "the unofficial but efficient coordinating organization that each week brought together the representatives of the principal national and international conferences" called "the conference of twenty-two" (1964: 5).

45. Quoted in Grootaers, *Actes et Acteurs*, 141.

46. DM Minutes 2:4, September 24, 1965, PC, Latin.

47. "Report to the U.S. Hierarchy of the DM," September 18, 1964, DOH 3(5).

48. DM Minutes 1:4, September 17, 1965, PC, Latin.

49. CIC 2.

50. CIC 1.

51. Irish bishop Conway and told Caporale, "We did not attend the informal group meetings, the bishops of England substituted for us, and we were kept informed by them" (CIC 2). German bishop Hengsbach told Caporale, "Each Monday we had a meeting of German and Austrian bishops [and other] German-speaking bishops: bishops from Switzerland, the missionary German bishops . . . and some bishops from Nordic countries" (CIC 2).

52. Falconi, *Pope John*, 185.

53. CTC 2.

54. Ibid.

55. Guglielmi CHT, emphasis added.

56. CIC 2.

57. CIC 7.

58. CIC 7a.

59. Primeau to Tirot, February 4, 1966, PC 21(7). While Primeau does not explicitly refer to the DM, it seems likely that he was thinking of it (nowhere else did he come into such regular and direct contact with bishops from other parts of the world). This is especially likely since he was writing the letter for publication—and the DM was careful to never refer to themselves by name publicly (Alberigo and Komonchak, *History of Vatican II*, 2:208).

60. McGrath, "La creazione della coscienza di un popolo latinoamericano," 140.

61. Guimarães, *In the Murky Waters of Vatican II*, 93.

62. Superior generals are the heads of religious orders. Lefebvre, also an archbishop, was the superior general of the Holy Ghost Fathers (Alberigo and Komonchak, *History of Vatican II*, 2:197).

63. Estimates of the exact time Sigaud and Lefebvre began strategizing vary from the first week of the First Session (Wiltgen, *The Rhine Flows*, 89) to midway through it (Alberigo and Komonchak, *History of Vatican II*, 2:197), but sources agree that Sigaud and Lefebvre did not officially form a group with Carli until the beginning of the Second Session (Wiltgen, *The Rhine Flows*, 89; Alberigo and Komonchak, *History of Vatican II*, 2:1997, 197–98; Perrin, "Il 'Coetus Internationalis Patrum,'" 175).

64. Berto to Carli, November 6, 1963, FCrl 15.30, and November 13, 1963, FCrl 15.31, Italian.

65. Berto to Carli, March 13,1964, FCrl 17.1, Italian.

66. Berto to Carli, August 5, 1964, FCrl 15.35, Italian.

67. Alberigo and Komonchak, *Vatican II*, 2:116.

68. Lefebvre to Carli, May 3, 1965, FCrl 15.2, French.

69. In this sense, the CIP is best understood as a countermovement to the movement for progressive change being promoted by the DM during the Council. The CIP had all three of the conditions Meyer and Staggenborg identify as promoting the rise of countermovements (1996). They argue that, "first, the movement shows signs of success," which was certainly the case with the DM by the Second Session of the Council, "second, the interests of some populations are threatened by movement goals," as were the interests of conservatives, and third, "political allies are available to aid oppositional mobilization." The CIP had prominent political allies within the Roman Curia.

70. Alberigo and Komonchak, *Vatican II*, 2:198; Laurentin, *Bilan du concile*, 39–40; Perrin, "Il 'Coetus Internationalis Patrum,'" 174–75; Wiltgen, *Rhine Flows*, 149.

71. FSig 3.7.

72. Wiltgen, *Rhine Flows*, 274. For a more extensive discussion of the issue of communism at the Council, please see appendix B.

73. Caporale, *Vatican II*, 56.

74. CIC 1.

75. CIC 2.

76. CIC 1.

77. CIC 2.

78. Caporale, *Vatican II*, 75–77.

79. Quoted in Grootaers, *Actes et Acteurs*, 141.

80. CIC 1.

81. Snow et al., "Frame Alignment Processes," 467.

82. Wiltgen, *Rhine Flows*, 89–90.

83. Carli claimed that he spoke in the name of "thirty fathers from various nations," but Alberigo and Komonchak report that when the list of signatures was checked it contained only nine: Sigaud and Lefebvre and seven of their closest allies (*Vatican II*, 3:149–50).

84. Noël, "Gli incontri," 113.

85. Perrin, "Il 'Coetus Internationalis Patrum,'" 177; Alberigo and Komonchak, *Vatican II*, 2:197.

86. Lefebvre to Carli and other CIP sympathizers, February 14, 1964, FCrl 15.27, Latin.

87. Lefebvre to Sigaud, August 5, 1964, FSig 1.9, French.

88. Perrin, "Il 'Coetus Internationalis Patrum,'" 179–80.

89. CT.

90. Ganz, "Resources and Resourcefulness."

91. Quoted in Perrin, "Il 'Coetus Internationalis Patrum,'"182.

92. Lefebvre to Carli, December 27, 1964, FCrl 15.13, French.

93. Noël categorizes the DM's efforts in this regard as their "most significant success" ("Gli incontri," 112).

94. Veuillot to Council Moderators, October 14, 1964, EA 5.4.

95. Sigaud and de Castro Mayer to Council Fathers, September 15, 1964, FSig 2.19, Latin.

96. Lefebvre to Carli, August 20, 1965, FCrl 15.11, French, emphasis mine.

97. Cf. Perrin, "Il 'Coetus Internationalis Patrum,'" 179.

98. "Composition of Propaganda Congregation Made More Precise by Three Clauses," November 16, 1965, DWNS, DOH 4(13).

99. For example see the CIP Modi on Religious Liberty, November 18, 1965, FCrl 1.87, or the CIP Modi on The Church's Attitude toward Non Christian Religions, FCrl 15.28, Latin.

100. Cf. Laurentin, *Bilan du concile*, 123.

101. Wiltgen estimates that 510 signed the petition on Mary (*Rhine Flows*, 241), but I found a list with only 461 signatures in Sigaud's archive.

102. Ganz, "Resources and Resourcefulness," 1041.

103. Armstrong, "Crisis, Collective Creativity."

104. Sewell, "Bastille."

105. Komonchak, "The Conciliar Discussion on the Sources of Revelation," 20.

106. Ganz, "Resources and Resourcefulness," 1043.

107. Mansbridge, *Why We Lost the ERA*; Polletta, *Freedom*.

108. Stevens, *Kingdom of Children*.

109. CIC 2.

110. Ibid.

111. Rynne, *Vatican Council II*, 92.

112. Clemens, *The People's Lobby*, 63.

113. The reader should not come away from this analysis with the impression that the CIP was completely ineffective. At a very basic level, the CIP demonstrates that any organization is better than none. Though they were not effective at mobilizing or even communicating with voters, they were successful in one important way (and perhaps to them, the only legitimate way): pressuring the pope to qualify Council decisions, especially those which most conflicted with their theological views. The pope acceded to their demands on both Mary and collegiality. Indeed, the CIP's clearest victories are connected to these two issues (cf. Rynne, *Vatican Council II*, 407). But papal decisions, while directive, were not determinative for the Council: even with the pope's qualifications, both issues, especially

the status of Mary, which is explored in detail in chapter 5, were ultimately decided in ways that were interpreted as progressive victories.

114. Stevens, *Kingdom of Children*, 193.

115. Epstein, *Political Protest*.

116. Polletta, *Freedom*, 219.

117. Polletta, *Freedom*, 2.

118. Only one delegate per EC was allowed. As the Second Session started, members were asked to "invite no one to future meetings" without "the consent of all the members." DM Minutes 1:2, October 4, 1963, PC, Latin.

119. DM Minutes 1:2, October 4, 1963, PC, Latin.

120. DM Minutes 3:1, November 20, 1962, PC, Latin.

121. "Letter to representatives" from Etchegaray, October 12, 1963, PC.

122. Grootaers, *Actes et Acteurs*, 161.

123. The DM's emphasis on consensus also resulted from the phenomenological approach used by them and many others at the Council, which entailed "a style of reflection" that "primarily focuses on the *subjectivity* of whoever is inquiring" (Kobler, "An Introduction"). Understanding how their own experiences and subjective understandings of the Church and its place in the world differed from their colleagues' was a key goal for the DM.

CHAPTER FOUR

1. Brown, *Observer in Rome*, 174.

2. Casanova, *Public Religions*, 72.

3. Fesquet, *The Drama of Vatican II*, 606

4. Slayton, *Empire Statesmen: The Rise and Redemption of Al Smith*.

5. Komonchak, "Confessional State," 644; see also "Ecumenical Chronicle: Religious Liberty in Italy."

6. Alberigo and Komonchak, *Vatican II*, 2:523; Martina, "Historical Context," 17.

7. E.g., Oxnam, *The Church and Contemporary Change*, 58. These reports continued well into the Council. For example, see the "Ecumenical Chronicle" written just before the Fourth Session (1965, 176).

8. "The Roman Catholic Church in Spain and Religious Liberty," 95–96.

9. "Letters," 4.

10. Gill, *Rendering unto Caesar*, 415.

11. See Bates, "Religious Liberty: Recent Phases of the Problem," 374; "Ecumenical Chronicle: Religious Liberty from Day to Day."

12. "World Report," January–February 1960, 33.

13. Lowell, "Colombia: Land of Martyrs," 12.

14. Vol. 13, no. 4.

15. "World Report," March–April 1960, 33.

16. Carrillo de Albornoz, "Roman Catholicism and Religious Liberty" (vol. 12), 23–24, emphasis Carrillo de Albornoz'.

17. Carrillo de Albornoz, "Roman Catholicism and Religious Liberty" (vol. 11), 405, emphasis Carrillo de Albornoz'.

18. Ibid., 409.

19. Ibid., 408–9, note 2.

20. Father Augustin Léonard, quoted in ibid., 409, emphasis Carrillo de Albornoz'.

21. Albert Hartman, quoted in ibid., 418, emphasis mine.

22. Quoted in ibid., 419, emphasis mine.

23. "Ecumenical Chronicle: Religious Liberty from Day to Day," 477.

24. Wladimire d'Ormesson, a French diplomat with close ties to the Vatican, quoted in Carrillo de Albornoz, "Roman Catholicism and Religious Liberty" (vol. 11), 410, emphasis Carrillo de Albornoz'.

25. John Bennett, quoted in ibid., 408.

26. Quoted in ibid., 421, emphasis Carrillo de Albornoz'.

27. Martina, "Historical Context," 28–30.

28. Komonchak, "Confessional State," 648.

29. Carelton, "The Vatican Council and Issues of Religious Liberty," 459.

30. Stransky, "What the Council Will Do," 20.

31. Alberigo and Komonchak, *Vatican II*, 2:282.

32. Komonchak, "Confessional State," 647, 650.

33. Formed in July 1960, at the behest of Pope John XXIII, the SCU was both a preparatory and a conciliar commission—in fact, the only preparatory commission to survive the events of the First Session intact (though members were later added). It began with eighteen members; eight were later elected by the Council and four appointed by Paul VI. These thirty members of the hierarchy met weekly with the Protestant observers to discuss Council issues. More than two-thirds of the bishops on the SCU were from countries with a strong Protestant presence, as was the entire administrative staff, and its president Augustine Cardinal Bea.

34. Brown, *Observer in Rome*, 174.

35. DOH 5(13).

36. Olsen, "Catholicity," 25.

37. CIC 5.

38. Ibid.

39. CIC 7.

40. CIC 5.

41. Ibid.

42. Ibid.

43. Rynne, *Vatican Council II*, 107.

44. Ibid., 121.

45. Ibid., 145, 146.

46. Scatena, "Lo Schema sulla Libertà Religiosa."

47. The president of the Coordinating Commission, Cardinal Cicognani, a conservative member of the Curia, decided that the SCU could prepare the text on religious freedom, and then give it to the Doctrinal Commission, which would make recommendations for changes before it was officially added to the Schema on Ecumenism and promulgated to the assembly for discussion and vote. This in effect was a "graceful way of putting the question off until later," for there was no

way to guarantee that the Doctrinal Commission would actually give feedback to the SCU in time for the document to be discussed during the Second Session. Indeed, Cicognani promised Bea that the document would be "quickly printed for sending to the bishops," but though Bea sent him the text two days later, "nothing happened" (Alberigo and Komonchak, *Vatican II*, 3:279).

48. Alberigo and Komonchak, *Vatican II*, 3:278.

49. Stransky to Primeau, July 28, 1963, PC.

50. Rynne, *Vatican Council II*, 228; Alberigo and Komonchak, *Vatican II*, 3:280.

51. "Memorandum to Coordinating Commission, to the Board of Moderators and to Whomsoever May Pertain Decisions Regarding the Conciliar Agenda," October 21, 1963, PC.

52. National Catholic Welfare Conference (NCWC) document, undated, PC. See also "The Council and the Issue of the Free Exercise of Religion: The Urgency of the Issue," NCWC, October 22, DOH 1(22).

53. Though Ottaviani made numerous attempts to delay the decision by "making a great many long-winded explanations and offering a number of wild suggestions," after a series of meetings, the Commission, on November 11, voted eighteen to five in favor of reporting the text to the floor. Alberigo and Komonchak, *Vatican II*, 3:280–82.

54. DeSmedt, quoted in Rynne, *Vatican Council II*, 237.

55. "Cardinal Ritter Calls Religious Liberty Basis for Ecumenical Contacts," November 21, 1963, DWNS, DOH 2(9).

56. Rynne, *Vatican Council II*, 299.

57. Yzermans, *American Participation in the Second Vatican Council*, 636.

58. Fesquet, *The Drama of Vatican II*, 606.

59. *Vatican Council II*, 253–54, 267.

60. See Emmerson, "The Changing Face of Rome."

61. Carrillo de Albornoz, "Religious Liberty and the Second Vatican Council," 394.

62. Etchegaray to Primeau, January 13, 1964, PC, French.

63. The "relator" was a person closely connected to the document in question and responsible for presenting its overall argument and summarizing any changes that had been made since its last promulgation. The relator usually opened the discussion on any given document.

64. Rynne, *Vatican Council II*, 298–99.

65. Quoted in ibid., 627–28.

66. Rynne, *Vatican Council II*, 300.

67. "Cardinal Beran Begs Council Fathers Not to Weaken the Religious Liberty Declaration," September 20, 1965, DWNS, DOH 4(12).

68. "Intervention of Josef Cardinal Beran, Archbishop of Prague, on September 20, 1965, DOH 4(14), cf. Yzermans, *American Participation*, 621.

69. Rynne, *Vatican Council II*, 302.

70. Ibid., 405.

71. DM minutes 7:3, November 6, 1964, EA, Latin.

72. Rynne, *Vatican Council II*, 417.

73. The most significant of such efforts resulted in the declaration temporarily being taken out of progressives' control in the SCU and placed under the jurisdiction of a "special mixed commission" heavily weighted toward the conservative point of view. In response, seventeen cardinals submitted a petition to the pope deploring the "appearance of a violation of the rules of the Council." Paul then intervened and mandated that the declaration remain under the jurisdiction of the SCU (Rynne, *Vatican Council II*, 317–20; Alberigo and Komonchak, *Vatican II*, 4:180–91, 396; Fesquet, *Drama*, 422).

74. Rynne, *Vatican Council II*, 417–19.

75. Ibid.; cf. Alberigo and Komonchak, *Vatican II*, 4:397–401.

76. Outler, "Vatican II-Act Three," 261. The text of the petition: "Your Holiness: With reverence but urgently, very urgently, most urgently [*instanter, instantius, instantissime*], we request that a vote on the declaration on religious liberty be taken before the end of this session of the Council, lest the confidence of the world, both Christian and non-Christian, be lost." There are conflicting reports about the number of signatures progressives obtained for the petition. It seems likely that the document presented to the pope had approximately five hundred, but the final petition, which continued to circulate on the Council floor, had more than a thousand (Rynne, *Vatican II*, 419–20; Horton, *Vatican Diary 1964*, 178).

77. Grootaers *Actes et Acteurs*, 88–95; Rynne, *Vatican Council II*, 420.

78. Lefebvre to Carli, May 3, 1965, FCrl 15.2, French.

79. See the following letters from the Primeau Collection: Willebrands to Primeau, November 26, 1964; Bea to Primeau, December 18, 1964; Primeau to Elchinger, January 6, 1965; Primeau to Meyer, January 12, 1965.

80. Primeau to Meyer, January 12, 1965, PC.

81. Brown, "A Protestant Viewpoint," 443.

82. Muelder, "The Church in the Modern World," 113.

83. Quoted in Carrillo de Albornoz, "Religious Liberty and the Second Vatican Council," 394.

84. Rynne, *Vatican Council II*, 463–65.

85. CIP document, "Pro Suffragatione 5@," undated, PC 22(4), Latin.

86. Anderson, *Council Day book*, Session 4, 157.

87. Cuttriss, "Observer Reports on Council," 5.

88. Albert Hartman, quoted in Carrillo de Albornoz, "Roman Catholicism and Religious Liberty" (vol. 11), 418.

89. Max Pribilla, quoted in ibid.

90. Ibid.

91. This is why the French wrote to Primeau before the Fourth Session that the early drafts of the declaration had "a number of lacunae and serious faults." They did not consider the statement strong enough, and felt that it was too focused on the legal and political reasons in favor of religious freedom instead of freedom of conscience. (Elchinger to Primeau, February 16, 1965, PC, French; Murray, "This Matter of Religious Freedom," 42).

92. Primeau to Stransky, August 17, 1963, PC.

93. "American Bishop Asks for Statement by Council on Church-State Relations," October 7, 1963, DWNS, DOH 1(20).

94. "Cardinal Siri Believes Schema Defends Religious Liberty Indiscrimination," September 15, 1965, DWNS, DOH 4(11).

95. Max Pribilla, quoted in Carrillo de Albornoz, "Roman Catholicism and Religious Liberty" (vol. 11), 419.

CHAPTER FIVE

1. Moorman, *Vatican Observed*, 72.

2. McCarthy, *The Catholic Tradition*, 343.

3. Ibid.

4. Ibid., 347–57.

5. Berkouwer, *The Second Vatican Council*, 222.

6. McCarthy, *The Catholic Tradition*, 356.

7. Kinder, "Protestant–Roman Catholic Encounter," 338.

8. National Conference of Christian and Jews, "The Second Vatican Council."

9. See, for example, Baum, "Conflicts and the Council," in which he argues that the Marian movement and the liturgical movement could be integrated.

10. Komonchak, "U.S. Bishops' Suggestions for Vatican II," 361.

11. The antepreparatory commission received almost 600 vota requests that the Council clarify "the standing and role of Mary," most of which were requests that Mary be elevated and that her status as coredemptrix be defined (Alberigo and Komonchak, *Vatican II*, 2:480, 76).

12. Rynne, *Vatican Council II*, 159.

13. DOH 2(1).

14. Laurentin, "The Blessed Virgin at the Council," 2.

15. Primeau from Etchegaray, January 4, 1963, PC.

16. Alberigo and Komonchak, *Vatican II*, 3:96.

17. "Summary of the Arguments Presented for and against Including the Schema on the Blessed Virgin Mary in the Schema on the Church," *Concilio Ecumenico Vaticano II, Ufficio Stampa,* October 29, 1963, DOH 1(29).

18. Rynne, *Vatican Council II*, 212.

19. Rynne, *Vatican Council II*, 212; Alberigo and Komonchak, *Vatican II*, 2:212. Laurentin, "The Blessed Virgin at the Council," 4.

20. Moorman, *Vatican Observed*, 73. See also Alberigo and Komonchak, *Vatican II*, 3:97.

21. Alberigo and Komonchak, *Vatican II*, 3:97.

22. Rynne, *Vatican Council II*, 113.

23. Bernardo (illegible last name) to Sigaud, April 24, 1964, FSig 3.4, Portuguese.

24. Ibid.

25. Fesquet, *Drama*, 313.

26. Rynne, *Vatican Council II*, 105.

27. Alberigo and Komonchak, *Vatican II*, 3:98; Fesquet, *Drama*, 199; Rynne, *Vatican Council II*, 214.

28. "Council Fathers Not in Discord on Doctrine and Dignity of Virgin Mary," October 30, 1963, DWNS, DOH 2(9).

29. Yzermans, *American Participation*, 25.

30. Even progressive Spaniards were not immune to the legitimacy critiques. Early during the First Session, the Spanish bishop García Martínez asked "how much longer the Church was to be *embarrassed* by such 'relics' as Our Blessed Lady's milk and veil," and suggested that such things "be reverently buried and heard of no more" (Rynne, *Vatican Council II*, 58).

31. CIC 7.

32. Rynne, *Vatican Council II*, 161.

33. CIC 5. The translation/transcription is a bit rough here. It literally reads: "It is a question to avoid the scandal too to our faithful, while giving Mary the right place."

34. "Program for the Bishops' Meeting Monday, October 28, 1963," PC 32 (44c).

35. Yzermans, *American Participation*, 25–26 (bishop's name not given).

36. Komonchak, "US Bishops' Suggestions for Vatican II," 361.

37. Alberigo and Komonchak, *Vatican II*, 3:52.

38. Ibid., 369.

39. Consecration is an act which makes something sacred or an act "by which a person or thing is dedicated to the service and worship of God by prayers, rites, and ceremonies." A consecration is similar to, but more solemn and elaborate than, a blessing (*Catholic Encyclopedia* 1908 [2003]).

40. Alberigo and Komonchak, *Vatican II*, 3:175, n. 188.

41. I am being cautious with this estimate for a number of reasons. First, the copy of the petition I obtained (FSig 2.8) has only 461 signers, 10 percent less than the highest estimates of 510 (Wiltgen, *Rhine Flows*, 241). Second, the 461 includes eleven bishops who were members of Sigaud's "Pro-Consecration Committee" (FSig 3.14 and 3.28), who were not included among the signatures on my draft of the petition, probably because it was an earlier draft. I included them because it seems highly likely that their support was counted in the final tallies. Third, because my draft of the petition was handwritten, some of the names were impossible to decipher, and I consequently could only match 370 of them with the bishops in my database of Council votes. Thus, it is possible that as many as 150 of the bishops who voted conservatively on the Marian schema did indeed sign the petition, either a later draft, or this one, illegibly. However, even so, we can be certain that at least 700 bishops who were sympathetic to CIP concerns about Mary did not sign their petition, more than one hundred who did sign voted progressively against the separate schema, and twenty-seven signers failed to vote at all. Finally, I should note that though this petition was not titled, I am confident that it is indeed the petition on Mary for two reasons. First, in Sigaud's archive there are letters from five bishops indicating an intention to sign the petition, all of whom had legible signatures on the untitled document. Second, it is definitely not an earlier draft of the CIP's other major petition, which asked that the Council condemn communism (which was typed and summarized by country and continent), as only 27 percent of those who signed the communism petition also signed this one.

42. Brown, *Observer in Rome*, 74.

43. Berkouwer, *The Second Vatican Council*, 223.

44. Alfrink, "Editorial Information: Thoughts on Ecumenism," NCWC News Service, 5 (PC).

45. Brown, *The Ecumenical Revolution*, 298.

46. Wolf, "Anglican Observations of the Second Session of Vatican II," 18.

47. Alberigo and Komonchak, *Vatican II*, 2:367.

48. For example, see "Must the Marial Chapter of Vatican II Speak of Mediation?" DOC document no. 141, DOH 3(5).

49. McCarthy, *The Catholic Tradition*, 351.

50. Berkouwer, *The Second Vatican Council*, 235.

51. Laurentin, "The Blessed Virgin at the Council," 5.

52. Horton, *Vatican Diary 1964*, 28.

53. Ibid., 26–27.

54. Ibid., 119–20.

55. "Modi on the Blessed Virgin Mary," October 28, 1964, DOH 3(7). This modum was probably seen as a compromise meant to mollify the most ecumenically oriented progressives, who were not happy that the term "Mediatrix" was used at all, as well as insurance in case conservatives did submit enough modi to send the schema back to the drafting committee to mandate that it be revised. If the majority of modi canceled each other out (as was the case with the modi on this vote), some sort of revision would be attempted so that the majority would approve the schema the next time, but that revision would not be overwhelmingly conservative or progressive in nature.

56. Rynne, *Vatican Council II*, 444.

57. Ibid., 425; Alberigo and Komonchak, *Vatican II*, 3:332.

58. Brown, *The Ecumenical Revolution*, 166–67.

59. Blakemore, "A Protestant Views the Vatican Council," 2.

60. Bristol, "Comments on the Decree on Ecumenism," 109.

61. Brown, *The Ecumenical Revolution*, 176.

62. That Sigaud saw Paul's speech as a result of CIP pressure is indicated by what he wrote to one of his supporters, congratulating him "for the consecration that the Holy Father expressed by declaring Our Lady, "Mother of the Church," in the last solemn Session of the Vatican Council. Actually, Sigaud wrote, "in a certain way, this proclamation fulfills that which we hoped for. This is the interpretation given by the Holy Father in a letter written to me" (Sigaud to Kondor, June 2, 1965, FSig 3.3, Portuguese).

63. Sigaud to Frota, September 30, 1965, FSig 3.36, Portuguese.

64. Cicognani to Sigaud, January 16, 1965, FSig 3.29, Latin.

CHAPTER SIX

1. Originally published in *ACT*, the periodical for the Christian Family Movement. Quoted in McClory, *Turning Point*, 52.

2. McCarthy, *The Catholic Tradition*, 315.

3. De Vries, "Population Growth and Christian Responsibility."

4. "Ecumenical Chronicle: A Report on Responsible Parenthood and the Population Problem," 87.

5. Gaines, *The World Council of Churches*, 821–35. Kartachoff, "Orthodox Theology and the Ecumenical Movement," and Metropolitan James of Melita, "The Significance of the World Council of Churches for the Older Churches."

6. Dr. G.K.A. Bell, quoted in Gaines, *The World Council of Churches*, 828.

7. Ibid., 828–29.

8. For example, see Fagley, "Statements on Parenthood and the Population Problem: Part II," PC 4(1), p. 9.

9. Bayne, "Responsible Parenthood and the Population Problem," 30.

10. Ibid., 32.

11. This is not to say that the issue of birth control was entirely disconnected from ecumenical concerns. Robert McAfee Brown wrote that birth control became an ecumenical issue "when Catholic teaching to its own constituency determines public policy for non-Catholics, who run into difficulty when they attempt to establish birth-control clinics, for example, or include the dissemination of contraceptives in legislation to aid underdeveloped countries where over-population leads to famine" (Brown, *The Ecumenical Revolution*, 286). The point here is that Protestants did not see it as a major legitimacy problem which needed to be dealt with in order for the Roman Catholic Church to engage the ecumenical movement in greater dialogue.

12. Horton, *Vatican Diary 1965*, 120.

13. Brown, *The Ecumenical Revolution*, 286.

14. Fagley, "Doctrine and Attitudes of Major Religions in Regard to Fertility," 336.

15. The "pill," a synthetic form of progesterone that suppressed ovulation, was first developed in 1953 and approved by the FDA in 1960, just in time for the Council to have to deal with it (Kaiser, *The Politics of Sex and Religion*, 39).

16. For this chapter, I read and coded all articles on birth control in one major American Catholic periodical (*Catholic Mind*, a publication directed at educated, middle-class, professional American Catholics) from 1950 to 1970. The thirty-five articles were distributed in a U-shaped curve. In the period from 1950 to 1955, as the pill was first popularized, seven articles focused on birth control; the discussion waned during the next decade (only two articles between 1956 and 1960, four between 1961 and 1965) as the Church waited for Vatican II to make an official pronouncement. *Humanae Vitae* brought about a plethora of articles—twenty-one—between 1968 and 1970.

17. Letter dated June 5, 1962, PC.

18. Kaiser, *Politics*, 17.

19. Rynne, *Vatican Council II*, 369; Fesquet, *Drama*, 448.

20. Fesquet, *Drama*, 449.

21. Burns, "Abandoning Suspicion," 75; McClory, *Turning Point*.

22. "What Does the Family Expect from the Council?" 1965, DOH 4 (12).

23. Burns, "Abandoning Suspicion," 75; Gallup and Castelli, *The American Catholic People*, 6.

24. Rynne, *Vatican Council II*, 363.

25. Burns, "Abandoning Suspicion," 71.

26. Sen, *Food, Population and Development*, 7–17.

27. McClory, *Turning Point*, 41.

28. Demographers on the Papal Birth Control Commission reported that the populations in Catholic Mexico and Brazil were "growing at a staggering rate" (McClory, *Turning Point*, 116).

29. "Contraceptives—Again," 38–39.

30. Kaiser, *Politics*.

31. Rynne, *Vatican Council II*, 350.

32. Ibid., 359.

33. Conservatives who referred to birth control in their interventions, the majority of whom were from monopolistic countries such as Italy, Spain, and Ireland, questioned both the new focus on conjugal love, which, according to one Spanish bishop, smacked of eroticism (Fesquet, *Drama*, 479) and according to another, of hedonism ("Bishop Says Schema Sounds Materialistic on Subject of Family Planning," October 30, 1964, DWNS, DOH 6[16]).

34. Fesquet, *Drama*, 477.

35. "Maximos Saigh Calls Normal Conjugal Love and Conscience Contradictory Demands," October 29, 1964, DWNS, DOH 6(16).

36. Only one progressive, the Belgian leader Cardinal Suenens asked that the papal birth control commission be allowed to work more directly with the Council, in his intervention during the Third Session (McClory, *Turning Point*, 59–60).

37. Among the vast papers from the SCU in Daniel O'Hanlon's archive I found only one mention of informal talks being given on birth control, and that talk was given by the Catholic theologian John Noonan for the Protestant observers during the Fourth Session. It was thus not aimed at drumming up support for reform among the voting bishops (handwritten flyer titled "John Noonan," DOH 4(8).

38. For example, see the DM document titled "Summary of the Second Session of the Council" (EA 4.1.3, French), which summarizes the issues the Council had dealt with up to the end of the Second Session as well as the issues the DM felt still needed to be addressed. There is no mention of birth control.

39. Cf. Noël, "Gli incontri," 121.

40. DM minutes from the meeting on October 13, 1964, during the Third Session, meeting not numbered, EA 5.5, French.

41. The missionary bishops who mentioned birth control in their interventions were Bishops Joseph Nkongolo and Joseph Malula from the Democratic Republic of Congo, Archbishop Bernard Yago from Ivory Coast, Bishop Frans Simons from India, and Bishop Rudolf Joseph Stavermen from Indonesia (Fesquet, *Drama*, 475; Rynne, *Vatican Council II*, 362, 371).

42. Rynne, *Vatican Council II*, 509.

43. CIC 14.

44. McClory, *Turning Point*, 51.

45. CIC 3.

46. McCarthy, *The Catholic Tradition*, 316. Paul was clearly deeply conflicted about his decision. During an interview toward the end of the Fourth Session, when asked about birth control, he replied "The world is wondering what we think and we must give an answer. But what? The Church has never in her history confronted such a problem. This is a strange subject for men of the Church to be discussing, even humanly embarrassing. The commissions are in session and mountains of reports are piling up. There is a good deal of study going on. . . . Deciding is not as easy as studying. But we must say something. What? . . . God must truly enlighten us" (Fesquet, *Drama*, 658).

47. Seidler and Meyer, *Conflict and Change*, 93, 95 and 171.

48. The majority report from the Birth Control Commission argued that "The order of creation [i.e., natural law] does not require that all things be left

untouchable just as they are, but that they reach the end to which they have been ordered" (cited in McClory, *Turning Point*, 112).

49. McClory, *Turning Point*, 148.
50. "The Center Doesn't Hold."

RETHINKING THE COUNCIL

1. CIC 14a.
2. Câmara, CIC 14.
3. Boudreaux, CIC 14.
4. Smith, *Liberation Theology*, 97, paraphrasing Cleary, *Crisis and Change*.
5. Grootaers, *Actes et Acteurs*, 148.
6. Sewell, "Bastille," 844.
7. Burns, "Abandoning Suspicion," 74.

APPENDIX B

1. Many felt that this issue as brought to a vote was oddly worded, perhaps intentionally. Typically, the bishops would be asked to approve or reject a document, whereas in this case, they were asked whether an "interruption in the debate was needed." This may have confused those voters who were not paying close attention, because a "placet" vote, which would normally be used to approve a document, would in this case be a negative vote, indicating that the document needed more work (Alberigo and Komonchak, *History of Vatican II*, 2:249–66; Rynne, *Vatican Council II*, 90). Also, my totals for this vote vary by ten from the official Vatican tallies because five bishops recorded both a placet and non-placet. This was most likely because five bishops mis-punched their ID number on their punch cards on this early vote (when their numbers and the voting procedure were still unfamiliar), and their vote was thus recorded under the name of another bishop. The Vatican could count these votes in the final tallies they released because they only reported totals. I cannot include them because all votes are connected to names in my database and I have no way of knowing which vote was the valid one for each of the five bishops with two recorded (and opposing) votes.

2. The official totals for this vote were 1,114 placets to 1,074 non-placets (Alberigo and Komonchak, *History of Vatican II*, 3:95–98). I found that two bishops whose votes (one placet and one non-placet) were isolated on the last page of the vote tally were excluded from the Vatican's official totals, and I have included them.

3. Alberigo and Komonchak, *History of Vatican II*, 3:102–5. The Vatican Secret Archive confirms that the last page of the record of this vote seems to have been lost. As a result, fifteen bishops whose last names start with *Z* were missing. I extrapolated their votes using their votes on the Third Point on Collegiality (the two votes occurred at the same time and are highly correlated), and the totals in my database now match the official totals.

4. *The Times Index-Gazetteer of the World*.

5. The vast majority of voters for whom country-of-service information was not available were superior generals or heads of religious orders (n = 120). Analyses suggest that they voted similarly to the average for the assembly as a whole (63 percent of superior generals voted progressively on revelation, as compared to 64 percent of the total assembly; 49 percent of superior generals voted against the separate Marian schema as opposed to 51 percent of the total assembly).

6. The authors of the NCA seem to have generally lost interest in the variable, except in relation to those countries where the Church was persecuted (there was no change in the assessment of the situation in communist countries). More than half of the countries described as having "constitutional freedom" in earlier years also had no description of the legal situation of the Church by 1965 (n = 77).

7. Cf. Noël, "Gli incontri," 97, n. 1.

8. Not listed on the table are Roger Etchegaray (France), the DM secretary, and the following, who attended intermittently or not until the Third Session: John K. Amissah (Ghana), Arrieta (Costa Rica), William Brasseur (Philippines), Alberto Castelli (Italy), William Conway (Ireland), Eugene D'Souza (India), D. Herliby (Ireland), Marc Lallier (France), Léo Lemay (Malaysia), Stanislas Lokuang (China), Joseph Malula (Congo), Petrus Moors (Holland), Jérome Pillai (Ceylon), Nicolas Verhoeven (Indonesia), Karol Wojtyla (Poland), Dieudonné Yougbare (Upper Volta). Etchegaray to Primeau, January 4, 1963, PC; and DM Minutes 1:1, November 9, 1962, PC, Latin; 4:1, November 27, 1962, PC, Latin; 1:2 October 4, 1963, PC, Latin; 2:2, October 11, 1963, PC, Latin; 3:2, October 18, 1963, PC, Latin; Noël, "Gli incontri," 99–100, n. 8.

9. CIC 2.

10. See Blomjous, McCann, Scalais, and Zoa, CIC 2.

11. "To the world episcopate together in Rome for the fourth session of the Second Vatican Council," September 10, 1965, DOH 2(13).

12. DOC flyer, "International Council for the Development of Religious Information and Documentation," n. d., DOH 2(13), bold in original.

13. "Description of Services for 1964," November 10, 1964, DOH 2(13); "Report on the CCCC for the IV Session of Vatican II," DOH 8(11); and "DOC Series I, II and III," September 27, 1965, DOH 8(11).

14. It seems that the progressives' reluctance to condemn communism was at least partly a result of their interest in better relations with the Russian Orthodox Church. Some conservatives claim that the Communist Party allowed Russian Orthodox bishops to attend the Council with the understanding that the Council would not condemn communism (Martin, *The Jesuits*, 85–86; Guimāres, "The Pact of Metz"). For more on communism at the Council, see Wiltgen, *Rhine Flows*, 272–79, and Rynne, *Vatican Council II*, 476–77.

15. Froese and Pfaff (2005) note that the Church existed in high tension with the Communist Party in East Germany until 1976.

Appendix C

1. Adapted from the timeline created by Thomas E. Buckley, SJ, for his course titled "U.S. Catholics and Vatican II" at the Graduate Theological Union, fall 1997.

REFERENCES

Acta et documenta Concilio oecumenico Vaticano II apparando: Series prima (antepraeparatoria). Vatican City: Typis Polyglottis Vaticanis (Vatican Press), 1960–61.

"Actions of the Commission of the Churches on International Affairs and the Executive Committee of the World Council of Churches July 1965: Human Rights and Religious Liberty—Current Considerations." *Ecumenical Review* 17, no. 4 (1965): 384–86.

Alberigo, Giuseppe, and Joseph Komonchak, eds. *History of Vatican II*. Vol. 1, *Announcing and Preparing Vatican Council II: Toward a New Era in Catholicism*. Maryknoll, NY: Orbis Books, 1995.

———. *History of Vatican II*. Vol. 2, *The Formation of the Council's Identity: First Period and Intersession: October 1962–September 1963*. Maryknoll, NY: Orbis Books, 1997.

———. *History of Vatican II*. Vol. 3, *The Mature Council: Second Period and Intersession: September 1963–September 1964*. Maryknoll, NY: Orbis Books, 2000.

———. *History of Vatican II*. Vol. 4, *Church as Communion: Third Period and Intersession: September 1964–September 1965*. Maryknoll, NY: Orbis Books, 2003.

Anderson, Floyd. *Council Daybook: Vatican II, Sessions 1 and 2*. Washington, DC: National Catholic Welfare Conference, 1965.

———. *Council Daybook: Vatican II, Session 3*. Washington, DC: National Catholic Welfare Conference, 1965.

———. *Council Daybook: Vatican II, Session 4*. Washington, DC: National Catholic Welfare Conference, 1966.

Annuario Pontificio per l'anno. Vatican City: Typis Polyglottis Vaticanis (Vatican Press), 1962–66.

Armstrong, Elizabeth A. "Crisis, Collective Creativity, and the Generation of New Organizational Forms: The Transformation of Lesbian/Gay Organizations in San Francisco." In *Research in the Sociology of Organizations*, ed. Michael Lounsbury and Marc Ventresca, 361–95. Oxford: JAI Press, 2002.

———. *Forging Gay Identities: Organizing Sexuality in San Francisco, 1950–1994*. Chicago: University of Chicago Press, 2002.

Banaszak, Lee Ann. *Why Movements Succeed or Fail: Opportunity, Culture and the Struggle for Woman Suffrage*. Princeton, NJ: Princeton University Press, 1996.

Barth, Karl. "Thoughts on the Second Vatican Council." *Ecumenical Review* 15, no. 4 (1963): 355–67.

Bates, M. Searle. "Religious Liberty: Recent Phases of the Problem." *Ecumenical Review* 8, no. 4 (1956): 372–75.

Baum, Gregory. "Conflicts and the Council." *Commonweal*, September 21, 1962, 511–14.

———. "Montreal: Faith and Order." *Commonweal*, August 23, 1963, 505–11.

Bayne, Stephen F. "Responsible Parenthood and the Population Problem." *Ecumenical Review* 13, no. 1 (1960): 24–35.

Bea, Augustin Cardinal. *Ecumenism in Focus.* London: Geoffrey Chapman, 1968.

———. *Spiritual Profile.* Ed. Stjepan Schmidt. London: Geoffrey Chapman, 1971.

———. *Unity in Freedom: Reflections on the Human Family.* New York: Harper and Row, 1964.

Beisel, Nicola, and Tamara Kay. "Abortion, Race, and Gender in Nineteenth-Century America." *American Sociological Review* 69, no. 4 (2004): 498–518.

Bellah, Robert, Richard Madsen, William M. Sullivan, Ann Swidler, and Steven M. Tipton. *Habits of the Heart.* New York: Harper and Row Publishers, 1985.

Bellitto, Christopher M. *The General Councils: A History of the Twenty-One Church Councils from Nicaea to Vatican II.* Mahwah, NJ: Paulist Press, 2002.

Bender, Courtney. *Heaven's Kitchen: Living Religion at God's Love We Deliver.* Chicago: University of Chicago Press, 2000.

Benford, Robert D., and David A. Snow. "Framing Processes and Social Movements: An Overview and Assessment." *Annual Review of Sociology* 26 (2000): 611–39.

Berger, Mark T. *The Battle for Asia.* London: Routledge, 2003.

Berger, Peter. "A Market Model for the Analysis of Ecumenicity." *Social Research* 30, no. 1 (1963): 77–93.

Berkouwer, G. C. *The Second Vatican Council and the New Catholicism.* Grand Rapids. MI: William B. Eerdmans, 1965.

Bilheimer, Robert S. *Breakthrough: The Emergence of the Ecumenical Tradition.* Grand Rapids. MI: William B. Eerdmans, 1989.

Binder, Amy J. *Contentious Curricula: Afrocentrism and Creationism in American Public Schools.* Princeton: Princeton University Press, 2002.

Birmingham, David. *The Decolonialization of Africa.* Athens, OH: Ohio University Press, 1995.

Blakemore, W. B. "A Protestant Views the Vatican Council." *Chicago Sun-Times,* December 6, 1964.

Blanshard, Paul. *American Freedom and Catholic Power.* Boston: Beacon Press, 1949.

———. *Freedom and Catholic Power in Spain and Portugal: An American Interpretation.* Boston: Beacon Press, 1962.

Blau, Judith R., Kent Redding, and Kenneth C. Land. "Ethno-cultural Cleavages and the Growth of Church Membership in the United States, 1860–1930." *Sociological Forum* 8, no. 4 (1993): 609–37.

Blomjous, J. "Ecumenism in Africa: Reflections of a Bishop." *Ecumenist* 2, no. 2 (1964): 17–20.

Borgman, Erik. *Edward Schillebeeckx: A Theologian in His History.* 1999. Trans. John Bowden. London: Continuum, 2003.

Bourdieu, Pierre. "Genesis and Structure of the Religious Field." *Comparative Social Research* 13 (1991): 1–44.

Breault, Kevin D. "New Evidence on Religious Pluralism, Urbanism, and Religious Participation." *American Sociological Review* 54, no. 6 (1989): 1048–53.

Bristol, Oliver. "Comments on the Decree on Ecumenism: Enacted in the Second Vatican Council and Promulgated on November 21, 1964: VI." *Ecumenical Review* 17, no. 2 (1965): 107–9.

Brouwers, Jan A. "*Vatican II: Derniers préparatifs et première session: Activitiés conciliaires en coulisses.*" In *Vatican II commence . . . : approches francophones,* ed. É. Fouilloux. Bibliotheek Van De Faculteit Der Godgeleerdheid: Leuven, 1993.

Brown, Robert McAfee. *The Ecumenical Revolution: An Interpretation of the Catholic-Protestant Dialogue.* Garden City, NY: Doubleday, 1967.

———. *Observer in Rome.* Garden City, NY: Doubleday and Co., 1964.

———. "A Protestant Viewpoint: Apprehensions about the Council." *Commonweal,* December 1964, 442–45.

Burns, Gene. "Abandoning Suspicion: The Catholic Left and Sexuality." In *What's Left? Liberal American Catholics,* ed. Mary Jo Weaver. Bloomington: Indiana University Press, 1999.

———. "Commitments and Non-Commitments: The Social Radicalism of U.S. Catholic Bishops." *Theory and Society* 21, no. 5 (1992): 703–33.

———. "The Politics of Ideology: The Papal Struggle with Liberalism." *American Journal of Sociology* 95, no. 5 (1990): 1123–52.

———. "Voice, Exit, and Moving to the Margin: How Sex Trumps Catholic Social Doctrine." Paper presented at the annual meeting of the Eastern Sociological Society (Catholicism and Public Policy Panel), Washington, DC, March 2005.

Callahan, Daniel, ed. *The Catholic Case for Contraception.* London: Macmillan, 1969.

Caporale, Rock. *Vatican II: The Last of the Councils.* Baltimore: Garamond/Pridemark Press, 1964.

Carelton, Alford. "The Vatican Council and Issues of Religious Liberty." *Ecumenical Review* 14, no. 4 (1959): 456–59.

Carillo de Albornoz, A.F. "Reactions to 'Roman Catholicism and Religious Liberty.'" *Ecumenical Review* 13, no. 2 (1960–61): 228–34.

———. "Religious Liberty and the Second Vatican Council." *Ecumenical Review* 16, no. 4 (1964): 394–405.

———. "Roman Catholicism and Religious Liberty." *Ecumenical Review* 11, no. 4 (1959): 405–21.

———. "Roman Catholicism and Religious Liberty." *Ecumenical Review* 12, no. 1 (1959): 23–43.

Casanova, José. *Public Religions in the Modern World.* Chicago: University of Chicago Press, 1994.

The Catholic Encyclopedia: Classic 1914 Edition. New York: Robert Appleton Co., 1907–14. Computer edition by Kevin Knight, 2003.

Chaves, Mark. "Denominations as Dual Structures: An Organizational Analysis." *Sociology of Religion* 54, no. 2 (1993): 147–69.

———. *Ordaining Women: Culture and Conflict in Religious Organizations.* Cambridge: Harvard University Press, 1997.

———. "Secularization as Declining Religious Authority." *Social Forces* 72, no. 3 (1994): 749–74.

Chaves, Mark, and David E. Cann. "Regulation, Pluralism and Religious Market Structure." *Rationality and Society* 4, no. 3 (1992): 272–290.

Chaves, Mark, and Philip Gorski. "Religious Pluralism and Religious Participation." *Annual Review of Sociology* 27 (2001): 261–81.

Chaves, Mark, Peter J. Schraeder, and Mario Sprindys. "State Regulation of Religion and Muslim Religious Vitality in the Industrialized West." *Journal of Politics* 56, no. 4 (1994): 1087–97.

Chikeka, Charles O. *Decolonialization Process in Africa during the Post War Era, 1960–1990.* Lewiston, NY: Edwin Mellen Press, 1998.

Cleary, Edward L. *Crisis and Change: The Church in Latin America Today.* Maryknoll, NY: Orbis Books, 1985.

Clemens, Elisabeth S. "Organizational Repertoires and Institutional Change: Women's Groups and the Transformation of U.S. Politics, 1890–1920." *American Journal of Sociology* 98, no. 4 (1993): 755–98.

———. *The People's Lobby: Organizational Innovation and the Rise of Interest Group Politics in the United States, 1890–1925.* Chicago: University of Chicago Press, 1997.

Clemens, Elisabeth S., and James M. Cook. "Politics and Institutionalism: Explaining Durability and Change." *Annual Review of Sociology* 25 (1999): 441–66.

Coleman, John. *The Evolution of Dutch Catholicism, 1958–1974.* Berkeley: University of California Press, 1978.

"Contraceptives—Again." *Catholic Mind* 62 (January 1964): 38–40.

Curran, Charles E., ed. *Contraception: Authority and Dissent.* New York: Herder and Herder, 1969.

"Current Fact and Comment." *Sign* 41, no. 1 (1961): 33–35.

Cuttriss, Frank. "Observer Reports on Council." *Advocate,* February 10, 1966, 3–5.

Demerath, Nicholas J., Peter Dobkin Hall, Rhys Williams, and Terry Schmidt. *Sacred Companies.* New York: Oxford University Press, 1998.

De Vries, E. "Population Growth and Christian Responsibility." *Ecumenical Review* 13, no. 1 (1960): 36–41.

Dietzfelbinger, Wolfgang. "Vestigia Ecclesiae." *Ecumenical Review* 15, no. 4 (1962): 368–76.

Dillon, Michele. *Catholic Identity: Balancing Reason, Faith, and Power.* Cambridge: Cambridge University Press, 1999.

———. *Debating Divorce: Moral Conflict in Ireland.* Lexington: University Press of Kentucky, 1993.

DiMaggio, Paul. "The Relevance of Organization Theory to the Study of Religion." In *Sacred Companies,* ed. Nicholas J. Demerath, Peter Dobkin Hall, Rhys Williams, and Terry Schmidt. New York: Oxford University Press, 1998.

DiMaggio, Paul J., and Walter W. Powell. "The Iron Cage Revisited: Institutional Isomorphism and Collective Rationality in Organizational Fields." *American Sociological Review* 48 (1983): 147–60.

Dobbelaere, Karel, and Liliane Voyé. "Western European Catholicism since Vatican II." *Religion and the Social Order* 2 (1991): 205–31.

Dornbusch, Sanford M., and Roger D. Irle. "The Failure of Presbyterian Union." *American Journal of Sociology* 64, no. 4 (1959): 352–55.

Dugan, George. "U.S. Catholics Begin Reforms in the Mass: Switch to English for 45 Million Hailed as Successful." *New York Times,* November 30, 1964.

Durkheim, Émile. 1912. *The Elementary Forms of Religious Life.* Trans. Karen Fields. New York: Free Press, 1995.

Dussel, Enrique. *A History of the Church in Latin America: Colonialism to Liberation*. Grand Rapids, MI: William B. Eerdmans, 1981.

Ebaugh, Helen Rose. "Vatican II and the Reconceptualization of the Church." *Religion and the Social Order* 2 (1991): 267–84.

———. "Vatican II and the Revitalization Movement." *Religion and the Social Order* 2 (1991): 3–19.

Eisenstadt, S. N. "Social Change, Differentiation and Evolution." *American Sociological Review* 29, no. 3 (1964): 375–86.

"Ecumenical Chronicle: Notes on Roman Catholic Writings Concerning Ecumenism." *Ecumenical Review* 8, no. 2 (1956): 191–97.

"Ecumenical Chronicle: Religious Liberty from Day to Day." *Ecumenical Review* 13, no. 4 (1961): 477–88.

"Ecumenical Chronicle: Religious Liberty in Italy." *Ecumenical Review* 13, no. 4 (1961): 489–93.

"Ecumenical Chronicle: Report of the Executive Committee to the Central Committee, At Paris, 1962." *Ecumenical Review* 15, no. 1 (1962): 67–81.

"Ecumenical Chronicle: Report of the General Secretary to the Central Committee: Relations with the Roman Catholic Church." *Ecumenical Review* 17, no. 2 (1965): 165–71.

"Ecumenical Chronicle: A Report on Responsible Parenthood and the Population Problem." *Ecumenical Review* 12, no. 1 (1959): 85–92.

"Ecumenical Chronicle: The Roman Catholic Church and the First Assembly of the World Council of Churches." *Ecumenical Review* 1, no. 2 (1949): 197–201.

"Ecumenical Chronicle: The Roman Catholic Church and the Present Inter-Confessional Situation." *Ecumenical Review* 16, no. 4 (1964): 444–50.

Ellingson, Stephen. "Theories of Religious Change and the Sociology of Religion: From Crisis to Commonplaceness." Paper presented at the annual meeting of the Society for the Scientific Study of Religion, October 19, 2001.

Ellis, John Tracy. *American Catholicism*. Chicago: University of Chicago Press, 1955.

Emmerson, W. L. "The Changing Face of Rome—What Does It Mean?" *Liberty* 59, no. 1 (1964): 20–34.

Epstein, Barbara. *Political Protest and Cultural Revolution: Nonviolent Direct Action in the 1970s and 1980s*. Berkeley: University of California Press, 1991.

Etchegaray, Roger. "Interventi scritti," in *Paolo VI e la collegialità episcopale*. Rome: Edizioni Studium, 1995.

Fagley, Richard. "Doctrines and Attitudes of Major Religions in Regard to Fertility." *Ecumenical Review* 17, no. 4 (1965): 332–44.

Falconi, Carlo. *Pope John and the Ecumenical Council: A Diary of the Second Vatican Council, September–December 1962*. Trans. Muriel Grindrod. Cleveland and New York: World Publishing Company, 1964.

Fesquet, Henri. *The Drama of Vatican II: The Ecumenical Council, June, 1962–December, 1965*. Trans. Bernard Murchland. New York: Random House, 1967.

Fitzpatrick, Joseph P. "The Church and Social Issues: Institutional Commitments." *Religion and the Social Order* 2 (1991): 155–68.

Finke, Roger. "The Illusion of Shifting Demand: Supply-Side Interpretations of American Religious History." In *Retelling U.S. Religious History*, ed. Thomas Tweed, 108–24. Berkeley: University of California Press, 1997.

———. "Innovative Returns to Tradition: Using Core Teachings as the Foundation for Innovative Accommodation." *Journal for the Scientific Study of Religion* 43, no. 1 (2004): 19–34.

Finke, Roger, and Kevin Dougherty. "The Effects of Professional Training: The Social and Religious Capital Acquired in Seminaries." *Journal for the Scientific Study of Religion* 41 (2002): 103–20.

Finke, Roger, Avery M. Guest, and Rodney Stark. "Mobilizing Local Religious Markets: Religious Pluralism in the Empire State, 1855 to 1865." *American Sociological Review* 61, no. 2 (1996): 203–18.

Finke, Roger, and Laurence R. Iannaccone. "Supply-Side Explanations for Religious Change." *Annals* 527, no. 1 (1993): 27–39.

Finke, Roger and Rodney Stark. *The Churching of America: Winners and Losers in Our Religious Economy, 1776–1990*. New Brunswick: Rutgers University Press, 1992.

———. "Religious Economies and Sacred Canopies: Religious Mobilization in American Cities, 1906." *American Sociological Review* 53, no. 1 (1988): 41–49.

———. "Reply: Religious Choice and Competition." *American Sociological Review* 63, no. 5 (1998): 761–66.

Flannery, Austin. *Vatican Council II: Constitutions, Decrees, Declarations*. Northport, NY: Costello Publishing Co., 1996.

Fligstein, Neil. "Markets as Politics: A Political-Cultural Approach to Market Institutions." *American Sociological Review* 61, no. 4 (1996): 656–73.

Fogarty, Gerald P. *American Catholic Biblical Scholarship: A History from the Early Republic to Vatican II*. San Francisco: Harper and Row, 1989.

Foy, Felician A., ed. *The 1942 National Catholic Almanac*. Paterson, NJ: St. Anthony's Guild, 1942.

———. *The 1955 National Catholic Almanac*. Paterson, NJ: St. Anthony's Guild, 1955.

———. *The 1966 National Catholic Almanac*. Paterson, NJ: St. Anthony's Guild, 1966.

Freeman, Jo. "The Tyranny of Structurelessness." *Berkeley Journal of Sociology* 17 (1972–73): 151–64.

Froese, Paul and Steven Pfaff. "Explaining a Religious Anomaly: A Historical Analysis of Secularization in Eastern Germany." *Journal for the Scientific Study of Religion* 44, no. 4 (2005): 397–422.

Gaines, David P. *The World Council of Churches: A Study of Its Background and History*. Peterborough, NH: Richard R. Smith Co., 1966.

Gallup, George, and Jim Castelli. *The American Catholic People*. Garden City, NY: Doubleday, 1987.

Ganz, Marshall. "Resources and Resourcefulness: Strategic Capacity in the Unionization of California Agriculture 1959–1966." *American Journal of Sociology* 105, no. 4 (2000): 1003–62.

Gifford, Prosser, and Wm. Roger Louis. *Decolonialization and African Independence: The Transfers of Power, 1960–1980*. New Haven: Yale University Press, 1988.

Gill, Anthony. "Government Regulation, Social Anomie and Protestant Growth in Latin America: A Cross-National Analysis." *Rationality and Society* 11, no. 3 (1999): 287–316.

———. *Rendering unto Caesar: The Catholic Church and the State in Latin America*. Chicago: University of Chicago Press, 1998.

———. "Rendering unto Caesar: Religious Competition and Catholic Political Strategy in Latin America, 1962–79." *American Journal of Sociology* 38, no. 2 (1994): 403–25.

Glock, Charles Y., and Rodney Stark. *Christian Beliefs and Anti-Semitism*. New York: Harper and Row, 1966.

Godement, François. *The New Asian Renaissance*. New York and London: Routledge, 1997.

Gómez de Arteche y Catalina, Salvador. *El II Concilio Vaticano: Una historica asamblea parlamentaria: La formacion de grupos parlamentarios en el desenvolvimiento y la obra del II Concilio Vaticano*. Ph.D. dissertation, Universidad Complutense de Madrid, n.d.

Gonnet, Dominique. *La liberté religieuse à Vatican II: La contribution de John Courtney Murray*. Paris: Editions du Cerf, 1994.

Goodwin, Jeff, and James Jasper. "Caught in a Winding, Snarling Vine: The Structural Bias of Political Process Theory." *Sociological Forum* 14, no. 1 (1999): 27–54.

Gorski, Philip S. "Historicizing the Secularization Debate: Church, State and Society in Late Medieval and Early Modern Europe, ca. 1300 to 1700." *American Sociological Review* 65, no. 1 (2000): 138–67.

Gould, Andrew. *Origins of Liberal Dominance: State, Church and Party in Nineteenth-Century Europe*. Ann Arbor: University of Michigan Press, 1999.

Greeley, Andrew. *The American Catholic: A Social Portrait*. New York: Basic Books, 1977.

———. *The Catholic Revolution: New Wine, Old Wineskins, and the Second Vatican Council*. Berkeley: University of California Press, 2004.

———. "The Second Vatican Council—Occurrence or Event? Towards a Social Historical Reconsideration." *Commonweal*, September 1998.

Grootaers, Jan. *Actes et acteurs à Vatican II*. Leuven: University Press, 1998.

Guimarães, Atila Sinke. 1997. *In the Murky Waters of Vatican II*. 2 ed. Rockford, IL: Tan Books and Publishers, 1999.

———. "The Pact of Metz: Why Didn't the Last Ecumenical Council Condemn Communism?" http://www.traditioninaction.org/HotTopics/a007ht.htm.

Hamberg, Eva M., and Thorleif Pettersson. "The Religious Market: Denominational Competition and Religious Participation in Contemporary Sweden." *Journal for the Scientific Study of Religion* 33, no. 3 (1994): 205–16.

Hennesy, James. *American Catholics: A History of the Roman Catholic Community in the United States*. New York: Oxford University Press, 1981.

Horton, Douglas. *Vatican Diary 1962: A Protestant Observes the First Session of Vatican Council II*. Philadelphia: United Church Press, 1964.

———. *Vatican Diary 1963: A Protestant Observes the Second Session of Vatican Council II*. Philadelphia: United Church Press, 1964.

———. *Vatican Diary 1964: A Protestant Observes the Third Session of Vatican Council II*. Philadelphia: United Church Press, 1965.

Horton, Douglas. *Vatican Diary 1965: A Protestant Observes the Fourth Session of Vatican Council II*. Philadelphia: United Church Press, 1966.

Hout, Michael, and Andrew M. Greeley. "The Center Doesn't Hold: Church Attendance in the United States, 1940–1984." *American Sociological Review* 52, no. 3 (1987): 325–45.

Hout, Michael, Andrew Greeley, and Melissa J. Wilde. "The Demographic Imperative in Religious Change in the United States." *American Journal of Sociology* 107, no. 2 (2001): 468–500.

Huebsch, Bill. *Vatican II in Plain English: The Council*. Allen, TX: Thomas More, 1997.

Hunt, Robert P., and Kenneth L. Grasso. *John Courtney Murray and the American Civil Conversation*. Grand Rapids, MI: William B. Eerdmans, 1992.

Iannaccone, Laurence R. "The Consequences of Religious Market Structure: Adam Smith and the Economics of Religion." *Rationality and Society* 3, no. 2 (1991): 156–77.

———. "Religious Markets and the Economics of Religion." *Social Compass* 39, no. 1 (1992): 123–31.

———. "Why Strict Churches Are Strong." *American Journal of Sociology* 99, no. 5 (1994): 1180–211.

Of Melita, metropolitan James. "The Significance of the World Council of Churches for the Older Churches." *Ecumenical Review* 9, no. 1 (1956): 16–18.

Jeffrey, Robin. *Asia: The Winning of Independence*. New York: St. Martin's Press, 1981.

Jelen, Ted, and Clyde Wilcox. "Context and Conscience: The Catholic Church as an Agent of Political Socialization in Western Europe." *Journal for the Scientific Study of Religion* 37, no. 1 (1998): 28–40.

Johnson, Curtis D. "Supply-Side and Demand-Side Revivalism? Evaluating the Social Influences on New York State Evangelism in the 1830s." *Social Science History* 19, no. 1 (1995): 1–30.

Jung, Eva-Maria. "Roman Catholic Impressions of the Evanston Assembly." *Ecumenical Review* 7, no. 2 (1955): 117–26.

Kane, John J. *Catholic-Protestant Conflicts in America*. Chicago: Regnery Press, 1955.

Kaiser, Robert Blair. *The Politics of Sex and Religion: A Case History in the Development of Doctrine, 1962–1984*. Kansas City, MO: Leaven Press, 1987.

Kartachoff, Antione. "Orthodox Theology and the Ecumenical Movement." *Ecumenical Review* 8, no. 1 (1955): 30–35.

Katzenstein, Mary Fainsod. *Faithful and Fearless: Moving Feminist Protest inside the Church and Military*. Princeton: Princeton University Press, 1998.

Kaufman, Philip S. *Why You Can Disagree and Remain a Faithful Catholic*. New York: Crossroad Publishing Company, 1989.

Kelly, James R. "Catholic Sexual Ethics since Vatican II." *Religion and the Social Order* 2 (1991): 139–54.

Kerwin, Jerome G. *Catholic Viewpoint on Church and State*. Garden City, NY: Hanover House, 1960.

Kinder, Ernst. "Protestant-Roman Catholic Encounter: An Ecumenical Obligation." *Ecumenical Review* 7, no. 4 (1955): 338–46.

Kniss, Fred. "Ideas and Symbols as Resources in Intrareligious Conflict." *Sociology of Religion* 57, no. 1 (1996): 7–23.

Kobler, John Francis. "An Introduction to the Thought of Vatican II." *Chicago Studies* 44, no. 1 (2005): 82–100.

Koet, Josefa, Leideke Galema, and Marion Van Assendelft. *Hearth of Unity*. Rome: Fratelli Palombi Editori, 1996.

Komonchak, Joseph A. "The Conciliar Discussion on the Sources of Revelation." Department of Religious Studies, Catholic University of America, 1999.

———. "The Constitution on the Liturgy." Department of Religious Studies, Catholic University of America, 1999.

———. "Convening Vatican II: John XXIII Calls for a Council." *Commonweal*, February 12, 1999, 10–12.

———. "The Elections to the Conciliar Commissions." Department of Religious Studies, Catholic University of America, 1999.

———. "Initial Reactions to Pope John XXIII's Announcement of an Ecumenical Council." Department of Religious Studies, Catholic University of America, 1999.

———. "Introduction: Episcopal Conferences under Criticism." In *Episcopal Conferences: Historical, Canonical and Theological Studies*, ed. Thomas J. Reese. Washington, DC: Georgetown University Press, 1989.

———. "Popes Pius XI and Pius XII and the Idea of an Ecumenical Council." Department of Religious Studies, Catholic University of America, 1999.

———. "Religious Freedom and the Confessional State: The Twentieth-Century Discussion." *Extrait de la Revue d'Histoire Ecclésiastique* 95, no. 3 (2000).

———. "U.S. Bishops' Suggestions for Vatican II." *Cristianesimo nella Storia: Studies in History Exegesis and Theology* 15 (1994): 313–71.

———. "Vatican II as an 'Event.'" Fourth Annual DeLubac Lecture in Historical Theology, Catholic University of America, 1999.

Kosnik, Anthony, William Carroll, Agnes Cunningham, Ronald Modras, and James Schulte. *Human Sexuality: New Directions in American Catholic Thought*. New York: Paulist Press, 1977.

Küng, Hans. *The Council, Reform and Reunion*. New York: Sheed and Ward, 1961.

Küng, Hans, Yves Congar, and Daniel O'Hanlon, eds. *Council Speeches of Vatican II*. Glen Rock, NJ: Deus Books, 1964.

Kurtz, Lester R. *The Politics of Heresy: The Modernist Crisis in Roman Catholicism*. Berkeley: University of California Press, 1986.

Land, Kenneth C., Glenn Deane, and Judith R. Blau. "Religious Pluralism and Church Membership: A Spatial Diffusion Model." *American Sociological Review* 56, no. 2 (1991): 237–49.

Laurentin, René. *Bilan du concile: Histoire—textes—commentaries avec une chronique de la quatrième session*. Paris: Editions du Seuil, 1966.

———. "The Blessed Virgin at the Council." Marian Library Studies, no. 109. Dayton, OH: Marian Library of the University of Dayton, 1964.

Lawson, Matthew P. "The Holy Spirit as Conscience Collective." *Sociology of Religion* 60, no. 4 (1999): 341–61.

Lechner, Frank J. "Secularization in the Netherlands?" *Journal for the Scientific Study of Religion* 35, no. 3 (1996): 252–64.

Lee, Robert. *The Social Sources of Church Unity: An Interpretation of Unitive Movements in American Protestantism*. New York: Abingdon Press, 1960.

"Letters." *Liberty* 55, no. 2 (1960): 4.

Lindbeck, George A. *Dialogue on the Way: Protestants Report from Rome on the Vatican Council*. Minneapolis: Augsburg Publishing House, 1965.

Lissner, Will. "Cathedral Leads in New Liturgy." *New York Times*, November 30, 1964, p. 29.

Love, Thomas T. *John Courtney Murray: Contemporary Church-State Theory*. Garden City, NY: Doubleday and Co., 1965.

Lowell, C. Stanley. "Colombia—Land of Martyrs." *Liberty* 56, no. 2 (1961): 12–15.

Mansbridge, Jane J. *Why We Lost the ERA*. Chicago: University of Chicago Press, 1986.

March, James G., and Johan P. Olsen. *Rediscovering Institutions: The Organizational Basis of Politics*. New York: Free Press, 1989.

Martin, John Levi. "Power, Authority, and the Constraint of Belief Systems." *American Journal of Sociology* 107, no. 4 (2002): 861–904.

Martin, Malachi. *The Jesuits: The Society of Jesus and the Betrayal of the Roman Catholic Church*. New York: Simon and Schuster, 1987.

Martina, Giacomo. "The Historical Context in Which the Idea of a New Ecumenical Council Was Born." In *Vatican II: Assessment and Perspectives Twenty Five Years After*, Ed. René Latourelle. vol. 1. Mahwah, NJ.: Paulist Press, 1988.

Maury, Phillippe. "Ecumenical Chronicle: Survey of Press Comments on the Third Assembly, Part II: Roman Catholic Comments." *Ecumenical Review* 14, no. 4 (1962): 480–87.

McAdam, Doug. *Political Process and the Development of Black Insurgence, 1930–1970*. Chicago. University of Chicago Press, 1982.

McAdam, Doug, Sidney Tarrow, and Charles Tilly. *Dynamics of Contention*. Cambridge: Cambridge University Press, 2001.

McBrien, Richard P. *Catholicism*. New York: HarperCollins Publishers, 1994.

McCarthy, Timothy G. *The Catholic Tradition: Before and After Vatican II, 1878–1993*. Chicago: Loyola University Press, 1994.

McClory, Robert. *Turning Point: The Inside Story of the Papal Birth Control Commission, and How Humanae Vitae Changed the Life of Patty Crowley and the Future of the Church*. New York: Crossroad Publishing Co., 1997.

McEnroy, Carmel. *Guests in Their Own House: The Women of Vatican II*. New York: Crossroad Publishing Co., 1996.

McGrath, Marcos. "La creazione della coscienza di un popolo latinoamericano: Il CELAM ed il concilio Vaticano II." In *L'evento e le decisioni: Studi sulle dinamiche del concilio Vaticano II*, ed. Maria Teresa Fattori and Alberto Melloni. Bologna: Il Mulino, 1997.

McGrath, Mark G. "Impressions of the Council." *America* 113, no. 6, (1965): 182–83.

McInerny, Ralph M. *What Went Wrong with Vatican II: The Catholic Crisis Explained*. Manchester, NH: Sophia Institute Press, 1998.

McVeigh, Rory, Daniel J. Meyers, and David Sikkink. "Corn, Klansmen and Coolidge: Structure and Framing in Social Movements." *Social Forces* 83, no. 2 (2004): 653–90.

Mehl, Roger. "The Ecclesiological Significance of the World Council from a Roman Catholic Standpoint." *Ecumenical Review* 9, no. 3 (1957): 240–52.

————. "The Ecumenical Situation." *Ecumenical Review* 16, no. 1 (1963): 1–13.

Meyer, David S., and Debra C. Minkoff. "Conceptualizing Political Opportunity." *Social Forces* 82, no. 4 (2004): 1457–92.

Meyer, David, and Susan Staggenborg. "Movements, Countermovements, and the Structure of Political Opportunity." *American Journal of Sociology* 101, no. 6 (1996): 1628–60.

Meyer, John W., and Brian Rowan. "Institutionalized Organizations: Formal Structure as Myth and Ceremony." *American Journal of Sociology* 83, no. 2 (1983): 340–63.

Meyer, John W., John Boli, George M. Thomas, and Francisco O. Ramirez. "World Society and the Nation-State." *American Journal of Sociology* 103, no. 1 (1997): 144–81.

Miller, John H., ed. *Vatican II: An Interfaith Appraisal.* Notre Dame, IN: University of Notre Dame Press, 1966.

Miller, Kent. "Competitive Strategies of Religious Organizations." *Strategic Management Journal* 23, no. 5 (2002): 435–56.

Mizruchi, Mark S., and Lisa C. Fein. "The Social Construction of Organizational Knowledge: A Study of the Uses of Coercive, Mimetic, and Normative Isomorphism." *Administrative Science Quarterly* 44, no. 4 (1999): 653–83.

Monsma, Stephen V., and J. Christopher Soper. *The Challenge of Pluralism: Church and State in Five Democracies.* New York: Rowan and Littlefield Publishers, 1997.

Moon, Dawne. *God, Sex, and Politics: Homosexuality and Everyday Theologies.* Chicago: University of Chicago Press, 2004.

Moorman, John. *Vatican Observed: For Anglicans.* London: Darton, Longman and Todd, 1967.

Morris, Aldon D. *The Origins of the Civil Rights Movement: Black Communities Organizing for Change.* New York: Free Press, 1984.

Morrison, Charles Clayton. *The Unfinished Reformation.* New York: Harper and Brothers, 1953.

Muelder, Walter G. "The Church in the Modern World: A Critique of Schema XIII." *Ecumenical Review* 17, no. 2 (1965): 113–26.

————. "From Sect to Church." *Christendom* 10 (Autumn 1945): 450–62.

Mumford, Stephen D. *American Democracy and the Vatican: Population Growth and National Security.* Amherst, NY: Humanist Press, 1984.

Murray, John Courtney. *Religious Liberty: An End and a Beginning.* New York: Macmillan Co., 1966.

————. *We Hold These Truths: Catholic Reflections on the American Proposition.* New York: Sheed and Ward, 1960.

Neufeld, Karl Heinz. "In the Service of the Council: Bishops and Theologians at the Second Vatican Council." In *Vatican II: Assessment and Perspectives Twenty Five Years After,* ed. René Latourelle, vol. 1. Mahwah, NJ: Paulist Press, 1988.

Neuhouser, Kevin. "The Radicalization of the Brazilian Catholic Church in Comparative Perspective." *American Sociological Review* 54, no. 2 (1989): 233–44.

Noël, Pierre C. "Gli incontri delle conferencze episcopali durante il Concilio. Il <<gruppo della Domus Mariae>>." In *L'evento e le decisioni: Studi sulle dinamiche del concilio Vaticano II*, ed. Maria Teresa Fattori and Alberto Melloni. Bologna: Il Mulino, 1997.

Noonan, John T., Jr. *Contraception: A History of Its Treatment by the Catholic Theologians and Canonists*. Cambridge: Harvard University Press, 1965.

———. "Contraception and the Council." *Commonweal* 83 (March 11, 1966): 657–62.

"Notes on Contributors and Articles." *Ecumenical Review* 7, no. 4 (1955): 418.

Núñez, Emilio A., and William D. Taylor. *Crisis in Latin America: An Evangelical Perspective*. Chicago: Moody Press, 1989.

O'Brien, David. *Public Catholicism*. New York: Macmillan, 1989.

O'Collins, Gerald. "Revelation Past and Present." In *Vatican II: Assessment and Perspectives Twenty-Five Years After*, ed. René LaTourelle, vol. 1. Mahwah, NJ: Paulist Press, 1988.

O'Hanlon, Daniel J. "Faith and Order Conference." *America* 109, no. 6 (1963): 138–41.

Olsen, V. Norskov. "Catholicity: Who Has Greater Claim to It—Catholics or Protestants?" *Liberty* 58, no. 1 (1963): 23–26.

Olson, Daniel V. A. "Religious Pluralism and U.S. Church Membership: A Reassessment." *Sociology of Religion* 60, no. 2 (1999): 149–73.

———. "Religious Pluralism in Contemporary U.S. Counties." *American Sociological Review* 63, no. 5 (1998): 759.

Olson, Daniel V.A., and C. Kirk Hadaway. "Religious Pluralism and Affiliation among Canadian Counties and Cities." *Journal for the Scientific Study of Religion* 38, no. 4 (1999): 490–508.

O'Malley, John W. "Developments, Reforms, and Two Great Reformations: Towards a Historical Assessment of Vatican II." *Theological Studies* 44, no. 3 (1983): 373–406.

Orsi, Robert Anthony. *The Madonna of 115th Street: Faith and Community in Italian Harlem, 1880–1950*. New Haven: Yale University Press, 1985.

Outler, Albert C. "Vatican II—Act Three." *Christianity and Crisis* 24, no. 21 (1964): 260–64.

Oxnam, G. Bromley. *The Church and Contemporary Change*. New York: Macmillan, 1950.

Patillo-McCoy, Mary. "Church Culture as a Strategy of Action in the Black Community." *American Sociological Review* 63, no. 6 (1998): 767–84.

Pawley, Bernard C. *An Anglican View of the Vatican Council*. New York: Morehouse-Barlow Co., 1962.

Perl, Paul, and Daniel V. A. Olson. "Religious Market Share and Intensity of Church Involvement in Five Denominations." *Journal for the Scientific Study of Religion* 39, no. 1 (2000): 12–31.

Perrin, Luc. "Il 'Coetus Internationalis Patrum' e la minoranza conciliare." In *L'Evento e le decisioni: Studi delle dinamiche del Concilio Vaticano II*, ed. Maria Teresa Fattori and Alberto Melloni. Bologna: Il Mulino, 1997.

Piven, Frances Fox, and Richard A. Cloward. *Poor People's Movements: Why They Succeed, How They Fail*. New York: Vintage Books, 1979.

Polletta, Francesca. *Freedom Is an Endless Meeting: Democracy in American Social Movements*. Chicago: University of Chicago Press, 2002.

Pottmeyer, Hermann J. *Towards a Papacy in Communion: Perspectives from Vatican Councils I and II*. New York: Crossroad Publishing Co., 1998.

Rao, Hayagreeva. "Caveat Emptor: The Construction of Nonprofit Consumer Watchdog Organizations." *American Journal of Sociology* 103, no. 4 (1998): 912–61.

Rao, Hayagreeva, Calvin Morrill, and Mayer N. Zald. "Power Plays: How Social Movements and Collective Action Create New Organizational Forms." *Research in Organizational Behavior* 22 (2000): 237–81.

Reese, Thomas J. *Episcopal Conferences: Historical, Canonical, & Theological Studies*. Washington, DC: Georgetown University Press, 1989.

"The Roman Catholic Church in Spain and Religious Liberty." *Ecumenical Review* 1, no. 1 (1948): 95–96.

Rouse, Ruth, and Stephen Charles Neill. *A History of the Ecumenical Movement, 1517–1948*. London: SPCK, 1954.

Rynne, Xavier. *Vatican Council II*. New York: Farrar, Straus and Giroux, 1968.

Scatena, Silvia. "Lo schema sulla libertà religiosa: Momenti e passagi dalla preparazione del Concilio alla Seconda Intersessione." In *Experience, Organisations and Bodies at Vatican II*, ed. M. T. Fattori and A. Melloni. Leuven: Bibliotheek van de Faculteit Godgeleerheid, 1999.

Schmitt, Karl M. *The Roman Catholic Church in Modern Latin America*. New York: Alfred A Knopf, 1972.

Scott, W. Richard, Martin Ruef, Peter J. Mendel, and Carol A. Caronna. *Institutional Change and Healthcare Organizations: From Professional Dominance to Managed Care*. Chicago: University of Chicago Press, 2000.

Seidler, John, and Katherine Meyer. *Conflict and Change in the Catholic Church*. New Brunswick: Rutgers University Press, 1989.

Sen, B. R. *Food, Population, and Development*. New York: Food and Agriculture Organization of the United Nations, 1965.

Sengers, Erik. "'Although We Are Catholic, We Are Dutch.'—The Transition of the Dutch Catholic Church from Sect to Church as an Explanation for Its Growth and Decline." *Journal for the Scientific Study of Religion* 43, no. 1 (2004): 129–39.

———. "'You Don't Have to Be a Saint or a Practicing Catholic . . .': Higher Tension and Lower Attachment in the Dutch Catholic Church since 1970." *Antonianum* 77 (2003): 529–45.

Sewell, William. "Historical Events as Transformations of Structures: Inventing Revolution at the Bastille." *Theory and Society* 25, no. 6 (1996): 841–81.

———. "A Theory of Structure: Duality, Agency, and Transformation." *American Journal of Sociology* 98, no. 1 (1992): 1–29.

———. "Three Temporalities: Toward an 'Eventful' Sociology." In *The Historic Turn in the Human Sciences*, ed. Terrence J. McDonald. Ann Arbor: University of Michigan Press, 1996.

Skydsgaard, K. E. *One in Christ: Protestant and Catholic*. Philadelphia: Muhlenberg Press, 1957.

Slayton, Robert A. *Empire Statesmen: The Rise and Redemption of Al Smith*. New York: Free Press, 2001.

Smith, Christian. *American Evangelicalism: Embattled and Thriving*. Chicago: University of Chicago Press, 1998.

Smith, Christian, ed. *Disruptive Religion: The Force of Faith in Social Movement Activism.* New York: Routledge, 1996.

———. *The Emergence of Liberation Theology: Radical Religion and Social Movement Theory.* Chicago: University of Chicago Press, 1991.

———. *Resisting Reagan: The U.S. Central America Peace Movement.* Chicago: University of Chicago Press, 1996.

Snow, David A., and Robert D. Benford. "Master Frames and Cycles of Protest." In *Frontiers in Social Movement Theory*, ed. Aldon D. Morris and Carol McClurg Mueller. New Haven: Yale University Press, 1992.

Snow, David A., E. Burke Rochford Jr., Steven K. Worden, and Robert D. Benford. "Frame Alignment Processes, Micromobilization and Movement Participation." *American Sociological Review* 51, no. 4 (1986): 464–81.

"Some Roman Catholic Voices about the First Assembly." *Ecumenical Review* 1, no. 2 (1949): 202–12.

Sperry, Willard L., ed. *Religion and Our Divided Denominations.* Cambridge: Harvard University Press, 1945.

Spina, Tony. *The Pope and the Council.* New York: A. S. Barnes and Co., 1963.

Stark, Rodney. "Do Catholic Societies Really Exist?" *Rationality and Society* 4, no. 3 (1992): 261–71.

———. "Europe's Receptivity to New Religious Movements: Round Two." *Journal for the Scientific Study of Religion* 32, no. 4 (1993): 389–97.

Stark, Rodney, and Roger Finke. *Acts of Faith: Explaining the Human Side of Religion.* Berkeley: University of California Press, 2000.

Stark, Rodney, Roger Finke, and Laurence R. Iannaccone. "Pluralism and Piety: England and Wales, 1851." *Journal for the Scientific Study of Religion* 34, no. 4 (1995): 431–44.

Stark, Rodney, and Laurence R. Iannaccone. "Response to Lechner: Recent Religious Declines in Quebec, Poland and the Netherlands: A Theory Vindicated." *Journal for the Scientific Study of Religion* 35, no. 3 (1996): 265–71.

Steensland, Brian. "Cultural Categories and the American Welfare State: The Case of Guaranteed Income Policy." *American Journal of Sociology* 111, no. 5 (2006): 1273–1326.

Stevens, Mitchell L. *Kingdom of Children: Culture and Controversy in the Home-schooling Movement.* Princeton: Princeton University Press, 2001.

Stransky, Thomas. "What the Council Will Do." *Sign*, October 1962, 17–21.

Stryker, Robin. "A Political Approach to Organizations and Institutions." *Research in the Sociology of Organizations* 19 (2002): 169–91.

Swidler, Ann. "Cultural Power and Social Movements." In *Social Movements and Culture*, ed. Hank Johnston and Bert Klandermans. Minneapolis: University of Minnesota Press, 1995.

———. "Culture in Action: Symbols and Strategies." *American Sociological Review* 51, no. 2 (1986): 273–86.

———. *Talk of Love: How Culture Matters.* Chicago: University of Chicago Press, 2001.

Tarrow, Sidney. *Power in Movement.* Cambridge: Cambridge University Press, 1998.

Tilly, Charles. *Popular Contention in Great Britain, 1758–1834.* Cambridge: Harvard University Press, 1995.

Times Index-Gazetteer of the World. London: Times Publishing Co., 1965.

Todd, John M. *Catholicism and the Ecumenical Movement.* London: Longmans, Green and Co., 1956.

Tracy, Robert E., *American Bishop at the Council: Recollections and Projections.* New York: McGraw-Hill, 1966.

Turner, Victor Witter. *The Ritual Process: Structure and Anti-Structure.* New York: Aldine de Gruyter, 1995.

Underwood, Kenneth. *Protestant and Catholic: Religious and Social Interaction in an Industrial Community.* Boston: Beacon Press, 1957.

Vallier, Ivan. *Catholicism, Social Control, and Modernization in Latin America.* Englewood Cliffs, NJ: Prentice Hall, 1970.

———. "Church 'Development' in Latin America." In *The Roman Catholic Church in Modern Latin America*, ed. Karl M. Schmitt. New York: Alfred A Knopf, 1972.

Valsecchi, Ambrogio. *Controversy: The Birth Control Debate 1958–1968.* Washington, DC: Corpus Books, 1967.

Van der Bent, Ans Joachim. *Historical Dictionary of Ecumenical Christianity.* Metuchen, NJ: Scarecrow Press, 1994.

"Various Voices on Evanston: From the Roman Catholic Church." *Ecumenical Review* 7, no. 3 (1955): 261–79.

Verghese, Paul. "Aggiornamento and the Unity of All: An Eastern Orthodox View of the Vatican Council." *Ecumenical Review* 15, no. 4 (1963): 377–84.

Verweij, Johan, Peter Ester, and Rein Nauta. "Secularization as an Economic and Cultural Phenomenon: A Cross-National Analysis." *Journal for the Scientific Study of Religion* 36, no. 2 (1997): 309–24.

Vischer, Lukas. "Report on the Second Vatican Council." *Ecumenical Review* 16, no. 1 (1963): 43–59.

Visser't Hooft, W. A. *The Genesis and Formation of the World Council of Churches.* Geneva: World Council of Churches, 1982.

Wallace, Anthony F. C. "Revitalization Movements." *American Anthropologist* 58 (1956): 264–81.

Warner, Stephen R. "Work in Progress toward a New Paradigm for the Sociological Study of Religion in the United States." *American Journal of Sociology* 98, no. 5 (1993): 1044–93.

Weber, Max. *Economy and Society.* 1956. Vols. 1–2. Trans. and ed. Guenther Roth and Claus Wittich. Berkeley: University of California Press, 1978.

Wenger, Antoine. *Vatican II.* Vol. 1, *The First Session.* Trans. Robert J. Olsen. Westminster, MD: Newman Press, 1966.

"What Went Wrong?" *Time*, December 6, 1963.

Wilde, Melissa J. "From Excommunication to Nullification: Testing and Extending Supply-Side Theories of Religious Marketing with the Case of Catholic Marital Annulments." *Journal for the Scientific Study of Religion* 40, no. 2 (2001): 235–49.

Wilson, H. S. *African Decolonialization.* London: Edward Arnold, 1994.

Wiltgen, Ralph M. *The Rhine Flows into the Tiber: A History of Vatican II.* 1967. Rockford, IL: TAN Books, 1985.

Wolf, William J. "Anglican Observations of the Second Session of Vatican II." *Living Church*, January 12, 1964, pp. 10–18.

Wood, James R., and Mayer N. Zald. "Aspects of Racial Integration in the Methodist Church: Sources of Resistance to Organizational Policy." In *Social Movements in an Organizational Society*, ed. Mayer N. Zald and John D. McCarthy. New Brunswick: Transaction Publishers, 1994.

Wood, Richard L. *Faith in Action: Religion, Race, and Democratic Organizing in America*. Chicago: University of Chicago Press, 2002.

———. "Religious Culture and Political Action." *Sociological Theory* 17, no. 3 (1999): 307–32.

"World Report." *Liberty* 55, no. 1 (1960): 33–34.

"World Report." *Liberty* 55, no. 2 (1960): 32–33.

Wuthnow, Robert. *Communities of Discourse: Ideology and Social Structure in the Reformation, the Enlightenment, and European Socialism*. Cambridge: Harvard University Press, 1989.

———. *The Restructuring of American Religion*. Princeton: Princeton University Press, 1988.

———. "World Order and Religious Movements." In *Studies of the Modern World-System*, ed. A. Bergensen, New York: Academic Press, 1980.

Young, Michael P. "Confessional Protest: The Religious Birth of U.S. National Social Movements." *American Sociological Review* 67, no. 5 (2002): 660–88.

Yzermans, Vincent A. *American Participation in the Second Vatican Council*. New York: Sheed and Ward, 1967.

Zald, Mayer N., and John D. McCarthy. "Religious Groups as Crucibles of Social Movements." In *Social Movements in an Organizational Society*, ed. Mayer N. Zald and John D. McCarthy, New Brunswick: Transaction Publishers, 1994.

Zaret, David. *The Heavenly Contract: Ideology and Organization in Pre-Revolutionary Puritanism*. Chicago: University of Chicago Press, 1985.

Zeilstra, Jurjen. *European Unity in Ecumenical Thinking, 1937–1948*. Zoetermeer, Netherlands: Uitgeverij Boekencentrum, 1995.

INDEX

Page numbers in italics refer to figures or tables in the text.